CAPITAL GAINS TAX AND THE PRIVATE RESIDENCE

DEDICATION

For Sue, Helen and Adam Williams

CAPITAL GAINS TAX AND THE PRIVATE RESIDENCE

Third Edition

David E. Williams MA, FTII
Consultant, Smith & Williamson, Chartered Accountants, and formerly HM Senior Inspector of Taxes

Smith & Williamson

Disclaimer

This publication is sold on the understanding that the publisher is not engaged in rendering legal or accounting advice or other professional services. The publisher, its editors and any authors, consultants or general editors expressly disclaim all and any liability and responsibility to any person, whether a purchaser or reader of this publication or not, in respect of anything and of the consequences of anything, done or omitted to be done by any such person in reliance, whether wholly or partially, upon the whole or any part of the contents of this publication. While this publication is intended to provide accurate information in regard to the subject matter covered, readers entering into transactions on the basis of such information should seek the services of a competent professional adviser.

Legislative and other material

While copyright in all statutory and other materials resides in the Crown or other relevant body, copyright in the remaining material in this publication is vested in the publisher.

The publisher advises that any statutory or other materials issued by the Crown or other relevant bodies and reproduced or quoted in this publication are not the authorised official versions of those statutory or other materials. In their preparation, however, the greatest care has been taken to ensure exact conformity with the law as enacted or other material as issued.

Crown copyright legislation is reproduced under the terms of Crown Copyright Policy Guidance issued by HMSO. Other Crown Copyright material is reproduced with the permission of the Controller of HMSO. European Communities Copyright material is reproduced with permission.

Ownership of Trade Marks

The trade mark is the property of

Commerce Clearing House Incorporated, Riverwoods, Illinois, USA.
(**CCH** INCORPORATED)

The trade mark **CRONER @ CCH** is the property of

Croner.CCH Group Ltd

ISBN 0 86325 577 9

First published 1991
Second edition 1993
Third edition 2002

© 1991, 1993, 2002 Croner.CCH Group Ltd

All rights reserved. No part of this work covered by the publisher's copyright may be reproduced or copied in any form or by any means (graphic, electronic or mechanical, including photocopying, recording, recording taping, or other information and retrieval systems) without the written permission of the publisher.
Typeset in the UK by Mendip Communications Ltd.
Printed in the UK by Chiltern Press Ltd.

Preface to the Third Edition

Previous editions of this book were published by CCH Editions in July 1991 and December 1993. For a few years under the previous Conservative administration it seemed possible that capital gains tax might be abolished, and this, plus other professional commitments, discouraged me from attempting a third edition. More recently, however, the growing complexity and importance of capital gains tax under Gordon Brown's Chancellorship, and the encouragement of a number of professional friends and contacts, have prompted me to think again.

This third edition therefore attempts to provide an authoritative update of the previous editions, and, like them, to provide professional advisers with a comprehensive survey of the capital gains tax legislation and suggestions for efficient planning. Once again, a basic knowledge of the UK tax system in general, and of CGT in particular, has been assumed.

Since the publication of the second edition, the Inland Revenue has made most of the material in its internal instruction manuals available to the general public and I have made substantial use of the very helpful sections of these manuals which deal with capital gains tax and the private residence. I have, however, indicated where I disagree with the manuals and it should be remembered that they are merely expressions of the internal views of the Inland Revenue, and not statements of the law.

I am particularly grateful to Elizabeth Roberts and Virginia Hopson who have given me much help in the preparation of this edition, and to all my Partners and colleagues at Smith & Williamson over the years for the benefit of stimulating discussions on this subject. My thanks also go to the publication team at CCH Information for their encouragement and help. As with the two previous editions, my final thanks go to Sue, Helen and Adam Williams whose support and tolerance has sustained me throughout.

David E Williams
June 2002
Smith & Williamson
1 Riding House Street
London
W1A 3AS

About the Author

The author, David E Williams, MA, FTII, was Tax Technical Partner of Smith & Williamson, Chartered Accountants, from 1987 until April 2002, and is now a Consultant to the firm. He is a former Council member of the Chartered Institute of Taxation and a former chairman of its Capital Taxes sub-committee. Before joining Smith & Williamson, he spent 15 years with the Inland Revenue, latterly as a Senior Inspector of Taxes. Smith & Williamson is an independent professional and financial services group which is one of the leading providers of investment management, financial advisory and accountancy services to private clients, professional practices and mid-sized corporates.

About the Publisher

CCH is part of the Wolters Kluwer Group. Wolters Kluwer is the leading international publisher specialising in tax, business and law publishing throughout Europe, the US and the Asia Pacific region. The group produces a wide range of information services in different media for the accounting and legal professions and for business.

All CCH publications are designed to be practical and authoritative reference works and guides and are written by our own highly qualified and experienced editorial team and specialist outside authors.

CCH publishes information packages including electronic products, loose-leaf reporting services, newsletters and books on UK and European legal topics for distribution world-wide. The UK operation also acts as distributor of the publications of the overseas affiliates.

CCH
SOUTH BAR HOUSE
SOUTH BAR STREET
BANBURY
OXFORDSHIRE OX16 9AB
UNITED KINGDOM

Telephone: +44 (0) 870 241 5726
Facsimile: +44 (0) 1295 819776

Part of the Wolters Kluwer Group

Abbreviations

The following abbreviations are used in this book:

AC	Law Reports, Appeal Cases, from 1891–(current)
All ER	All England Law Reports, from 1936–(current)
BTC	British Tax Cases (CCH), from 1982–(current)
BTR	British Tax Review
CA	Court of Appeal
CCAB	Consultative Council of Accounting Bodies
Ch	Law Reports, Chancery Division, from 1891–(current)
CGT	capital gains tax
CGT	(followed by numbers) Inland Revenue Capital Gains Tax Manual
CGTA	Capital Gains Tax Act
col.	column
EG	Estates Gazette
ESC	extra-statutory concession
FA	Finance Act
HMSO	Her Majesty's Stationery Office
ICAEW	The Institute of Chartered Accountants in England and Wales
ICTA	Income and Corporation Taxes Act
IHT	inheritance tax
IHTA	Inheritance Tax Act
IRLR	Industrial Relations Law Reports, from 1972–(current)
JPL	Journal of Planning and Environmental Law
JRA	job-related accommodation
LT	Law Times Reports, 1859–1947
MR	main residence
MR	Master of the Rolls
NI	Northern Ireland Reports
OMR	only or main residence
p.; pp.	page(s)
para(s).	paragraph(s)
PET	potentially exempt transfer
plc	public limited company

PRR	private residence relief
Pt.	Part
QB	Law Reports, Queen's Bench Division, 1891–1901; 1952–(current)
QBD	Law Reports, Queen's Bench Division, 1875–1890
R	Rex or Regina (i.e. the Crown)
s.; ss.	section(s)
Sch.	Schedule(s)
SP	statement of practice
subs.	subsection
TC	Tax Cases, from 1875–(current)
TCGA 1992	Taxation of Chargeable Gains Act 1992
TMA	Taxes Management Act
VAT	value added tax
V-C	Vice Chancellor
Vol.	Volume
VOM (followed by numbers)	Valuation Office Manual
WLR	Weekly Law Reports, from 1953–(current)

Dates in square brackets [ ] are part of the citation of a case and identify the appropriate volume. Thus, [1985] BTC 33 refers to the 1985 volume of *British Tax Cases*, p. 33. Dates in curved brackets or parentheses ( ) identify the year of the judgment. Thus, (1971) 46 TC 687 refers to Volume 46 of *Tax Cases*, 1971, p. 687.

Contents

	Page
Preface	v
About the Author	vi
About the Publisher	vii
Abbreviations	ix

1 Introduction   1

¶101	Historical background	1
¶102	Developments since 1965	1
¶103	Development of the law	2
¶104	Scope of this text	2
¶105	A cautionary note	3

2 The Legislation in Summary   4

¶201	Background and mechanism for relief	4
¶202	The principal relieving provision	4
¶203	The scope of the relief	5
¶204	The period of ownership	7
¶205	How much relief is available?	8
¶206	Partial business or investment use	10
¶207	Changes of status	10
¶208	Acquisition or expenditure for the purpose of disposal	11
¶209	Occupation under the terms of a settlement	11
¶210	Inland Revenue Manuals	11

3 The House Itself   13

WHAT IS A DWELLING-HOUSE?   13

¶301	Introduction	13
¶302	The concept in general law	13
¶303	Tax case law and dwelling-houses generally	14
¶304	CGT case law on dwelling-houses	15
¶305	Areas of practical difficulty	17

		Page
ACQUISITIONS AND EXPENDITURE WITH A VIEW TO DISPOSAL		23
¶306	Provisions of TCGA 1992, s. 224(3)	23
¶307	'Tainted' acquisitions	23
¶308	'Tainted' expenditure	28
AN INTEREST IN A DWELLING-HOUSE		30
¶309	Joint owners	30
¶310	Leasehold interests	32
¶311	Leasehold 'carve-outs'	32
¶312	Assignment of a life interest	32
¶313	Other types of interest – and the problem of licences	32
¶314	Successive or varying interests	33
PART OF A DWELLING-HOUSE		37
¶315	Definition of 'dwelling-house'	37
¶316	Fundamental considerations	37
¶317	Extensions to the main house, wings, flats, etc.	39
¶318	Unused or seldom used parts of the main house	40
¶319	Separate outbuildings	42
¶320	The CGT case law on subsidiary dwelling-houses	44
¶321	Current state of the law on subsidiary dwellings	54
¶322	Specific problem areas	58
¶323	Servants' houses – practical application of case law principles	63

4 The House and its Surroundings 67

THE SCOPE OF THE EXEMPTION FOR GARDEN AND GROUNDS		67
¶401	Definition of 'permitted area' within s. 222(1)(b)	67
¶402	Land	67
¶403	'Which the individual has'	67
¶404	'For his own occupation ...'	67
¶405	'... and enjoyment'	68
GARDEN OR GROUNDS		68
¶406	The everyday sense of the phrase	68
¶407	Grounds, paddocks and 'wild' land	68
THE PERMITTED AREA		70
¶408	The basic rule – 0.5 hectares	70

		Page
¶409	The extension of the basic rule – permitted areas exceeding 0.5 hectares	72
¶410	Establishing the permitted area in practice	80
¶411	Part disposals of land	87
¶412	Negotiations and contentious cases in practice	90

LAND ACQUIRED BEFORE THE HOUSE OR RETAINED AFTER ITS SALE — 97

¶413	Land acquired before the house	97
¶414	The terms of the ESC	98
¶415	Where the ESC may assist	98
¶416	Land retained and sold after the sale of the house	99
¶417	Crystallising an exempt gain on 'retained' land	101
¶418	Bringing land within the garden	102
¶419	Conclusion	102

5 The Multiple Owner — 104

RESIDENCE AND MAIN RESIDENCES — 104

¶501	The need for a distinction	104
¶502	Lack of definition of 'residence'	104
¶503	Main residence (in the absence of an election under s. 222(5))	105
¶504	Planning	107
¶505	Main residence by Revenue determination	108

MAIN RESIDENCE BY TAXPAYER'S ELECTION UNDER s. 222(5)(a) — 108

¶506	Is an election necessary?	108
¶507	An election is conclusive	109
¶508	In writing	109
¶509	The time limit	109

MARRIED COUPLES AND THE s. 222(5)(a) ELECTION — 112

¶510	Generally	112
¶511	Both spouses had a residence before marriage and continue to use both	113
¶512	Both spouses have more than one jointly owned residence before marriage	113
¶513	Only one spouse owned 'electable' properties before marriage	114
¶514	End of a marriage	115
¶515	An anachronistic rule?	116

		Page
PLANNING WITH THE s. 222(5)(a) ELECTION		117
¶516	Which property to elect?	117
¶517	The danger of delay	117
¶518	Remedial measures if time limit missed	117
¶519	Using the 'last 36 months' exemption and the 'variation' facility	118
¶520	Licences and interests of negligible value	119
¶521	Job-related accommodation	121
¶522	Losses	121

6 The Absentee Owner — 122

'PERIODS OF ABSENCE'		122
¶601	The definition	122
¶602	Practical pitfalls	122

THE THREE TYPES OF 'PERMITTED ABSENCE' IN s. 223(3)		123
¶603	Any three years – s. 223(3)(a)	123
¶604	Absence from the UK due to employment – s. 223(3)(b)	123
¶605	Other work-related absences – s. 223(3)(c)	125
¶606	The 'before and after' rule	128
¶607	Additive conditions	129
¶608	Effect of exceeding the specified periods	130
¶609	Sale of home to a relocation agency	130

JOB-RELATED ACCOMMODATION (JRA)		130
¶610	Background	130
¶611	Effect of relief	132
¶612	Scope for s. 222(5)(a) elections	132
¶613	Lettings irrelevant	133
¶614	Conditions for JRA relief	133
¶615	The self-employed	134
¶616	JRA relief and the permitted absences	135
¶617	Time limits and JRA	136

		Page
THE 'PERIOD OF OWNERSHIP'		136
¶618	The relevant dates	136

7 The Business User — 138

THE HOME AS OFFICE		138
¶701	Authority for restriction of relief by reference to usage	138
¶702	PRR contrasted with income tax 'expenses' rules	138
¶703	Schedule D usage	138
¶704	Schedule E usage	139
¶705	Roll-over relief	139
¶706	Retirement relief	140
¶707	Computational problems	140

THE LANDLORD		145
¶708	Residential lettings and s. 223(4)	145
¶709	The 'rent-a-room' scheme – interaction with PRR	150
¶710	Commercial lettings	151
¶711	Furnished holiday lettings	151

PROBLEMS FOR FARMERS AND LANDOWNERS		
¶712	The farmhouse	153
¶713	Estate management – the manor house	153
¶714	Workers' cottages	153
¶715	Exchanges of land	155

8 Trustees and Personal Representatives

THE EXTENT OF THE s. 225 EXEMPTION		156
¶801	Disposal of settled property	156
¶802	An asset within s. 222(1)	156
¶803	A person entitled to occupy under the terms of the settlement	157
¶804	Residential status of the property	158
¶805	User-related restrictions	160
¶806	Interaction with let property relief	160
¶807	Interaction with CGT legislation about trusts	161

AVOIDING AN INTEREST IN POSSESSION		161
¶808	The problem	161
¶809	Interest in possession	162
¶810	Avoiding the difficulty?	162

	Page
DOES THE s. 225 EXEMPTION HAVE OTHER PLANNING USES?	163
¶811 Use of a gift	163
DEATH	164
¶812 Generally	164
¶813 Occupation by beneficiary of estate	164
¶814 Post-death variations	165

9 Marital Breakdown and the Private Residence Relief
¶901 Generally — 167

SEPARATION PRIOR TO SALE — 167
¶902 Sale after both parties have left — 167
¶903 Inter-spouse transfers — 167
¶904 Concession for inter-spouse transfers — 169

OTHER PLANNING POSSIBILITIES — 170
¶905 Postponed sales and *Mesher* orders — 170
¶906 Deferred charges — 171
¶907 Formal Trusts — 172
¶908 Overview — 172

WHO OWNS THE MATRIMONIAL HOME? — 173
¶909 How the difficulty may arise — 173
¶910 Possible arguments — 173
¶911 Important distinctions – interest in property or proceeds? — 174

10 Miscellaneous Problem Areas — 175

PLANNING FOR LOSSES ON PRIVATE RESIDENCES — 175
¶1001 The problem — 175
¶1002 Allowable losses — 175
¶1003 Some planning opportunities — 175

RE-BASING OF CGT-ELECTIONS UNDER s. 35(5) AND THE PRIVATE RESIDENCE — 178
¶1004 Whether to elect — 178
¶1005 Effect on other assets — 179
¶1006 Time limit — 180

		Page
PROPERTY OVERSEAS		180
¶1007	No territorial limitation to PRR	180
¶1008	Double taxation relief	180
¶1009	Practical difficulties	180
¶1010	Effect of foreign law	181
¶1011	Let property	182
UK RESIDENTIAL PROPERTY OCCUPIED BY FOREIGN EXPATRIATES		182
¶1012	Conflict between CGT and IHT planning	182
¶1013	Ownership by a non-resident trust	182
¶1014	Ownership by a non-UK resident company	182
LIFETIME GIFTS OF THE PRIVATE RESIDENCE		183
¶1015	Business assets	183
¶1016	Gifts to discretionary trusts	185
THE ZIM PROBLEM AND PRIVATE RESIDENCES		185
¶1017	The problem	185
¶1018	The concession	185
¶1019	Implications for PRR	186
¶1020	Shares of profits on sales by relocation agencies	187
OCCUPATION BY A DEPENDENT RELATIVE		187
¶1021	Transitional reliefs still in force	187
¶1022	The conditions	187
¶1023	Interpretational problems	189
¶1024	Withdrawal of relief and the transitional rules	194
¶1025	Combination of s. 226 relief and conventional PRR	196
COMPULSORY PURCHASE AND PRIVATE RESIDENCES		196
¶1026	The general deferral relief	196
¶1027	Restriction where new asset is a dwelling-house	197
¶1028	Traps and problems	198
IMPLICATIONS OF PRR FOR COMPLETION OF TAX RETURNS		200
¶1029	Practical problems	200
¶1030	Suggested entries on returns	200
¶1031	Records	201

	Page
11 Interaction with Other Reliefs and Taxes	202
MORTGAGE INTEREST RELIEF	202
¶1101 The contrasting tests	202
RETIREMENT RELIEF	202
¶1102 Property used partly for trade	202
ROLL-OVER RELIEF	203
¶1103 Business use of a dwelling-house	203
¶1104 Taper relief	204
¶1105 Reverse premiums	206
INHERITANCE TAX (IHT)	206
¶1106 'Carve out' schemes involving the private residence	206
¶1107 Shared occupation schemes	207
¶1108 Stamp duty	207
VALUE ADDED TAX (VAT)	208
¶1109 Impact on dwelling-houses	208
THE COUNCIL TAX AND BUSINESS RATES	209
¶1110 Council tax and the factual main residence	209
¶1111 Property used in part for business	210
Appendix A: Taxation of Chargeble Gains Act 1992, s. 222–226	211
Appendix B: Inland Revenue Extra-Statutory Concessions	217
Appendix C: Inland Revenue Statements of Practice	225
Appendix D: ICAEW Technical Releases	231
Appendix E: Extracts from Inland Revenue Tax Bulletins	233
Case Table	245
Legislation Finding List	248
Index	252

1 Introduction

¶101 Historical background

Capital gains tax (CGT) was introduced by Harold Wilson's Labour Government in the *Finance Act* 1965, and applied to disposals on or after 6 April of that year. The earlier income tax liability on short-term capital gains (in force from 1962 to 1965) was of limited scope and normally had no application to an individual's residence (FA 1962, s. 11(3)). The introduction of a 'true' capital gains tax which, in principle, applied to all forms of property (CGTA 1979, s. 19(1)) made it necessary to enact a number of specific exemptions for a variety of social and political reasons. The private residence was one of the beneficiaries of this process.

Announcing the government's intention to introduce CGT in Parliament on 8 December 1964, the Chancellor of the Exchequer, James Callaghan, said that gains on the 'only or principal residence' would be exempt (*Hansard* Vol. 703, Written Answers col. 166). In his Budget speech the following spring, the Chancellor mentioned this exemption as one of only a few 'limited exceptions' to the tax (*Hansard* Vol. 710, col. 245). In Committee on the Finance Bill 1965, the Financial Secretary to the Treasury, Niall MacDermot, described the exemption as:

> '... a very important and substantial concession .... It is an example ... of the favouring in our tax system which we have, on both sides of the Committee, provided for the owner-occupier .... It is another example of how we have made home ownership a more attractive investment in many ways than other things .... The reasons for our exemption are to encourage home ownership, to avoid any feeling of resentment there might be ... if [the private residence] was subject to tax – and, also from a social point of view, to assist greater mobility, which is an important matter from a labour point of view.' (*Hansard* Vol. 713, col. 996–997.))

¶102 Developments since 1965

There have been few serious attempts since 1965 to suggest that any wholesale removal of 'Private Residence Relief' (called PRR for convenience throughout this text, and not, as is frequently and incorrectly the case, 'Principal Private Residence Relief') is likely or desirable, although its existence may well have distorted the economics of home ownership in the UK in recent years.

¶103 Development of the law

The legislation on PRR (originally in FA 1965, s. 29 and now in TCGA 1992, s. 222–226) has remained largely undisturbed (see ¶201) apart from three significant changes. In 1978 relief was extended to homes owned by employees who were required to live in 'job-related' accommodation (extended to certain self-employed people in 1983). There was a further extension in 1980 to allow relief for the letting of parts of the residence. This latter extension was shown to be rather wider in scope than was once thought to be the case by the Court of Appeal's decision in *Owen v Elliott (HMIT)* [1990] BTC 323 (see ¶708(3)). In 1988 the special relief for residences occupied by dependent relatives was withdrawn for the future (see ¶1021ff.) but significant transitional reliefs were provided, and this legislation still has some relevance for practitioners. Private residences, like other potentially chargeable assets, benefited from the re-basing of CGT to 31 March 1982 which took effect for disposals after 5 April 1988, and from the introduction of taper relief from 6 April 1998.

Three detailed changes were made in the *Finance Act* 1991: the most important was the increase from 24 months to 36 months, in the automatic period of deemed main residence status at the end of the ownership period (see ¶205(1)).

The courts have contributed to the development of the law mainly in the string of cases about servants' houses (examined in detail at ¶315), and the significant extension of the scope of PRR applicable to trustees effected by the High Court in *Sansom (Ridge Settlement Trustees) v Peay (HMIT)* (1976) 52 TC 1 (see ¶801). In one of the most difficult practical areas of PRR – the question of its application to land held with the residence (see ¶408) – the courts remained silent for 36 years until the rather unhelpful decision in *Longson v Baker (HMIT)* [2001] BTC 356 which is discussed in ¶409.

¶104 Scope of this text

Many other problems are encountered in practice, however, and the aim of this text is to examine the legislation and case law in detail with a view to unravelling these as well as the areas mentioned above.

The discussion begins (Chapter 2) with a short exposition of the statute law.

Attention is then turned (Chapter 3) to the fundamental question of what constitutes a dwelling-house, with particular reference to the occasions where a particular property may lack that status, and to the problem of its extent where subsidiary dwellings are concerned. Consideration of the difficult problem of associated land ensues (Chapter 4).

Attention is then focused on the use of the dwelling-house and the difference between residential and main residential status (Chapter 5), as well as the effect of absences from the property (Chapter 6). These are followed by an examination of the effect of business use and lettings (Chapter 7).

The next two sections consider the special problems of trustees and executors (Chapter 8) and of divorcing and separating couples (Chapter 9).

Finally, various specific problems are considered (Chapter 10) and the interaction between PRR and other reliefs and taxes is briefly surveyed (Chapter 11).

Appendices include texts of TGCA 1992, s. 222–226 and of all the relevant extra-statutory concessions, statements of practice, ICAEW Technical Releases and extracts from Revenue's *Tax Bulletin*, which are referred to in the text.

Several flow-charts have been included to provide a schematic guide to some of the more difficult sections of the legislation (see ¶304, ¶308, ¶408, ¶609, ¶1022).

There are references throughout this text to the texts of TCGA 1992, s. 222–226 and of all the relevant Inland Revenue Manual passages, extra-statutory concessions, statements of practice, etc. Extracts from some of these appear in the appendices. References to the Inland Revenue CGT Manual are preceded by 'CGT', and references to the Valuation Office Manual by 'VOM', followed in each case by the paragraph number(s) in those Manuals.

Throughout the text, examples are given wherever they are considered to be helpful, but where a conclusion may differ from the apparent view of the Inland Revenue this is clearly stated. In numerical examples the statutory indexation allowance has been ignored for the sake of simplicity, although its effect in practice is, of course, often highly significant especially where a property has been held since before 1 April 1982. Indexation stopped at 31 March 1998 and was replaced by taper relief: in the numerical examples, for simplicity, this relief is also ignored (except in the specific discussion in Chapter 11) and gains are stated before that relief.

Standard abbreviations have been used throughout and a list appears at pp. ix–x. A case table appears at p. 245. All statutory references are to TCGA 1992 unless otherwise stated.

¶105   A cautionary note

The writer has not attempted to do more than indicate his understanding of the legislation and to offer possible interpretations and planning hints where practicable. There is, of course, no substitute for detailed professional advice in each case in the light of its own particular facts. If that maxim is true of taxation advice generally, it is perhaps never more true than of advice concerning what, for many clients, is their most valuable single asset.

2 The Legislation in Summary

There follows a straightforward exposition of the legislation governing PRR which is intended to do no more than to make the subsequent discussion intelligible. Cross-references are given to the commentary in the following chapters, and defined terms in the legislation are given in italics.

¶201 Background and mechanism for relief

Fortunately, the PRR legislation has suffered less than most areas of CGT from the effects of frequent revision and, following the 1992 consolidation, is now conveniently self-contained in TCGA 1992, s. 222–226. The provisions of s. 226, which dealt with property occupied as the sole residence of a dependent relative, were repealed as regards the future by FA 1988, s. 111 (a discussion of these rules appears at ¶1021ff.).

For convenience, throughout this text reference is made to the 'claiming' of PRR and to the person entitled to the relief as the 'claimant'. However, the legislation (with the exception of the rule about dependent relatives) does not in fact speak of 'claims', and prescribes no time limit. The tax compliance implications are discussed at ¶1031.

¶202 The principal relieving provision

The legislation affords relief from CCT by providing that a gain shall not be a chargeable gain:

(1) if it is a gain to which TCGA 1992, s. 222 applies; *and*

(2) broadly, to the extent that the dwelling-house or part thereof has been the individual's *only or main residence* (OMR) during his *period of ownership* (s. 223(1)).

This immediately highlights the point that the relief is, in principle, a relief for individuals only, but there are special rules for disposals by trustees and personal representatives (see ¶209 and Chapter 8).

It will follow that wherever a gain would be exempt under this rule, a loss will not be allowable (s. 16(2)).

From 6 April 1998, where part of a gain remains taxable after PRR because

¶201

relief is not fully due, taper relief is given as the final step in the calculation (s. 2A, and see ¶1104).

It is then necessary to move to s. 222 to consider the disposals to which the relief applies. Having delineated the scope of the relief, the remaining subsections of s. 223, analysed in Chapter 6, deal with situations where it may not extend to the whole of the gain.

¶203 The scope of the relief

(1) Principal qualifying gains
The principal gains within the scope of PRR are gains which:

(a) accrue to an individual (though see Chapter 8 as to relief for trustees and personal representatives); *and*

(b) are attributable to the disposal of, or of an interest in, an asset within (2) below (TCGA 1992, s. 222(1)).

A gain is only within the scope of the relief 'so far as' it is attributable to a disposal within (b). This raises some interesting possibilities in marital breakdown situations which are discussed at Chapter 10.

(2) Principal qualifying assets
The assets which qualify for PRR are:

(a) a dwelling-house or part of a dwelling-house, providing that it is, or has at any time in the disponer's *period of ownership*, been his *only or main residence* (s. 222(2)(a)); or

(b) land which the individual has for his own occupation and enjoyment with that residence as its garden or grounds up to the permitted area (s. 222(2)(b)).

Pausing there, this subsection contains several major problems of interpretation which are discussed in depth in Chapter 3 and 4. In particular, there is no definition of a 'dwelling-house' or 'part' of such a house. The concept of an 'only or main residence' is also capable of artificial deeming (see ¶506).

Nevertheless, it is already possible to see the scope of PRR: it is to extend to the house itself (s. 222(2)(a)) and to its surroundings, to a limited extent (s. 222(2)(b)). The scope of the latter, relating to the surroundings, is discussed in Chapter 4.

(3) The permitted area
In order to limit the scope of PRR on the surroundings of the house, the rules introduce the concept of the *permitted area*. This is, in principle, an area of 0.5 hectares inclusive of the site of the house (s. 222(2)), but in any particular case, the

appeal commissioners may determine a larger area as the permitted area, if they are satisfied that, regard being had to the size and character of the house, that larger area is required for its reasonable enjoyment as a residence (s. 222(3)). For disposals prior to 19 March 1991 the basic 'permitted area' was one acre (FA 1991, s. 93).

Where only part of the land occupied with a residence is within the ambit of s. 222(1), the part which is to enjoy the benefit of that subsection is to be the part which, if the remainder were separately occupied, would be the most suitable for occupation and enjoyment with the residence (s. 222(4)).

(4) Only or main residence

There is, in principle, no definition of an OMR for PRR purposes, but if, for any period, the claimant has more than one residence as a question of fact (as to which see ¶501), he is allowed to 'determine the question' which of them is his OMR, and therefore within the scope of PRR, by giving written notice to the inspector within two years of the end of that period (or, if later, by 5 April 1967). He then has the right to give a further such notice, varying the first, with the variation having effect for any period beginning not earlier than, two years before the giving of the further notice (s. 222(5)(a)).

Until 5 April 1996, any issue as to which of several residences was the OMR, which was not concluded by a claimant's notice as just described, had to be concluded by the determination of the inspector (old s. 222(5)(b)), against which the claimant could appeal to the general or special commissioners. When self-assessment was introduced from 1996/97, responsibility for making this determination passed, in effect, to the taxpayer, subject to the Revenue's power of enquiry into his return – see the commentary at the end of Chapter 10.

A married couple living together (see the definition at ¶514(6)) as such can have only one OMR between them, either in fact or by election as just described, and a s. 222(5) election must be given by both spouses if it affects both of them (s. 222(6)(a)).

The problem of when an election under s. 222(5)(a) is available is discussed generally at ¶506, and in relation to married couples at ¶510. Planning possibilities with the election are discussed at ¶518.

(5) Job-related accommodation

One of the few important modifications of the PRR provisions since their inception was the extension of the relief in 1978 to 'job-related' accommodation, in order to cater for those who are required to live in 'tied' property during their working lives and purchase property (called in what follows 'secondary' property) for use during holidays or after retirement. The extension applies to the *period of ownership* of a dwelling-house during which the claimant resides elsewhere in accommodation which is for him 'job-related'. Provided that he intends in due course to occupy the

¶203

'secondary' property as his OMR, residential occupation is imputed, for all PRR purposes, to the period during which the claimant actually resides in the 'job-related' property. It is to be noted that this still leaves open the possibility of a s. 222(5)(a) election since the imputation is only of *residential* occupation, not occupation as an OMR. The effect of the extension is thus to open up the possibility of a PRR claim for such a 'secondary' home even though it may have none of the attributes of a residence while the claimant is actually residing elsewhere for work reasons (s. 222(8)).

The definition of 'job-related' accommodation is imported from the income tax legislation applicable for mortgage interest relief purposes (see ICTA 1988, s. 356) (s. 222(8)). All the categories of such accommodation which qualify for interest relief may, in principle, lead to the claimant's 'secondary' home qualifying for PRR. However, where the 'tied' accommodation is occupied by reason of an obligation entered into by someone carrying on a Sch. D, Case I or II activity on rented premises – a tenant publican is the most obvious example – the PRR extension only confers residential occupation status on the 'secondary' home from 6 April 1983 (s. 222(9)).

Some problems of interpretation in this regard are discussed at ¶610.

¶204 The period of ownership

Section 223(1) of TCGA 1992 effectively exempts from CGT a gain which falls within s. 222 (see ¶203) and the exemption is total if the property has been the OMR (either in fact or by election) throughout the *period of ownership*. It is therefore necessary to define this concept and the legislation does this both by reference to the legal interest which has subsisted and the period of time which the relief covers.

(1) Temporal limitation

When the original PRR provisions were introduced in FA 1965 they took as their 'base line' for the period of ownership 6 April 1965 (see FA 1965, s. 29(13)(b)). This was appropriate because gains attributable to periods before that date were excluded from the CGT computation, either by time apportionment or by an election under FA 1965, Sch. 6, para. 25: equally, occupation before that date could confer no relief even if ownership had continued afterwards.

On the general re-basing of the tax introduced by FA 1988, the 'base line' was accordingly moved forward to 31 March 1982 for disposals on or after 5 April 1988 (s. 223(7)). However, exemption for factual residence which ceased before 1 April 1982 may be preserved, as discussed at ¶618.

(2) Different interests at different times

Since it is possible for PRR to be due on a disposal of a lesser interest than a freehold interest, a rule is provided for measurement of the period of ownership where the claimant has had different interests at different times. In such a case the period of ownership is taken to begin when the first acquisition occurred on which there was allowable expenditure for CGT purposes in calculating the gain on the disposal to which PRR applies (s. 222(7)).

The difficulties which can arise with such cases are discussed at ¶309.

(3) Husband and wife – successive interests

A rule is also provided to deal with the case where one spouse passes his or her interest to the other, whether in lifetime or on death and (apparently) whether by sale or gift. The claimant spouse can, in this case, benefit from the period of ownership of the original owner spouse (s. 222(7)(a)) and any OMR status of the property for the original owner is imputed to the claimant in such a case (s. 222(7)(b)).

For a discussion of possible difficulties here, see ¶314(3).

¶205 How much relief is available?

A gain may be wholly exempt if OMR status covers the entire *period of ownership* (see ¶204).

Rules are also provided in TCGA 1992, s. 223 to deal with cases where OMR status does not cover the entire period of ownership.

(1) OMR status only lacking during the last three years of ownership

To cater for the common case where the vendor of a property cannot dispose of it before acquiring a new home, total exemption, if otherwise available, is not lost in relation to disposals after 18 March 1991, when OMR status is only lacking for all or part of the last 36 months of ownership (s. 223(1), final phrase). This 'grace' period was only 12 months for disposals before 6 April 1980 (FA 1980, s. 80(2)), and 24 months for disposals between 6 April 1980 and 18 March 1991 (FA 1991, s. 94(1)). There is a power to amend this final period by statutory instrument (s. 223(5)). This power cannot, according to ministerial assurances given during the 1991 Finance Bill Committee Stage, be used retrospectively, and it has also been stated that reasonable notice of any future change would be given (see *Hansard*, Standing Committee B, 13 June 1991, col. 312–313).

For the implications of re-basing in this area, see ¶618.

(2) Longer absences

There are also rules which allow limited relief for longer *periods of absence*. The basic rule, in s. 223(2), exempts a fraction of the gain which can conveniently be expressed by:

$$\frac{A+B}{C}$$

(where A is the aggregate of the periods within the period of ownership during which OMR status existed in fact or by election: B is the last 36 months of ownership in so far as it is not included in A: *and* C is the length of the period of ownership).

(3) Additional periods of deemed OMR status

In determining the amount of relief available, whether for the whole of the gain (see ¶205 and (1) above) or in accordance with the prescribed formula (see (2) above), certain *periods of absence* may be regarded as periods of OMR status, provided that both before and after the period there was a time when the property was the claimant's OMR (s. 223(3), final words). These periods may be additive, as is clear from the words 'and in addition' which link subparagraphs (a), (b) and (c) of s. 223(3). Thus a claimant could, if he satisfied the relevant conditions, benefit from all of them in respect of a single disposal. The requirement for there to be a subsequent period when the property was the claimant's OMR can strictly only be satisfied if the claimant reoccupies the property – the extension of relief where OMR is lacking in the last three years of ownership (see (1) above) does not provide deemed OMR status. However, see ¶606(3) for circumstances where a concession may assist.

The permissible periods are:

(a) any period not exceeding three years, whether continuous or not (s. 223(3)(a)) – no particular reason for the absence is necessary;

(b) any period throughout which the claimant worked in an employment or office, all the duties of which were performed outside the UK (s. 223(3)(b)) – this period can be of unlimited duration;

(c) any period not exceeding four years (continuous or otherwise) throughout which the claimant was prevented from residing in the property in consequence of:

    (i) the situation of his place of work, *or*

    (ii) any condition imposed by his employer requiring him to work elsewhere, being a condition reasonably imposed to secure the effective performance by the employee of his duties. (s. 223(3)(c)).

(4) Period of absence

This is a defined term for the purpose of the rule just set out. It means a period:

(a) during which the property was not the claimant's OMR; and

(b) throughout which he had no residence or main residence eligible for PRR (s. 223(3), final words).

The problems of 'absentee' owners in taking advantage of these additional reliefs are considered in Chapter 6.

¶206 Partial business or investment use

(1) Business use
Where part of a property for which PRR is claimed is used exclusively for the purpose of a trade, profession or vocation, TCGA 1992, s. 224(1) requires an apportionment of the gain, and PRR applies only to the gain apportioned to the part which is not so used.

Problems in this area are discussed at ¶701.

(2) Use for residential letting
Without special provision, where a dwelling-house was let to residential tenants for part of the period of ownership PRR would be restricted through loss of OMR status for that period, subject to any extended relief available under s. 223 for deemed OMR status or for the final 36 months (see ¶205). Such, indeed, was the position for disposals before 6 April 1980.

However, for later disposals, a significant extension was introduced by FA 1980, s. 80(1) and now found in s. 223(4).

This extended relief applies where there is a gain to which s. 222 applies but the property has been wholly or partly let, at any time in the period of ownership (see ¶618), by the claimant as residential accommodation. The letting may have occurred or begun before 6 April 1980.

The chargeable gain which would otherwise accrue is calculated (as to the method, see ¶708(4)). It is then compared with:

(a) the gain which is covered by PRR; *and*

(b) £40,000 (or £20,000 for disposals between 6 April 1983 and 18 March 1991, and £10,000 for disposals before 6 April 1983) and only the excess, if any, over the lower of these amounts is taxable. In many current disposals inflation of values means that, in effect, the first £40,000 of such 'investment' gains is tax-free.

For a discussion of the implications and difficulties of this provision, see ¶708.

¶207 Changes of status

(1) Change of occupation
The legislation contemplates the situation where during the period of ownership

there is a change in what is occupied as the claimant's residence. Here, TCGA 1992, s. 224(2) requires the appeal commissioners to adjust the PRR due in any manner they consider just and reasonable. The draftsman has given one example of such a situation – the reconstruction or conversion of a building but this is expressly stated not to be exhaustive of the application of the subsection.

(2) Change of use
A similar power to that in ¶207(1) is conferred on commissioners where there have been changes in the use of part of the property, whether for a business (see ¶206) or for any other reason (s. 224(2)).

Changes of the types mentioned above are discussed at ¶707 below.

¶208 Acquisition or expenditure for the purpose of disposal
Two significant restrictions on PRR are contained in TCGA 1992, s. 224(3).

(1) 'Tainted' acquisitions
Private residence relief is not to apply at all to a gain if the acquisition in question was made wholly or partly for the purpose of realising a gain from the disposal of the property or part thereof, or the interest concerned.

(2) 'Tainted' expenditure
Section 224(3) has a second limb which denies PRR to a gain in so far as it is attributable to expenditure incurred after the beginning of the period of ownership and wholly or partly for the purpose of realising a gain on the disposal.

These very important restrictions are discussed in detail at ¶306.

¶209 Occupation under the terms of a settlement
Generally, PRR is only available to an individual by reference to his own occupation of a dwelling-house. However, TCGA 1992, s. 225 extends the relief to a trustee in respect of property which would qualify under the rules in s. 222, and which was the OMR of a person entitled to occupy it under the terms of a settlement, throughout the period of ownership of the trustees.

This special relief is assimilated to the rules in s. 222–224 by taking references to the individual as references to the trustee except where occupation is in issue; and if a s. 222(5) election is made to determine which of a number of residences is the OMR, it is to be made jointly by the trustees and the occupier.

For a discussion of the operation of this extension to PRR, see Chapter 8.

¶210 Inland Revenue Manuals
The Inland Revenue has for some years published its internal Manuals (with some omissions). These are often extremely helpful to practitioners, although it needs to

be remembered that they represent only the Department's view of the law. The Revenue's CGT Manual contains a very full treatment of PRR (CGT 64200-65681). The Valuation Office's manuals also contain useful information and guidance on the views which district valuers are likely to adopt. Both texts will be referred to frequently in the following commentary, with more detailed mention of those passages where the author disagrees with the official view. (References to 'CGT' and 'VOM', followed by a number, indicate paragraph numbers in the CGT and Valuation Office Manuals respectively).

3 The House Itself

WHAT IS A DWELLING-HOUSE?

¶301 Introduction
Since PRR is only available, in relation to a dwelling-house, where a gain accrues on the disposal of such a house which is the residence of the individual concerned (TCGA 1992, s. 222(1)(a)), it is first necessary to ask what is covered by the expression 'dwelling-house'.

¶302 The concept in general law
The search must start in general law since the draftsman has supplied no definition for CGT purposes. In everyday speech a dwelling-house is simply a place where somebody 'dwells, makes his abode or lives', according to the *Concise Oxford Dictionary*; the derivation of 'dwell' and cognate words indicates an apparent root meaning conveying *resting* in a particular position or place, which was the significance of the Old English word 'dwellan', and was not originally confined to contexts involving houses. Some traces of this wider meaning still survive in the metaphorical expression 'to dwell on a subject', meaning to linger over it. Some connotation of stability and some degree of permanence therefore seem inseparable from the word.

It is important to note that TCGA 1992, s. 222(1)(a) speaks of a dwelling-house which is a residence. The significance of 'residence' will be discussed at ¶501, where it will be stressed that the mere fact that a man owns a dwelling-house does not itself make that house his residence. One reason for the reference to a 'dwelling-*house*' in s. 222(1)(a) is to distinguish the physical premises which attract the relief from those which do not, such as commercial buildings and offices. However, it is also likely that the reference to a 'dwelling-house', and not merely to a 'dwelling', is deliberate, and that it serves to emphasise the importance of permanence; thus:

> 'It may ... be said that, generally, a "house" is a structure of a permanent character ... structurally severed from other tenements (and usually, but not necessarily, under its own separate roof) that is used, or may be used, for the

habitation of man, and of which the holding (as distinct from lodgings) is independent' (see *Stroud's Judicial Dictionary* Vol. 2, p. 1187(8)).

This concept may be further elucidated by cases in general law where a distinction was necessary between a dwelling-house and other types of accommodation.

Thus, for example, (1) a house where people live or which is physically capable of being used for human habitation was held to be a dwelling-house for the purposes of rating, even though it was actually used for a business (*Lewin v End* [1906] AC 299); but (2) not every property where people may eat or sleep is thereby a dwelling-house, since eating and sleeping may take place in all kinds of places if necessity arises (*Macmillan & Co Ltd v Rees* [1946] 1 All ER 675, a case under the Rent Restriction Acts which arose out of the use of an office for sleeping accommodation during wartime conditions in London); (3) the courts have been flexible when confronted by changing fashions in housing, as was shown by several early cases where flats, furnished rooms, and tenements were held to be dwelling-houses (e.g. *Re Hecquard* (1889) 24 QBD 71, which concerned furnished rooms, and *London County Council v Rowton House Co* (1897) 77 LT 693, which concerned common lodging houses).

As to the last-mentioned point, there is even older authority for a liberal interpretation of what constitutes a dwelling-house – the seventeenth century jurist Lord Coke wrote: 'A chamber or room, be it upper or lower, wherein any person doth inhabit or dwell, is *domus mansionalis* [i.e. a dwelling-house] in law' (3 Inst. 64–5). Thus no difficulty is likely to be experienced in regarding a flat or even a single bed sitting room as a dwelling-house for PRR purposes if that is its true function. Disposals of such small 'dwellings' may, in principle, be exempt, even though they may not involve the sale of any accompanying land; s. 222 (1)(a) and (b) are alternative heads of relief, joined by 'or', not 'and'.

¶303 Tax case law and dwelling-houses generally

Most of the non-CGT case law on the definition of dwelling-houses arose under the former inhabited house duty, which was in force in various forms, with interruptions of a few years, from 1778 to 1924. In a context which imposed tax liability rather than afforded tax relief, a narrow construction was to be expected (on the principle explained by Lord Thankerton in *IR Commrs v Ross and Coulter & Ors* [1948] 1 All ER 616 whereby the courts will prefer the meaning more favourable to the subject where a taxing Act is capable of two alternative meanings).

The inhabited house duty cases were further complicated by the need to decide where, in multi-occupied buildings such as tenement blocks, the boundaries between one taxpayer's dwelling and another's lay. The latter point is rarely material for PRR so long as it is clear from the facts that the taxpayer in question is entitled to occupy only part of such a property, since only that part can be his residence. The main relevance of the inhabited house duty cases for present purposes is the emphasis laid on the double-barrelled concept of 'dwelling-house': both a 'house' *simpliciter*, as distinct from a factory, shop, office, etc., and a 'dwelling' with its connotation of a place for eating, sleeping and all the ordinary incidents of life.

In *Riley v Read* (1879) 1 TC 219, Sir Fitzroy Kelly, the Lord Chief Baron said: 'In my judgment the meaning of the words "to dwell" is really to live in a house; that is, to live there day and night; to sleep there during the night, and to occupy it for the purposes of life during the day.' Thus a 'doss house' was not an inhabited dwelling-house merely because it contained beds where indigent travellers spent the night, being compelled to move on in the morning (a situation which will be recognised by those who have read George Orwell's *Down and Out in Paris and London*) since 'dwelling' required more than mere shelter for the night (*London County Council v Cook* (1905) 5 TC 173). This reinforces the point that, in speaking of a dwelling-house, one is referring to a place capable of being used as somewhere to live in the widest sense, and not a place designed and equipped merely for sleeping, or merely for eating, or merely for entertainment and relaxation.

¶304　CGT case law on dwelling-houses

In the context of a relieving provision in a taxing Act it must be expected that the courts will take a broad view of what constitutes a dwelling-house, and this has, indeed, been the approach adopted in the two PRR cases which have arisen on the point. Both involved unconventional 'dwellings' (see ¶303), and the point at issue was whether they could be regarded as 'houses'; it is arguable that neither would have arisen had the draftsman written merely 'dwelling' instead of 'dwelling-*house*'.

In neither of these cases did the court experience much difficulty. *Makins v Elson (HMIT)* (1976) 51 TC 437 concerned a mobile caravan (mobile at least in its original design) located on a plot of land which the taxpayer had recently purchased with the benefit of outline planning permission for the construction of a dwelling-house. What were described as 'essential services' – water, electricity and a telephone – were 'installed'; the inference being that these were actually connected to the caravan. However, apart from levelling the site, no further building work seems to have been done. The owner lived in the caravan from August 1970 to May 1973 and then sold the plot with planning permission, together with the caravan. During this time he had no other residence.

The Crown contended that although the caravan was his main residence, PRR was not due since it was a chattel, not fixed to the land and legally a separate asset from the land. The taxpayer, who appeared in person in the High Court, was allowed to add further facts to those found by the commissioners (who had rejected his claim on the grounds that a house in the course of erection could not be considered to be a dwelling-house and that the temporary occupation of the caravan was irrelevant); these were that a telephone line had been connected to the caravan in 1972, and that the caravan had been jacked up on some kind of support. Foster J quoted with approval some words of Lord Denning MR in a rating case involving caravans (*Field Place Caravan Park Ltd v Harding* [1966] 3 All ER 247) to the effect that residential caravans and their pitches were so similar to small bungalows that they should be rated in the same way.

In very few words, the judge went on to dismiss the Crown's contention on the grounds that having regard to the connected services and the fact that its wheels were not on the ground, the caravan was a dwelling-house. He did not address the 'chattel' point but it may be inferred that he regarded a chattel as capable of being a dwelling-house if it was so used.

In *Moore v Thompson (HMIT)* [1986] BTC 172, the facts were much more complicated and were still being hotly disputed even in the High Court. Essentially the position was similar to that in *Makins*, but the central point was the commissioners' finding that the caravan in question was never a dwelling-house capable of being regarded as the main residence of the taxpayer despite an election to that effect under s. 222(5)(a) (*Moore v Thompson* at p. 176). Millett J found that the commissioners were entitled to come to that conclusion, with the result that PRR was not due (p. 178). The judge, however, went on to consider (p. 179) whether, even if the commissioners had found that the caravan had been a dwelling-house, it could have been the taxpayer's main residence, and held on the facts that it could not have been so regarded.

It appears that in contrast to *Makins*, the caravan, though also parked on land owned by the taxpayer, remained on its road wheels and that main services were never connected to it, although it had limited planning consent for residential use and some kind of lavatory. Before Millett J the taxpayer contended that the caravan had, in fact, been jacked up on breeze blocks, and that its axle was broken so that it could not have been moved. However, the judge, while holding that the Commissioners had been entitled to come to the conclusion reached in respect of the caravan, added that it was clear that a caravan could be a dwelling-house: whether it was depended on a consideration of all the relevant facts (p. 178).

Thus, where the asset disposed of is capable of use as a dwelling – a completed and fully habitable house or flat, or, following the 'caravan' cases, less conventional structures – no doubt should arise that it is a dwelling-house. The problem in *Moore v Thompson*, from the taxpayer's viewpoint, appears to have been that the caravan never, on the facts, acquired the necessary degree of permanence which seems to be inseparable from the notion of a dwelling-house (see ¶302). The significance of the two caravan cases lay chiefly in the question of whether their sites qualified for PRR. It is, of course, chiefly in the site of such a

¶304

'dwelling-house' that any significant financial value will normally lie rather than in the caravan itself, though the disposal of the latter raises problems of its own which are discussed below (¶305(6)). The reason for ascertaining whether the caravans could be said to be dwelling-houses and if so, whether they were the only or main residences of the taxpayers in question, was that only thus could PRR possibly be due on the land on which they stood.

The next section considers other areas where difficulties might still be encountered.

A flow chart is attached to this Chapter (on p. 18) which may be useful in deciding what constitutes a dwelling house for PRR purposes.

¶305 Areas of practical difficulty

(1) Unconventional accommodation
The 'caravan' cases (see ¶304) indicate that the concept of a dwelling-house is not confined to bricks and mortar, and that design and construction are immaterial in themselves. Caravans and chalets may thus qualify, so long as they are stationary and actually support the full range of activities encapsulated in the notion of a dwelling (see ¶303). It is thus possible that some unmodified touring caravans, lacking eating, cooking or sanitary facilities, might not qualify, and the same might apply to small structures such as beach houses or huts. It is also clear that the previous history of a building is irrelevant here and that what matters is its status in the hands of the taxpayer in question; dwelling-houses converted from structures which were previously warehouses, barns, windmills, churches or lighthouses, for example, are no less dwelling-houses for PRR purposes.

In the case of caravans the prospects of success will be enhanced if the caravan has been immobilised, e.g. by removing the road wheels, towing attachments and brake lights, and if the setting has been made more permanent by providing a hard standing for the vehicle and (as in *Makins v Elson (HMIT)* (1976) 51 TC 437) connecting essential mains services. The absence of such features (as in *Moore v Thompson (HMIT)* [1986] BTC 172) is likely to make it very difficult for the taxpayer to persuade the inspector or the commissioners that his home can sensibly be described as a 'dwelling-house'.

(2) Unfinished houses
A house which is not structurally complete may still be capable of occupation as a dwelling (although in some cases this may be unlawful under planning legislation); a man who has bought a building plot and is building himself a house may be prepared to move in much earlier than would a purchaser buying from a builder, especially if he has no other home to sell and few family ties. He might, for example, move in (at any rate in the summer) before central heating had been

Capital Gains Tax and the Private Residence

WHAT IS A DWELLING-HOUSE?

At the date of the disposal in question:[1]

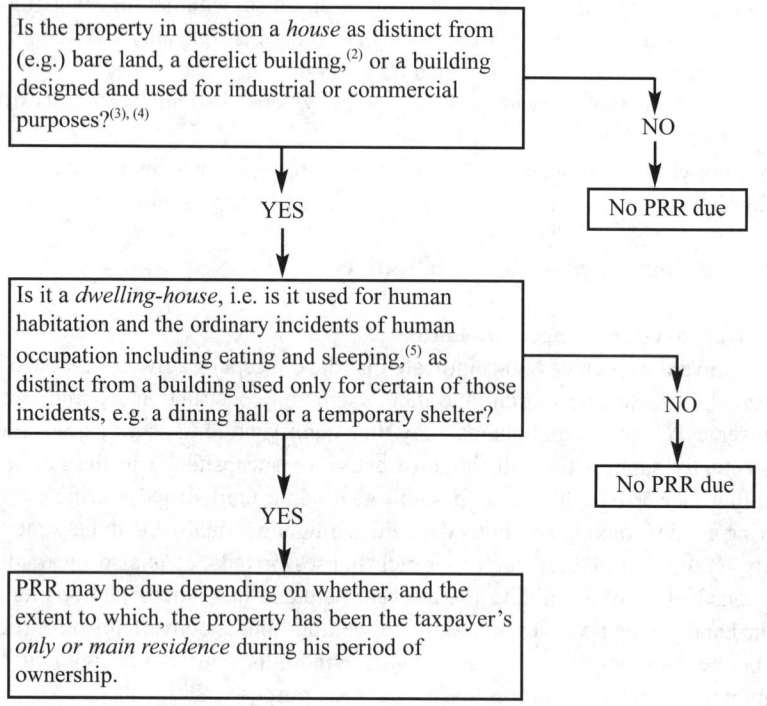

NOTES

(1) Earlier status and use as a dwelling-house during the taxpayer's ownership may afford partial relief even if used for some other purpose at the date of disposal (s. 224(2)).
(2) But see *Re 1–4 White Row Cottages, Bewerley* (1991) Ch 441 for a case where cottages abandoned for some 20 years were held to remain dwelling-houses for Commons Registration purposes.
(3) Or a distinct part of a house, such as a flat or apartment (*Re Hequard* (1889) 24 QBD 71).
(4) A caravan could be a 'house' for the purposes of CGT private residence relief (PRR) in certain circumstances, depending on the degree to which it has been adapted for permanent occupation and probably the extent to which it has been immobilised and has mains services (*Makins v Elson* (1971) 51 TC 437 and contrast *Moore v Thompson (HMIT)* [1986] BTC 172). Query whether a houseboat could also be so regarded, mutatis mutandis?
(5) See, e.g. *Riley v Read* (1879) 1 TC 219 (a temporary 'doss house' held not to be a dwelling-house for Inhabited House Duty).

installed, before the kitchen had been fitted out or before garages and outbuildings had been completed. Such a property would be, for him, a dwelling-house in fact regardless of any lack of comfort. However, in such cases it will be very important to document the occupation by memoranda or photographs and letters notifying a change of address to the usual third parties (including the inspector!).

This kind of case does not usually excite Revenue interest unless the house is sold while still uncompleted, perhaps because the owner has run out of funds to finish it; if he eventually occupies the completed house in the normal way the inspector is unlikely to query the initial period of occupancy. See, however, ¶414 and ¶415 regarding the period between the acquisition of the site and completion of the house.

(3) Destroyed, abandoned or derelict houses

Section 222(1)(a) of TCGA 1992, speaks of the 'disposal of a dwelling-house', implying that for PRR to be due, the asset in question must be a dwelling-house at the point of disposal. To take the most extreme case, if, prior to disposal, the house is razed completely to the ground, so that what is disposed of is the bare site, no PRR at all would seem to be due.

However, in such a case it would be open to the owner to make a claim under s. 24(1) and (3) to regard the 'entire loss, destruction, dissipation or extinction' of the building as a *disposal* in its own right. By such a claim (to be made within six years of the destruction) he would be deemed to have disposed of the dwelling-house and could crystallise whatever PRR was due to him. Although he would also be deemed immediately to reacquire the site at market value, and could thus face tax on any future gain made on it, this would clearly be preferable to losing PRR altogether.

Accidental destruction of, or damage to, the house will normally give rise to recoveries under an insurance policy. In principle this will be a disposal for CGT purposes by s. 22(1)(b), subject to the possibility of making a claim under s. 23(1) where the proceeds are applied to restoration, either wholly or excepting only a 'small' part (in practice not more than five per cent of the total capital sum). The effect of this claim is that there is no disposal on the receipt of the policy moneys, and instead they are deducted from base cost on a subsequent disposal. These provisions will only have any practical effect, of course, where PRR is not due, or not wholly due, e.g. if the property is a second home or there have been absences beyond the 'permitted' periods (see ¶601ff.).

The position where a dwelling-house is abandoned and becomes derelict is a question of fact. It was held in *Re 1–4 White Row Cottages, Bewerley* [1991] Ch 441 that four houses which had been abandoned for some 20 years, and were no longer fit for human habitation, nevertheless remained dwelling-houses for the purposes of the *Common Land (Rectification of Registers) Act* 1989. In that case the court had to consider whether the properties in question had been dwelling-houses at all times since 5 August 1945. They had been occupied from that date to 1968 in two cases and 1971 and 1972 in the other cases. Mummery J held that after vacation they did not cease to exist, nor were they converted to other uses such as shops, warehouses or offices. In the ordinary everyday sense of the word, which he held to be the right sense in the relevant Act (there being no statutory definition), the judge found that they did not cease to be dwelling-houses simply because they were not inhabited.

It seems that where such an issue arose in a PRR case a similar view could be sustained. There would necessarily have been occupation as the taxpayer's only or main residence at some point in the period of ownership in order to found a claim in the first place, and in the absence of other uses since vacation of the property, the fact that a house had become, as in the *Bewerley* case, 'empty and neglected and ... tumbledown' ([1991] Ch at p. 446G) would not appear to deprive it of its character as a dwelling-house when disposed of.

(4) Change of use of the property

A possible trap may be involved if there is a positive conversion of the *entire* property to non-domestic use before sale. Although there are provisions, in s. 224(2), to cater for changes in what is occupied as the residence of the owner during his period of ownership (see ¶707(3)) these appear to rest on the premise that the disposal is still capable of coming within s. 222(1) as the disposal of a dwelling-house. On a strict interpretation the total cessation of domestic use followed by conversion to a non-domestic purpose will forfeit any PRR, even for the last three years of ownership.

> **Example 1**
>
> Peter is a general medical practitioner who bought a small town house in 1996. He lived on the upper floor while using the ground floor as a surgery and dispensary until 2000. In 2000 he took in a partner, Adrian, who lives elsewhere, but uses one of the upstairs rooms to see patients; the house remains Peter's property. In 2000 Peter married Angela, who had a larger house of her own on the outskirts of town. As Angela does not wish to leave that house and his practice is expanding, Peter decides to move into Angela's house and the upstairs rooms of the town house are converted into further surgery and waiting room space. After conversion the town house is no longer suitable for domestic use since it no longer has any kitchen or bathroom facilities, and its front garden has been turned into a car park for patients.
>
> When the town house is sold it seems likely that it will no longer be a dwelling-house at all but a commercial property. On a strict analysis it is thought that Peter will be ineligible for any PRR even for the period from 1996 to 2000 when it was undoubtedly his home. In practice he may find that the inspector allows

¶305

partial relief under s. 224(2) but it might have been preferable to retain, say, one room as a flat for occasional use so that at least part of the property remains a dwelling-house until disposal.

It is sometimes argued that s. 224(2) can support an alternative calculation of the chargeable gain in a case where the whole of a property is unoccupied for a period during which it is renovated or otherwise altered, followed by normal residential occupation until sale. As has already been seen (¶205(2)), s. 223(2) prescribes 'straight-line' apportionment of the overall gain in such cases between periods of absence and actual occupancy (¶205(3)). This may lead to what is sometimes regarded as an unreasonable result.

Example 2
Alice bought a semi-derelict house for £50,000 in 1998. She owned her only residence elsewhere. From 1998 to 2001 the house was refurbished and made habitable at a cost of £60,000. In 2001 Alice sells her other house and moves into the refurbished property. She occupies it as her only residence until she sells it in 2005 for £300,000. In 2001 a reputable surveyor values the house, after completion of the refurbishment, at £150,000.

The 'straight-line' method prescribed by s. 223(2) would produce a taxable gain (ignoring indexation) of 3/7 × (300,000 – (50,000 + £60,000)), i.e. £81,428 – since Alice occupied the house for four out of the seven years of ownership. It would be tempting to argue, however, that s. 224(2) could be invoked, on the grounds that there had been 'a change in what is occupied' as Alice's residence 'whether on account of a reconstruction or conversion of a building or for any other reason', and thus that 'the relief given by section 223' should be adjusted 'in such manner as the commissioners concerned may consider to be just and reasonable'. On that basis, Alice might argue that the computation should be based on the valuation in 2001, producing a taxable gain of (£150,000 – (£50,000 + £60,000)), i.e. £40,000 with the balance being exempt.

The Revenue rejects this interpretation of s. 224(2), and maintains that this subsection can only apply where there is a 'change' in the degree of positive occupation of the same property – as illustrated in Example 1 above. (See CGT 64771.) On this view, s. 224(2) cannot provide an escape route from straight-line apportionment over time, as prescribed in s. 223(2), in cases such as Alice's where a property has been wholly unoccupied as a residence. An alternative calculation on the above lines might, however, be possible where there is a variation, over time, in the degrees of residential occupation and business use – see the Example at ¶707(4) – and where s. 224(3), regarding 'tainted' expenditure, applies (see ¶308).

¶305

(5) Houseboats

The 'caravan' cases seem capable of supporting a claim to PRR on a houseboat if the general tests for dwelling-house status set out at ¶302–¶304 are met. It does, however, seem to be essential that the houseboat should have been adapted so as make it suitable for use as a permanent home.

As with caravans, a claim will be easier to mount if the boat is immobilised, e.g. by removing its engines and steering gear, and if main services are laid on. However, it is interesting to speculate whether a PRR claim could have been made for the yacht in the old income tax case of *Bayard Brown v Burt* (1911) 5 TC 667, where the issue was whether the taxpayer was resident in the UK. He had, at the time of the case, lived on a yacht moored in Colchester harbour for some 20 years – the yacht being ready to put to sea at an hour's notice. There was no suggestion that this retention of mobility derogated from the permanence of his attachment to the UK. Although PRR obviously imposes different tests it is not impossible that after such a long time the yacht could have been said to be the taxpayer's dwelling-house in fact, even though it was also still a 'boat' in the full sense of the word.

Again as with caravans, the most valuable item in connection with a houseboat is likely to be the land used for mooring, where this is sold along with the vessel. If the latter could be shown to be the taxpayer's only or main residence, in principle there seems no reason why this land should not attract PRR provided that it constitutes the 'grounds' (or possibly even the garden) held by the taxpayer with the 'residence' for his own occupation and enjoyment, and it will usually cover much less than 0.5 hectares (see s. 222(1)(b) and the discussion at ¶401ff.).

(6) Interaction with the CGT chattel exemption

The fact that a gain on the disposal of an asset which is tangible movable property (a chattel) *and* a wasting asset is not a chargeable gain (see s. 45(1)) prompts one to ask how, if at all, this provision interacts with PRR in cases involving caravans or houseboats when considering the treatment of any gain on the caravan or vessel itself, as distinct from its site or moorings.

In *Makins v Elson (HMIT)* ((1976) 51 TC 437 at p. 441B) the Crown contended that because the caravan was a chattel, it cannot ipso facto have also been a dwelling-house. Foster J in that case did not specifically reject that view, and in *Moore v Thompson* the point does not seem to have been raised. Some doubt might have been present in both cases as to whether the vehicles were still really 'movable' property, and it is arguable that a totally immobilised caravan or houseboat has lost that quality. This appears to be the Revenue's view (CGT 64326 and 64329), although in the case of houseboats they may still regard them as chattels if occupied for less than six months.

If an asset is a chattel it is possible to argue that the exemption in s. 45(1) takes precedence over PRR, since s. 45(1) prevents a chargeable gain from accruing (it begins with the words 'Subject to the provisions of this section, no chargeable gain shall accrue ...') whereas PRR mitigates a gain which would otherwise be chargeable to tax (s. 223(1) beginning with the words 'No part of a gain to which s. 222 applies shall be a chargeable gain ...').

Section 45(1) only operates on a chattel which is also a wasting asset; that term is defined in s. 44(1) as an asset with a predictable useful life of 50 years or less when acquired by the person making the disposal in question. Most caravans will fall into that category, though houseboats – especially 'vintage' vessels such as converted canal barges or Thames sailing barges – are more likely to have a predictable life of more than 50 years on acquisition.

If s. 45(1) applies to the asset in question it may be worthwhile to invoke the exemption in priority to PRR, especially if there has been a substantial period of absence which could not be protected under s. 223(2) or (3) (see ¶603); chattel exemption would then be fully due whereas only partial PRR would be available. There seem to be no good grounds on which such a contention could be rejected. The really bold client who also owned a conventional residence could also make an election under s. 222(5)(a) in relation to the latter property.

The other form of chattel exemption for CGT, contained in s. 262, does not depend on the asset being 'wasting' as defined, but since it is confined to disposal proceeds not exceeding £6,000 its usefulness in this context is likely to be limited.

ACQUISITIONS AND EXPENDITURE WITH A VIEW TO DISPOSAL

¶306   Provisions of TCGA 1992, s. 224(3)

The provisions of TCGA 1992, s. 224(3) seek to confine PRR to the occupation of a dwelling-house as a dwelling-house, and therefore attack cases where the taxpayer's acquisition, or some later expenditure on the property, was 'wholly or partly' for the purpose of realising a gain. For convenience, these cases are described in what follows as 'tainted' transactions.

¶307   'Tainted' acquisitions

(1)   The circumstances attacked
Private residence relief is denied altogether where the acquisition of the property or an interest therein was made wholly or partly for the purposes of realising a gain on its disposal. In that event none of the gain attracts PRR, for any part of the period of ownership, whatever the position about periods of occupancy or elections under TCGA 1992, s. 222(5)(a) (see ¶506).

24   *Capital Gains Tax and the Private Residence*

(2) Acquisitions 'for the purpose ...' – 'Sole purpose' acquisitions
If a man acquires a house but never resides in it at any time, however fleeting, he will obtain no PRR, whatever his purpose in acquiring it may have been, because it will never have been his main residence and s. 223(1) will not apply. By definition, therefore, s. 224(3) attacks purchases with a mixed or dual purpose, or those with a single purpose – that of realising a gain on disposal – accompanied by a different and incidental result; a period of residential use. The latter situation – the 'sole purpose' acquisition – which naturally tends to be a function of a rapidly rising and active residential market, is considered in the following example. The former situation – the 'dual purpose' acquisition – is difficult to identify and deal with and is considered at ¶307(3).

Example 1
At a time of very high house prices in the South East in 2001, Julian decided to buy a new flat in a warehouse conversion in London. It was on offer for £500,000 but a friend who was an estate agent in the area advised Julian that within three weeks the developer would be releasing the next phase of similar flats at £600,000 each. Julian completed the deal quickly and spent a week 'camping out' in his new (unfurnished) flat before putting it on the market at £575,000, just as the developer increased the price of new flats as predicted. Julian sold the flat within a day or two for his asking price.

Leaving aside for the moment the question of whether Julian's profit is a trading profit assessable under Case I of Sch. D (of which more in (5)), this is almost certainly a case where s. 224(3) could be invoked by the Revenue. Julian's purchase was wholly motivated by the prospect of achieving a gain on sale and his brief occupation of the flat, even if sufficient to make it a residence in fact (itself doubtful), was no more than an incidental result of the transaction, which would fall to be disregarded for tax purposes.

(3) 'Wholly or partly ...' – 'Dual purpose' acquisitions
In contrast to the rules governing expenditure 'for the purpose of a trade' in ICTA 1988, s. 74(a), s. 224(3) also bites on a *partially* 'tainted' acquisition, i.e. one which has a dual or multiple purpose, as distinct from one with a single 'tainted' purpose and an incidental 'untainted' result. Thus even a subsidiary purpose of realising a gain on disposal will in strictness disqualify the whole gain for PRR.

Example 2
Jason, another friend of Julian in the previous example, was interested in the same development at a slightly earlier period, in 1999, before the market became so active. He took a longer view and decided that although short-term prospects for gains were uncertain, the long-term outlook was encouraging. He

¶307

also liked the area and his company was about to relocate its offices nearby. Thus he bought a flat in early 1999 for £400,000 and moved in fully. By mid-2000 he decided that the time was ripe for a sale and sold his flat for £500,000.

On the strictest and most mechanical analysis of s. 224(3) it seems that Jason too might forfeit all PRR on his gain, because he had a dual purpose at outset and more than half an eye on resale at a profit, even though he might have remained in his flat quite happily in the event of the market remaining sluggish. If, however, he could demonstrate that the possibility of a profit was no more than an incidental attraction in 1999, he would probably escape with his gains intact. The fact that the move was also very convenient for his work should be helpful to him here; if his work was on the other side of London, and especially if his previous home was much more convenient both for his working and social life, his task would be harder.

(4) Practical implications
In practice the Revenue would be unlikely to invoke s. 224(3) in cases like Jason's (Example 2). So long as there is no evidence to suggest that the taxpayer is carrying on a trade of property dealing or an adventure in the nature of a trade, it is recognised that most people have an eye for capital appreciation when buying a home, without running a risk of denial of PRR under s. 224(3) (see CGT 65211–65212). This is a sensible recognition of reality, although the risk of action under s. 224(3) should not be forgotten by those who turn properties over very rapidly in a rising market.

(5) Relationship between s. 224(3) and other provisions
Further indications of the theoretically swingeing effect of s. 224(3) can be deduced from the fact that in practice, if the Revenue could assemble sufficient evidence to succeed under the subsection, it might also be well on the way to success in showing that the taxpayer was carrying on a trade of dealing in property (or, which would suffice equally well, an adventure in the nature of trade). It would follow that an assessment under Case I of Sch. D might well be sustainable.

An individual who acquires a property with the predominant intention of selling it within a short time at a profit may very well, on the classic 'badges of trade' identified by the 1955 Royal Commission on the Taxation of Profits and Income, be a trader; he has no intention to use the property as his home (any such use being incidental, and possibly inserted as a cosmetic feature in the inspector's view) or as a source of investment income (there may be little or no rental market and no attempt to exploit one if it exists); he may have begun to seek a buyer almost as soon as he has made his purchase; and he may be unable to fund the purchase unless he can sell at a rapid profit (especially if it must be financed by high borrowings). Any suggestion that he was seeking a 'hedge' against property price

¶307

inflation may meet the same fate as the dealer in bullion in *Wisdom v Chamberlain (HMIT)* (1968) 45 TC 92. Repetition of the exercise may increase the risk of trading status.

The prospects of Revenue success on these lines have perhaps been slightly dented since the High Court's decision in *Marson (HMIT) v Morton and related appeals* [1986] BTC 377, where an isolated purchase of land followed by its sale at a profit a few months later was held not to be a trading transaction.

Sir Nicholas Browne-Wilkinson V-C in that case remarked (at p. 387) that it is no longer self-evident that land which produces no income must necessarily have been acquired with a view to resale; but it would be optimistic to hope that commissioners will be persuaded that no such motive existed if most of the other 'badges of trade' are present.

However, the Revenue has the option of running a 'trading' argument or alternatively arguing that relief is precluded by s. 224(3). In *Kirkby v Hughes (HMIT)* [1993] BTC 52, involving a builder, they successfully argued for trading in respect of the sale of a property which had been renovated and sold, but occupied by the builder only 'at some time' while he was still living with his parents. By contrast, *Goodwin v Curtis (HMIT)* [1996] BTC 501, involving a former property consultant, saw an attempt to obtain PRR on a house which was acquired by a company controlled by the taxpayer on 7 March 1985; on 1 April the company sub-sold it to the taxpayer; on 11 April he started to advertise it for resale; and on 3 May he sold it for a profit of some £100,000. The property was a farmhouse and the taxpayer's principal interest was in acquiring the farmyard, which had outline residential planning permission, for development purposes. Even though for his brief period of ownership the taxpayer ate and slept at the property throughout the week, the commissioners concluded from all the facts, including several other transactions in the same period and the taxpayer's need to sell the farmhouse to raise finance, that his occupation of the farmhouse lacked the requisite degree of permanence and expectation of continuity to attract PRR. They rejected a Revenue contention that he was trading, but held that s. 224(3) precluded relief and this was upheld in the High Court. Sir John Vinelott held that they had been right to 'take the view that the farmhouse could not be said to have been occupied by the taxpayer as his home'.

If the facts seem equally to support both the application of s. 224(3) and the existence of trading, trading status could in fact be advantageous to the taxpayer. If he has borrowed money to finance the deal, interest relief should be available against the Case I profit whereas it would not be available against a capital gain (without PRR). The Case I profits could also be pensionable earnings under a personal pension scheme which could further reduce the tax bill, and it may be possible to deduct some reasonable remuneration, e.g. to a spouse. The position would be neutral as regards professional fees which would be deductible under either computation. It is also necessary to consider whether there are income tax losses or capital losses which could shelter the taxable surplus under either method. For disposals after 5 April 1998 the availability of CGT taper relief also has to be considered. Where there is no trading, but also no PRR because of s. 224(3), non-business taper relief may be available to reduce the effective tax rate below 40 per cent, although in the context of rapidly acquired and resold properties a relief which requires a minimum of three years' ownership is unlikely to be significant. The same is likely to be true of indexation relief for periods up to 31 March 1998.

If the Revenue decides not to argue for liability under Case I of Sch. D on the facts, the alternative of using ICTA 1988, s. 776 will not be available. That section enables the Revenue to tax as income, under Case VI of Sch. D, a *capital* gain on the disposal of land acquired with the 'sole or main object' of realising a gain on disposal. A transaction which is not on capital account, such as a trading one, automatically falls outside s. 776 on first principles. The section goes further, however, by saying that it cannot apply if PRR would apply to such a gain but for the application of s. 224(3). Section 776 could not, therefore, have applied to the profits made by either of the taxpayers in *Kirkby v Hughes* or *Goodwin v Curtis* – the former made a trading profit and the latter occupied the house for a short time but made a non-exempt gain caught by s. 224(3). In effect, if a profit takes the form of a capital receipt there can be no question of s. 776 applying (see the Revenue's acceptance of this at CGT 65221).

Revenue practice is also not to use s. 776 in simple cases of purchase and resale, because such transactions should either be capable of characterisation as trading or at least adventures in the nature of trade, or be straightforward capital transactions to which s. 776 cannot apply – although s. 224(3) might (see Revenue Inspectors' Manual para. 4723). It is, therefore, unlikely that taxpayers will encounter a serious risk of s. 776 liability unless the facts are complex and, probably, unless commercial developers are involved at some point.

The exclusion of s. 776 works generally to the taxpayer's advantage, since a s. 776 liability under Case VI attracts none of the mitigating reliefs described above for Case I, and no indexation or taper relief either. ICTA 1988, s. 776(9) in terms applies only to individuals, and it appears that it does not apply to trustees, although no particular policy reason for such a distinction is evident.

It is, however, clear that if the special circumstances of ICTA 1988, s. 776(9) do not apply, so that there is no question of any PRR being due, and the circumstances go beyond a simple sale at market value of all the vendor's interest, ICTA 1988, s. 776 is available as a weapon to the Revenue in a case involving a dwelling-house, either against an individual or against trustees. The exclusion of trustees from ICTA 1988, s. 776(9) suggests that even where trustees make a disposal which ranks for relief under s. 225 (see ¶801ff.), or where s. 225 is excluded or restricted by an acquisition or expenditure within s. 224(3), the Revenue could nevertheless seek income tax liability under ICTA 1988, s. 776 if the case fell within the scope of that section. Whether such an approach would in fact be adopted by the Revenue is unclear, but trustees may need to be especially careful where these income tax provisions could in theory bite.

(6) Acquisitions other than by transactions at arm's length

It seems generally to be accepted that if a property is acquired other than by an arm's length transaction, e.g. by gift, inheritance or appointment from a trust, an attack under s. 224(3) is unlikely to succeed. This reasoning rests on the premise that such acquisitions come to the taxpayer as unsought windfalls, so that he cannot be said to have any purpose in making them, and thus the circumstances necessary for the application of the subsection do not apply.

The leading authority here is *McClelland v Commissioner of Taxation for Australia* [1971] 1 WLR 191, a Privy Council case where it was held (by a majority) that a taxpayer had not engaged in an adventure in the nature of trade in relation to an inherited property sold to raise capital; the Australian legislation in point required an acquisition 'for the purpose of profit making by sale'.

So, in relation to s. 224(3) it may be argued that the acquisition of property by the bounty of another person must necessarily be devoid of any purpose, since 'purpose' presupposes some positive act by the acquirer. However, caution may be called for in cases where the taxpayer effectively engineered the acquisition, perhaps by taking the initiative in accelerating an appointment from a trust (especially if he was himself a trustee) or a gift to himself in the owner's lifetime of an asset which was destined to come his way on the owner's death. The argument based on *McClelland* is most likely to succeed where the gift was either genuinely unsought (if in the donor's lifetime or from a trust) or resulted from a will.

¶308 'Tainted' expenditure

The second leg of TCGA 1992, s. 224(3) attacks expenditure on a property incurred after the beginning of the period of ownership and wholly or partly for the purpose of realising a gain on disposal. Whereas the first leg denies any PRR at all, the second leg restricts PRR in so far as the eventual gain is attributable to such 'tainted' expenditure.

(1) 'Wholly or partly for the purpose ...'

As with the rule about 'tainted' acquisitions, this rule is so widely drawn that in strictness any gain on a dwelling-house, continuously occupied by the disposer as his only residence, could be dissected by reference to improvements carried out with a view, even in part, to realising a gain on eventual sale, and PRR could be restricted by reference to the gains attributable to any such improvements. The rule lacks even an exclusion for 'revenue' expenditure as distinct from capital; so in theory an owner who obtains a higher price merely because he has had the property tastefully redecorated prior to putting it on the market could suffer a restriction.

(2) In practice
The taxpayer's answer to such a challenge, if made, might be to demonstrate that when the work was contracted for, the sale was not in contemplation; this would be a reasonable assertion if no agent had been instructed or other positive steps taken at that time. If the expenditure was on revenue account, such as repairs or redecoration, an equally convincing answer might be that his purpose was to prevent deterioration of the property and to keep it serviceable, any improvement in the sale price being incidental (see ¶307(3)); if the work was overdue that might be a tenable argument, and in any event it must always be very doubtful whether any element in the sale price can be directly attributed to such work, except perhaps in an extreme case of a property which was very run down and barely saleable in its unrepaired and unredecorated state. It can also be argued that there are few true 'improvements' (as distinct from minor repairs and redecoration) which are not undertaken predominantly for the convenience and amenity of the owner; since nobody can be certain how long it will take to sell a property or even whether it can be sold at all at an acceptable price, the owner must have had the benefit to himself from the work principally in mind.

As with 'tainted' acquisitions (see ¶307(4)) this is an area where the Revenue's practice may be more liberal than the strict letter of the law. No restriction of PRR is made solely because expenditure has been incurred in obtaining planning permission or the release of a restrictive covenant (see CGT 65243).

The two situations where the 'tainted expenditure' rules seems in practice to be invoked are the acquisition by a leaseholder of a superior interest in the property, and conversions into flats, followed in each case by sale (CGT 65245). A payment to a tenant to move out of a partly let residence may also suggest a s. 224(3) situation (and may arise as part of a conversion scheme, see CGT 65268).

There seems little doubt that a leaseholder who acquires a freehold or other superior interest in his residence, and immediately sells on the enhanced interest, has incurred the additional costs for no purpose other than the realisation of a gain. This has become more common since the *Leasehold Reform Housing and Urban Development Act* 1993 gave many tenants the right to 'enfranchise' their leases by acquiring the freehold (usually through a company) or taking long extensions to the term. As with other situations, however, it will be a question of fact whether s. 224(3) can be invoked. Tenants may wish to enfranchise to give themselves additional security (or borrowing power), and any disposal may be far from their thoughts. The example at CGT 65257, which shows a tenant with 63 years of his lease to run acquiring the freehold in February 1992 and selling it in March 1993, might not naturally seem an automatic candidate for s. 224(3) but for the statement that he 'decides to sell' before acquiring the freehold. In real life this would need to be established by evidence.

The case for applying s. 224(3) to the second situation – conversion into flats – may be more clear cut, but advisers should consider whether some or all of the costs might have been incurred for reasons other than the prospect of a sale; for example to create a 'granny flat' or accommodation for live-in staff. If this can be shown, there should be no s. 224(3) restriction. Otherwise, there are worked examples at CGT 65270–71 of cases where conversion was clearly with a view to sale. Again, in real life everything will depend on the evidence.

The legislation is silent on the method of attributing gains to expenditure, but in practice inspectors compare the gain which actually arises with the gain which would have been made without the relevant expenditure, arguing that the excess of the former over the latter is taxable (CGT 65246). The examples at CGT 65257, 65270 and 65271 are interesting in that they start by taking the estimated value of the property in its 'unimproved' state – either the leasehold before enfranchisement, or the house before conversion – and the excess of sale proceeds over that value becomes the 'tainted' and therefore taxable gain. This is in contrast to the method used by the Revenue where s. 224(2) has to be considered because there have been changes in what is occupied as the dwelling house (see Example 2 (Alice) at ¶305 above).

A flow chart to illustrate the application of the various provisions about trading or otherwise non-exempt transactions involving private residences is on p. 31.

AN INTEREST IN A DWELLING-HOUSE

¶309 Joint owners

In addition to referring to the disposal of a dwelling-house, TCGA 1992, s. 222(1)(a) also refers to the disposal of 'an interest in a dwelling-house'. As well as covering leasehold interests (see ¶310), this appears in practice to cover the position of joint owners of a freehold property.

The Revenue published a short statement about joint ownership in its *Tax Bulletin*, May 1992, pp. 20–21. This says that in its view 'joint owner-occupiers of a property who are not husband and wife' will 'generally' be entitled to PRR on the footing that they each have unrestricted access to the whole property. Although the statement is headed 'Joint but unrelated owner occupiers', what is said of joint owner-occupiers who are not married to each other seems equally true, in law, of a married couple (and despite the heading, of joint occupiers who are related, e.g. two sisters). The statement also distinguishes physically partitioned property,

The House Itself 31

TRADING OR OTHER NON-EXEMPT DISPOSALS

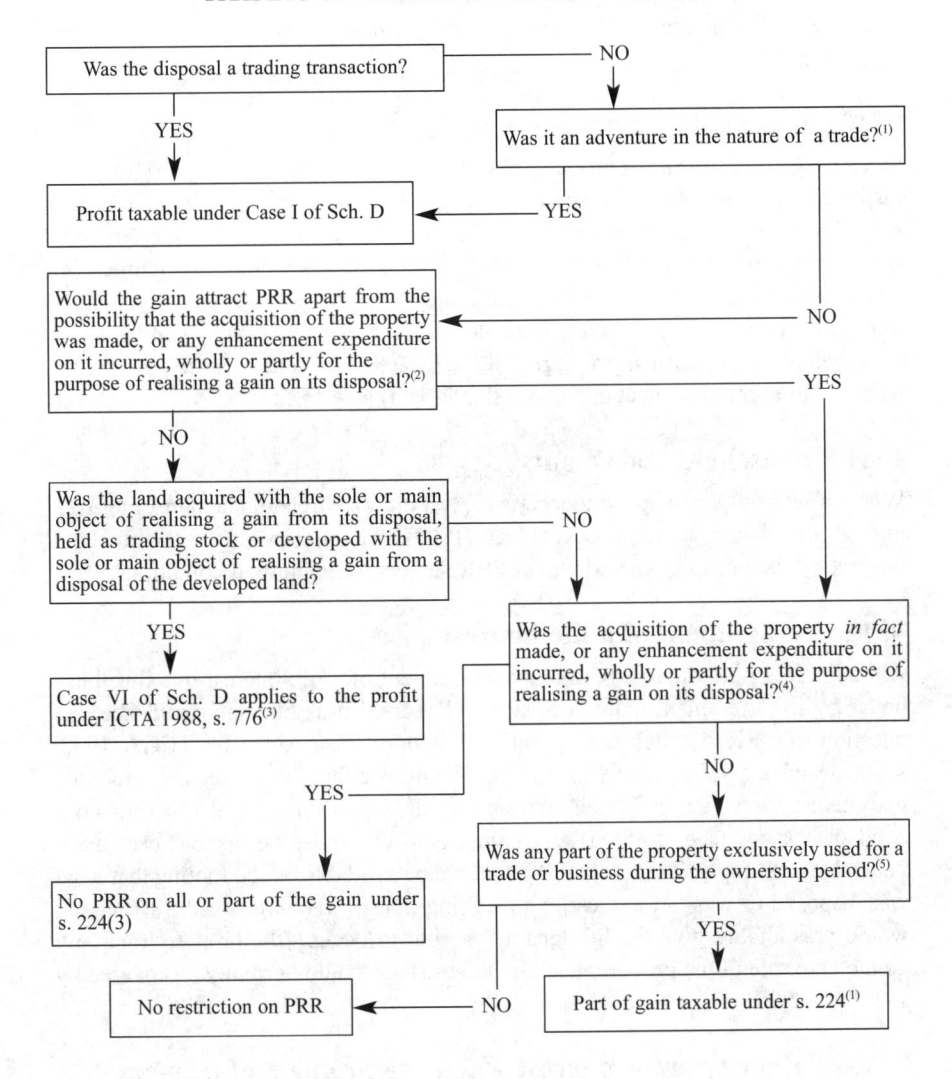

```
┌─────────────────────────────────────┐         NO
│ Was the disposal a trading          ├─────────────────┐
│ transaction?                        │                 │
└──────────────┬──────────────────────┘                 ▼
               │ YES              ┌──────────────────────────────────────┐
               ▼                  │ Was it an adventure in the nature of │
┌─────────────────────────────┐   │ a trade?[1]                          │
│ Profit taxable under Case I │◄──│                                      │
│ of Sch. D                   │YES└──────────────┬───────────────────────┘
└─────────────────────────────┘                  │
                                                 │ NO
┌──────────────────────────────────────┐         │
│ Would the gain attract PRR apart     │         │
│ from the possibility that the        │◄────────┘
│ acquisition of the property was      │         NO
│ made, or any enhancement expenditure │
│ on it incurred, wholly or partly for │─────────────────┐
│ the purpose of realising a gain on   │         YES     │
│ its disposal?[2]                     │                 │
└──────────────┬───────────────────────┘                 │
               │ NO                                      │
               ▼                                         │
┌──────────────────────────────────────┐                 │
│ Was the land acquired with the sole  │                 │
│ or main object of realising a gain   │     NO          │
│ from its disposal, held as trading   ├─────────────┐   │
│ stock or developed with the sole or  │             │   │
│ main object of realising a gain from │             │   │
│ a disposal of the developed land?    │             │   │
└──────────────┬───────────────────────┘             ▼   │
               │ YES                ┌──────────────────────────────────────┐
               ▼                    │ Was the acquisition of the property  │
┌─────────────────────────────┐     │ *in fact* made, or any enhancement   │
│ Case VI of Sch. D applies   │     │ expenditure on it incurred, wholly   │
│ to the profit under ICTA    │     │ or partly for the purpose of         │
│ 1988, s. 776[3]             │     │ realising a gain on its disposal?[4] │
└──────────────┬──────────────┘     └──────────────┬───────────────────────┘
               │                                   │ NO
               │ YES                               ▼
               │                    ┌──────────────────────────────────────┐
               └───────────────────►│ Was any part of the property         │
                                    │ exclusively used for a trade or      │
                                    │ business during the ownership        │
                                    │ period?[5]                           │
                                    └──────────────┬───────────────────────┘
┌─────────────────────────────┐                    │ YES
│ No PRR on all or part of    │                    ▼
│ the gain under s. 224(3)    │     ┌──────────────────────────────────────┐
└─────────────────────────────┘     │ Part of gain taxable under s. 224(1) │
                                    └──────────────────────────────────────┘
┌─────────────────────────────┐         NO
│ No restriction on PRR       │◄────────────────┐
└─────────────────────────────┘
```

Notes

(1) See definition in ICTA 1988, s. 832
(2) See s. 776(9)
(3) See s. 776(2) and the discussion in ¶307(5) and (6) of this text. The gain must be of a *capital* nature. See also IR Inspectors' Manual para. 4723.
(4) See s. 224(3) and the discussion in ¶308 of this text.
(5) See s. 224(1) and discussion in ¶701ff. of this text. Section 224(1) may also apply if exclusive use was for an employment in a trading business.

¶309

where PRR is, naturally, only due to each owner on his or her separate dwelling area (see ¶715). In practice, fortunately, this topic does not seem to give rise to any real difficulties.

¶310 Leasehold interests

Since for CGT all forms of property may be assets (see TCGA 1992, s. 21(1)), the disposal of a leasehold interest in a dwelling-house may, in principle, give rise to a taxable gain, just as may the disposal of a freehold interest. In practice, only substantial leasehold interests are likely to attract a lump sum on assignment (or possibly on the grant of a sub-lease), but if they do so the PRR legislation operates in exactly the same way as for a freehold disposal. However, there can be a trap even where the interest is of negligible value (e.g. a mere monthly or weekly tenancy) in relation to elections under s. 222(5)(a) (see ¶522).

¶311 Leasehold 'carve-outs'

Where a lease of a private residence is carved out of a freehold as part of an IHT mitigation scheme, (a topic covered at ¶1105), the sale or gift of the freehold interest by the occupier should attract PRR subject to the normal conditions.

¶312 Assignment of a life interest

Although it is possible to envisage the assignment of a life interest in a dwelling-house by the life tenant under a trust who has used it as his main residence, the question of PRR on such a disposal will seldom arise, since by TCGA 1992, s. 76(1) such a disposal is exempt from CGT unless either the life tenant purchased his interest for value, or the circumstances fall within the special rules for non-resident trustees (see s. 85). If any gain would otherwise be taxable because s. 76(1) does not apply, it seems that PRR would be available on the footing that what was disposed of was 'an interest in a dwelling-house'; the terms of the settlement would presumably give the life tenant the right to occupy the property (and any gain on the sale of the property itself by the trustees would normally be covered by s. 225, see ¶801).

¶313 Other types of interest – and the problem of licences

Given the exceptionally wide scope of 'assets' for CGT, it is possible that other types of interest in a dwelling-house could attract PRR if they are capable of disposal. The person entitled to such an interest, and to whom gains accrue, should therefore be entitled to the relief. An interesting example of this possibility is discussed at ¶911 in the context of marital breakdown.

The width of the concept of an asset for CGT may also mean that a tenant will require PRR to avoid an otherwise taxable gain when he receives a capital sum from the landlord to vacate his private residence. Such a receipt would normally give rise to a chargeable gain under s. 22(1)(c), but it is likely that the gain would be held to have been derived from an 'interest' in the dwelling-house under s. 222(1)(a). Some such sums may not be taxable in any event (e.g. where statutory compensation is paid for disturbance on the surrender of a tenancy it may be derived from statute rather than any disposal of the tenant's 'interest'), see *Drummond (HMIT) v Brown* [1984] BTC 142.

Another type of 'interest' which could figure in a PRR claim is that of the holder of rights under a restrictive covenant which benefits a main residence, usually because it entitles him to prevent development on adjoining land (see CGT 64604). A capital sum received for the release of such a covenant would be a disposal (s. 22(1)(c)), but is regarded as that of an interest in the residence and thus PRR would in principle be due, subject to all the applicable conditions.

Special problems surround properties occupied only under licence – for example where there is no exclusive right to occupy any particular accommodation (as in a hotel or nursing home), where the right to occupy is granted in consideration for services as an employee, or where it is granted without consideration. Since 1994 (see the *Tax Bulletin* for October that year) the Revenue has regarded licencees of this type as not owning an interest which is subject to CGT at all, and therefore unable to claim PRR by reference to such an interest. A taxpayer is, of course, unlikely to realise a gain on a disposal of such a licence, because it would normally have no value. However, the Revenue's stance means that he would be unable to use the property occupied under licence to support an election in favour of another property as his OMR (see ¶506 below). This may be a special problem for employees in job-related accommodation (see ¶610).

A common trap is to regard the shares in a company which owns a domestic residence as an interest in the dwelling-house. On first principles this is not the case since a shareholder does not own the assets of a company. This can have important implications for non-domiciled clients tempted to hold UK homes through offshore companies (see ¶1014). It is also relevant for the resident-owned companies which are typically formed to hold either the head lease, or the common areas, in apartment blocks. When occupational leases are assigned in such cases, a share in the company is normally transferred between the same parties, but whereas the leasehold interest may attract PRR, the share cannot do so.

¶314 Successive or varying interests

Section 222(7) of TCGA 1992, provides a rule to deal with situations where the nature of an individual's interest changes over time. This is further elaborated where there are inter-spouse transfers. It operates by extending the 'period of ownership' which is relevant to the calculation of the relief. In no circumstances however, can account be taken of events before 1 April 1982 (see s. 223(7) and the discussion at ¶618), or (for a disposal before 6 April 1988) 6 April 1965.

(1) Different interests at different times

Where a taxpayer has had different interests at different times, his 'period of ownership' is measured from the first acquisition taken into account in computing gains to which PRR would apply. This rule applies for all PRR purposes (see (2)) and its chief beneficiaries are leaseholders who later acquire their freeholds.

Example 1

Jane acquired a long lease of her flat in 1995 at a premium. In 2000 she was able to buy the freehold. Section 222(7) enables her 'period of ownership' to start in 1995 since if she had sold the lease before 2000, the premium paid in 1995 would have been deductible in computing any gain, apart from PRR. She occupies the flat as her only residence at all times. If she sells the flat in September 2002, the whole of her gain is exempt; and the final 36 months for the purposes of s. 223(1) begins in September 1999, even though at that time she did not own the freehold which she eventually sells. It follows that Jane could have moved out in September 1999 and never re-occupied the flat without any effect on PRR.

If Jane, in the above example, had occupied her flat merely on a monthly tenancy at a rent from 1995 to 2000, the analysis would have been different. Because the rental payments would not have been deductible on a taxable disposal of the flat, her period of ownership for s. 223(1) would not have begun until 2000. She could have obtained PRR on a sale of the freehold only if the flat had been her main residence from 2000 until the sale.

A further point to be noted here is that in the calculation required under s. 223(2) or (3) where there have been absences, the denominator of the fraction is to be determined by the period from the acquisition of the freehold, not the monthly tenancy (see ¶618).

Example 2

Jonathan took a monthly tenancy of a flat, paying no premium, in April 1993. In April 1996 he bought the freehold and in April 2002 he sells it and realises a gain of £180,000. However, from April 1994 to April 1998, he was employed full-time overseas. He reoccupies the property when he returns to the UK. This absence is, in principle, covered by s. 223(3)(b), but since s. 222(7) cannot apply to extend his period of ownership back beyond April 1996, that period is only six years (1996–02). His permitted absence which enters into the calculation is therefore only the two years from 1996 to 1998, not the four years from 1994 to 1998, and the computation will be as follows:

	£
Gain as above	180,000
Final 36 months exempt:	
3/6 × 180,000 =	(90,000)
Two years' permitted absence:	
2/6 × 180,000 =	(60,000)
Taxable gain	30,000

It would be incorrect to base the 'final 36 months' fraction on 3/9, or the permitted absence on 4/9, of the total gain.

Similar considerations and calculations would, of course, apply if the tenant in this example acquired a long lease rather than a freehold (see ¶310).

(2) Other effects of extending the ownership period

The extension of the 'period of ownership' under s. 222(7) is to apply for the purposes of s. 223–226 inclusive, i.e. for *all* PRR purposes. It follows that where the period of ownership is extended under the subsection, any non-domestic use of the property, or any 'tainted' expenditure, which occurred before the acquisition of the larger interest eventually sold, will entail a restriction of PRR (see s. 224(2) and ¶701, and s. 224(3) and ¶308). Conversely, of course, this effect does not operate where the period is not extended because there was no earlier interest which could have produced deductible expenditure for CGT in the absence of PRR, as in Example 2 above.

(3) Inter-spouse transfers and s. 222(7)

Disposals of assets between spouses living together have no immediate CGT cost (see s. 58(1)), but in the context of PRR, s. 222(7)(a) provides that the transferee spouse's period of ownership begins with that of the transferor spouse, even if that period began before the parties were married. The subsection adds that in particular this is to apply where the transfer takes place on death. Moreover, by s. 222(7)(b), on a disposal by the transferee, that spouse can count any period of residential occupation of the property by the transferor as if it was his or her own, regardless of the true position and regardless of the fact that part of that period may have fallen before the parties were married. The absence of the transferor from the property is also attributed to the transferee. This rule does not affect the base cost of the transferee spouse, which is in effect the relevant fraction of the transferor's cost for a lifetime gift (s. 58(1)), or of the probate value for a transfer on death (s. 62(1)); however, it can produce unexpected results, favourable or otherwise (as pointed out at CGT 64955).

¶314

Example 3

Wilfred bought a house in 1991 and lived there continuously until 1995 when he married Mabel, who moved in with him. On marriage he gave Mabel a half share in the freehold. The couple plan to sell the house in 2002. Mabel will be taxable on any taxable gain on her share but by s. 222(7)(a), that share is deemed to have been acquired in 1991 and by s. 222(7)(b), Wilfred's occupation from 1991 to 1995 is attributed to her, so that Mabel's entire gain attracts PRR. Without the rule in s. 222(7)(b), Mabel's gain would be based on a half share of the 1991 base cost (under s. 222(7)(a)) but she would not obtain PRR for the period before her marriage.

If Wilfred had been absent for work related reasons from 1992 to 1994, it appears that Mabel could, on her own disposal, count that period as a period of deemed occupation by her, exactly as could Wilfred in computing his own gains by s. 223(3)(c).

The position on death is also worth an illustration:

Example 4

Fred bought a house in 1983 when he was single. He lived in it continuously until 2002 when he dies. In 1989 he married Elsie and she then moved in with him and he gave her a 50 per cent interest, for which her base cost is 50 per cent of his own 1983 cost because this is a no gain/no loss inter-spouse transfer. In his will in 2002 he leaves his 50 per cent interest to Elsie, who sells the house in 2004. Her CGT base cost for the inherited 50 per cent is the probate value in 2004, but her period of ownership is deemed to have started when Fred's started, in 1983. So even though there were six years (1983–89) when she did not live in the house, her whole gain will attract PRR because she is deemed to have lived there from 1983 to the date of sale.

Suppose, however, that Fred had another house from 1983 to 1989 and had elected for that to be his main residence until his marriage, when he sold it. Elsie cannot claim PRR on the marital home for the period from 1983 to 1989 because although her ownership is deemed to have started in 1983, Fred's 'absence' from 1983 to 1989 is also deemed to be hers. Here the rule in s. 227(7)(b) works against her, and her exempt gain on the inherited 50 per cent will suffer a restriction for those six years (roughly 6/21 of the gain on that share will be taxable – i.e. 21 years of deemed ownership 1983–04, six years of non-occupation 1983–89).

Of course, the subsection does not apply to transfers between unmarried couples even if they are living together.

¶314

(4) Effect of marital breakdown on s. 222(7)

It must be stressed that s. 222(7) operates only while the couple in question are married and living together as man and wife. It cannot assist in relation to transfers after permanent separation or divorce (see Chapter 9). In such cases the transferee spouse cannot strictly extend his or her period of ownership or of occupation beyond the actual period in each case. (However, there are useful Revenue concessions which may assist in practice – see ¶904.)

PART OF A DWELLING-HOUSE

¶315 Definition of 'dwelling-house'

A subject which has caused great difficulty to practitioners and the courts since the introduction of CGT has been the question of how far a 'dwelling-house' can be said to extend. Since TCGA 1992, s. 222(1)(a) specifically mentions the disposal of part of a dwelling-house as a disposal to which PRR can apply, it is necessary to ask how far the dwelling-house extends. Does it, for instance, include part of a house which is unoccupied, or a self-contained wing occupied by elderly relatives or staff of the owner? Does it include physically separate buildings such as garages and storehouses, or garden buildings? And does it include separate buildings which are themselves dwelling-houses, perhaps occupied by staff or servants, such as lodge-houses and gardeners' cottages?

It is a measure of the difficulty of this topic that the majority of the decided cases on PRR have been concerned with it. This section will analyse those cases in some detail but it is first necessary to consider some basic principles.

¶316 Fundamental considerations

(1) General law

As was noted in the discussion about the meaning of 'dwelling-house' itself (see ¶301ff.), general case law, and pre-CGT case law, are not always reliable guides here. In land law generally, the expression 'dwelling-house' in documents has been given a wide meaning; thus, in *Belfast Corporation v Kelso* [1953] NI 163, Black LJ observed: 'A conveyance or demise of a dwelling-house would normally be construed as including all the land within the curtilage of the house.' This would clearly encompass outbuildings as well as the main house itself (though the concept of the 'curtilage' has now assumed considerable importance in the context of subsidiary houses – see ¶321).

Numerous enactments down the years have drawn their definitions of 'house', 'private house' or 'dwelling-house' in similarly wide terms, for purposes including compulsory purchase, rating and public health. However, in the writer's respectful opinion, the right approach to the problem was conveniently summarised by Lawrence J in a case under the *Housing Act* 1957 as follows:

> 'The precise meaning of the word "houses" has frequently arisen for judicial consideration, but mostly in connection with other statutes or in other contexts. Decisions in relation to such other matters appear to me to afford very little, if any, assistance ... What seems to be clear is that the word has a distinct fluidity of meaning, and that it is best construed in relation to the context in which it is found and in relation to the objects and purposes of the Act or of the section of the Act in which it is used.'

(*Annicola Investments Ltd v Minister of Housing and Local Government* [1965] 3 All ER 850 at pp. 853–854.)

(2) The crucial question
The validity of this approach is apparent when s. 222(1)(a) is considered. Although a conveyancer would naturally regard the garden of a house, for example, as passing under a conveyance of the 'dwelling-house', the fact that the draftsman here has dealt with 'garden or grounds' as a separate head of exemption under s. 222(1)(b) indicates that we are dealing with a narrower concept in s. 222(1)(a). The question then arises whether 'dwelling-house' in s. 222(1)(a) is some kind of concept totally peculiar to this legislation, to be considered without regard to other legal contexts in which the expression occurs or whether it represents a kind of abridged version of the conveyancer's concept, including everything which a conveyancer would naturally include within the term *except* those matters covered in s. 222(1)(b), i.e. the garden and grounds.

This question has, in fact, been at the heart of the decided PRR cases on this topic. In general, the Revenue has argued for the former view, attempting to construct a specialised concept for these purposes only, seeking to confine the 'dwelling-house' to the main house itself and including as few other buildings as possible; conversely taxpayers, naturally, have attempted to widen the boundaries of the expression as far as they can.

(3) Tax case law other than CGT
When considering the question of the meaning of a 'dwelling-house' generally (see ¶303) reference was made to the former inhabited house duty. Although it must be doubtful whether a modern court would now give much weight to these cases, they may, nevertheless, also afford some useful hints as to how far a dwelling-house extends. It must, however, be remembered that the inhabited house duty cases concerned a charging provision rather than a relieving provision such as PRR, so

that a court interpreting the latter legislation might be expected to take a broader view. The inhabited house duty cases may be of most assistance when considering extensions and appendages to the main house (see ¶317).

(4) A question of fact – the approach of the appeal commissioners and the courts

Before turning to the detailed problems which have featured in the decided cases, it may be helpful to recall that under the appellate machinery of the UK tax system, the courts have a strictly limited role. An appeal to the High Court (or the Court of Session in Scotland) from a decision of the appeal commissioners may only be taken on a point of law (see TMA 1970, s. 56(1)). The court has no power to go behind the findings of fact made by the commissioners and appellants may not strictly adduce fresh facts in court (although judges sometimes allow unrepresented appellants some latitude, cf. the 'caravan' cases discussed at ¶304).

This means that the only question which the court may properly address is whether the commissioners were entitled to draw the conclusion which they in fact reached from the facts which they found. The court may not disturb that conclusion merely because the judge feels that, sitting as a judge of the facts, he might have decided the matter differently. The court may interfere only if it is apparent that the commissioners made an error of law in formulating their conclusion, or if the conclusion is so much at odds with the facts found that no reasonable tribunal could justifiably have reached it (see *Edwards (HMIT) v Bairstow & Harrison* (1955) 36 TC 207).

It is important to bear this principle in mind when examining the case law on PRR generally and particularly the cases shortly to be discussed. Since the facts of any two cases will always differ from one another in some degree, the case law cannot be read as if it set up a detailed array of immutable principles. The cases merely show the development of certain very broad tests which the courts have approved. If the decisions in some of the cases strike the reader as odd, it should be remembered that the courts were doing no more than asking whether the commissioners' conclusion was one which could reasonably have been drawn from the facts found.

The importance of the findings of fact will be mentioned again when considering the practical approach to contentious cases (see ¶323(3)).

¶317 Extensions to the main house, wings, flats, etc.

Some of the inhabited house duty cases concerned tenement blocks and flats, where numerous families lived within the same four outer walls; others concerned buildings which had been extended from their original boundaries so that the additions interacted with the original parts. These problems caused the courts little difficulty in the context of inhabited house duty, and they held that such additions

¶317

were part of the same dwelling-house as the original parts, especially if there were interconnecting doors or internal passageways at any level (see *Russell v Coutts* (1881) 1 TC 469, and *Grant v Langston* (1900) 4 TC 205).

In another case, a pair of terraced houses which had separate street doors and house numbers, and were occupied by two related families, was regarded as a single dwelling-house, on the grounds that an internal door had been inserted and through this the two families frequently passed, sharing the same kitchen and eating together (*A and GB Murdoch v Lethem* (1904) 5 TC 76).

Such a common sense approach is also likely to be used in PRR cases today where a main house has been extended to form a separate wing or annex; so long as it is clear that there is a single household with internal communication (though even the latter may not be essential) there is likely to be only one dwelling-house, all of which is considered together for PRR. The fact that the additional part could be the subject of a separate sale is irrelevant by comparison with the way in which the owner in question has used the whole property.

Annexes for elderly relatives will often be built on to modern houses with the intention that the relative should be able to enjoy privacy where required, yet be able to call on the owner's family for help in emergencies. There will normally be internal doors between the main house and the annex and the relative may share at least some meals with the owner's family. Such cases are really updated versions of the facts in *Murdoch*, and there seems little doubt that the whole property would be viewed as a single dwelling-house, and qualify for PRR on a sale by the owner (though see ¶320(5) regarding the apparently anomalous decision in *Green v IR Commrs* [1982] BTC 378).

¶318 Unused or seldom used parts of the main house

(1) Occupation of the whole

The fact that a large house may contain rooms or floors which are rarely, or not regularly, used or which have fallen into disuse should not normally entail any loss of PRR. Many people, especially the elderly, may no longer use the whole of their homes on a daily basis, perhaps because the home once housed a large family which has grown up and moved on. However, there is no doubt that the owner remains the legal occupier of the whole house, and even if some parts may be unfurnished it is most unlikely that he can be said no longer to reside in the whole house. This point would hardly merit a mention were it not for the Revenue's attempt to argue the opposite view in *Green v IR Commrs* [1982] BTC 378.

(2) The Revenue argument in Green

In *Green v IR Commrs*, a case on complex and special facts which raises a number of problems, the subject matter was a very large property acquired by the taxpayer in 1971, which had a central mansion house containing no fewer than 33 rooms, together with two wings each having a self-contained flat (the wings produced a separate problem, see ¶320(5)).

Much redecoration and other work was done by the taxpayer over several years, but by May 1975, when the property was sold, nearly the whole house had been furnished, even though earlier in that year only a few rooms seemed to be in actual occupation. One of the flats was occupied from 1971 to 1972 by an original co-owner who was then bought out by the taxpayer, after which it was occupied by a gardener and his family. The taxpayer's father also occupied some rooms until he died in 1973, and the taxpayer's son and daughter lived in part of the house for a time also.

The Revenue tried to persuade the commissioners that because the taxpayer had not actually used more than a few of the many rooms at any time, some restriction of PRR was called for. The commissioners rejected this view, and went on to reject a further Revenue argument that relief should be restricted on the grounds (called 'somewhat startling' by the court, see *Green v IR Commrs* at p. 383) that the central mansion house 'was bigger than the household required, and that those rooms which the members [of the household] did not normally occupy themselves constituted a part of the house which was not the residence of the occupier of the whole'.

The commissioners thus rejected the Revenue's invitation to make an apportionment of the sale consideration, under what is now s. 222(10), because they were not prepared to hold that only part of the mansion house was the main residence of the taxpayer.

They then went on, however, to *accept* a further invitation to adjust the relief under what is now s. 224(2) (see ¶707(3)) on a 'just and reasonable' basis, apparently deciding that there had been changes in what had been occupied as the taxpayer's residence.

The Court of Session held that the commissioners had been right to refuse the invitation to apportion under s. 222(10) since there was no evidence that any part of the mansion house was not the taxpayer's residence. But the court regarded their acceptance of the second invitation as incompatible with this finding. If there was no part of the mansion house which was not the taxpayer's residence, no 'changes' can have occurred which would have justified any apportionment; the court upheld the commissioners' rejection of the argument that the mansion house was bigger than the household required, and thus that some part was to be excluded from the taxpayer's residence.

(3) Conclusions

To justify the conclusion that unoccupied or rarely occupied parts of a house were not part of the residence of the owner, it seems that highly exceptional and unusual

¶318

facts would be required. Possible examples of situations which might support such a conclusion might be:

(a) the acquisition of a house which is clearly, from the outset, much too large for any conceivable present or future domestic use of the owner, with the intention of letting the surplus space or using it for a business; here, any vacant period before such other use began might not attract PRR. However, if the owners are a young married couple with no children, who is to say that they did not originally intend to start a large family but later changed their minds?

(b) physical alterations which render part of a house uninhabitable residentially, e.g. the blocking of internal access routes or the demolition of the roof. Neither situation is likely to be common.

There certainly seems to be little to justify the Revenue's argument, in *Green*, that in a large house some kind of arbitrary line can be drawn to exclude from the residence of the occupier those rooms which he and his family rarely or never use. Nor does there seem to be any warrant for saying that where part of a house is uninhabitable *on acquisition*, that part is ipso facto not part of the dwelling-house – and if there is clear evidence of an intention to make it habitable in the form of plans and planning consents, this would weigh heavily in the taxpayer's favour.

¶319 Separate outbuildings

(1) Outbuildings which are not dwelling-houses

Can a physically separate outbuilding be 'part of' the main house? It is clearly not a physical part of that house: but the courts have approached the problem by asking: 'Is this part of the dwelling-house which is the owner's residence?', or in effect 'Is this part of the residence?'

If 'residence' is equated, as it has been in the decided cases, with 'what the owner occupies as his home and the buildings which serve that occupation' the difficulty begins to disappear. Buildings such as garages, storehouses, boilerhouses, stables and garden buildings have normally come into existence for no other reason but to serve the owner's occupation.

The old inhabited house duty legislation included a lengthy list of outbuildings which were part of the dwelling-house for inhabited house duty purposes (see the quotation in *Paul v The Governors of the Godolphin and Latymer Girls' School* (1919) 7 TC 192). This list includes some buildings which strike a modern reader as archaic, e.g. brewhouses, wash houses, dairies and bakehouses; yet at the time of its enactment a country house in particular was in many respects a self-sufficient economic community, where many domestic requirements which today's householder pays tradesmen to supply (e.g. bread, fuel, milk or beer) were supplied by his own servants on his own premises, using his own raw materials, all of which required specialised outbuildings.

Other such buildings have been overtaken by technical advances (e.g. coach houses and stables have given way to garages). But despite these social and technical changes, those outbuildings which exist today, like their counterparts in earlier times, also generally serve the domestic purposes of the owner. In a modern house they will usually be few in number, perhaps no more than a garage and a garden shed; in an older house some of the older outbuildings may have been adapted for modern purposes. Functionally, however, they remain 'part of' the owner's residence, and, in principle, should attract PRR in exactly the same way as the main house.

Some practical problems may, however, still arise with stables and former agricultural buildings, which are discussed below at ¶322(4)–(5). Garden buildings pose a problem of statutory construction because of the differentiation of garden land from the dwelling-house in TCGA 1992, s. 222(1)(b), which is discussed at ¶322(6).

(2) Outbuildings which are themselves dwelling-houses – an overview
Before embarking on a detailed analysis of the relevant cases on subsidiary houses, it may be helpful to outline the way in which the thinking of the courts has developed from case to case.

The line adopted by the Revenue when CGT was first introduced was that a subsidiary dwelling-house, e.g. a servant's cottage or lodge house, could never rank for PRR because a separate dwelling-house could not, in the plain words of the Act, normally be 'part of' another dwelling. (It now appears that the Revenue has never actually abandoned that view, though it has not advanced the argument in later cases – see ¶321(2).)

This was the Crown's main argument in the first of the cases on this point, *Batey (HMIT) v Wakefield* (1981) 55 TC 550. As indicated below (¶320(1)) it was the illogicality of saying that an integral servant's flat in the main house ranked as part of that house, whereas a servant's cottage in the grounds did not, which persuaded the court to adopt a wider view (see, for example, *Batey (HMIT) v Wakefield* at p. 556H, per Browne-Wilkinson J). If both the integral flat and the separate house were occupied for the purpose of promoting the taxpayer's enjoyment of his main house as a residence, each was part of that residence and part of the dwelling-house, whether it was physically joined to the main house or not.

This approach led naturally to what has been described subsequently as the 'entity test' (picking up some words of Browne-Wilkinson J at p. 556G). It was necessary, according to Browne-Wilkinson J, to:

¶319

'identify the dwelling-house which is [the taxpayer's] residence. That dwelling-house may or may not be comprised in one physical building; it may comprise a number of different buildings. His dwelling-house and residence consists of all those buildings which are part and parcel of the whole, each part being appurtenant to and occupied for the purposes of the residence' (*Batey (HMIT) v Wakefield* at p. 556J).

The importance of this search for the domestic 'entity' was upheld by the Court of Appeal in *Batey*. If a subsidiary dwelling-house could be described as 'part and parcel' of the main dwelling-house then it was right to regard its sale as that of part of that house. The distance between the two houses was mentioned only in one sentence of the High Court's decision (p. 556A) and not at all in that of the Court of Appeal.

However, in the next case, *Markey (HMIT) v Sanders* [1987] BTC 176, Walton J substituted for the single 'entity' test two sub-tests, each of which had to be passed for PRR to be due on a subsidiary house. These were:

(a) that the occupation of that house must increase the taxpayer's enjoyment of the main house; and

(b) that the subsidiary house must be very closely adjacent to the main house.

This dual test approach was expressly rejected in the third case, *Williams (HMIT) v Merrylees* [1987] BTC 393. Here, Vinelott J reinstated the single, 'entity' test from *Batey* as the correct test, but held that its application required the examination of a range of factors, of which the proximity of the subsidiary house to the main house was only one, albeit a very important one. The re-statement of the 'entity' test by Vinelott J in *Merrylees* was followed in the High Court in *Lewis (HMIT) v Lady Rook* [1990] BTC 9. However, in the Court of Appeal ([1992] BTC 102) the court unanimously reversed the High Court's decision and held that a secondary dwelling could not be part of a main dwelling-house unless it was within the curtilage of, and appurtenant to, the main house, so as to be part of the entity which, together with the main house, constituted the dwelling-house occupied by the taxpayer as his residence.

This represents a major reversal of the trends of the earlier cases and its implications are considered more fully below at ¶320(4) and ¶321.

¶320 The CGT case law on subsidiary dwelling-houses

For an outline of the way in which the case law on subsidiary dwelling-houses has developed, see ¶319(2). The 'servants' houses' cases are set out below.

The House Itself

(1) Batey (HMIT) v Wakefield – the emergence of the 'entity' test

The first attempt to litigate on subsidiary dwelling-houses was in 1980. The taxpayer built a house for himself and his family in 1959 on 1.1 acres of land which he owned. After a number of burglaries in the area, including one suffered by him, he decided in 1966 to employ a resident caretaker and built for him a chalet bungalow, separated from the main house by only a tennis court and a hedge – apparently about 50 feet in length. (A full-sized tennis court would be 39 feet wide, including sidelines.) It had its own access from a separate road, and was separately rated from the main house. He sold the chalet bungalow in 1974, while retaining the remainder of the property. Exemption was claimed on the gain.

The Revenue lost in the High Court and the Court of Appeal. The most significant judgment was that of Browne-Wilkinson J in the High Court. First, he made it clear that one must look at all the buildings and not just the main house by observing that:

> 'if one looks at a man's residence it includes not only the physical main building ... but also the appurtenant buildings, such as the garage and buildings of that kind. One is looking at the group of buildings which together constitutes the residence ... subs 1(a) is including in the dwelling-house some other buildings which are appurtenant thereto, for example the garage, the potting shed and the summer house'.

He then passed on to look at separate dwelling-houses occupied by servants and said that they were essentially no different from the ancillary buildings such as the garage; Parliament could hardly have intended that an integral staff flat should be outside the exemption and there seemed no reason why a separate staff house should be treated differently:

> 'it appears to me ... that what one is looking at is the *entity*, the building which is the residence of the taxpayer, divided in such a way as is reasonable for its enjoyment for the time being. The test to be applied was "What is the residence of the taxpayer? ... What is the dwelling-house which is his residence?" This might comprise a number of different buildings, and the dwelling-house and residence consists of all those buildings which were part and parcel of the whole, each part being appurtenant to and occupied for the purpose of the residence'. [emphasis added]

In this case he decided that the test was passed and added 'bearing in mind the fact that the buildings are very closely adjacent' – words on which the Revenue was to place much weight in later cases.

The case went on to the Court of Appeal, where Fox LJ delivered the only reasoned judgment. The Crown seems merely to have repeated its earlier argument that one dwelling-house could never be part of another. This was rejected on

¶320

similar grounds to those used in the High Court; physical separation was irrelevant if the subject matter was part of the 'entity', or as Fox LJ put it, 'What has to be determined is the identity of the dwelling-house' (*Batey (HMIT) v Wakefield* (1981) 55 TC 550 at p. 560D). He did not offer any views of his own on the proximity point, but his statement that the extent of the dwelling-house 'is ... a matter of degree in every case' (*Batey (HMIT) v Wakefield* at p. 560E) may imply that he regarded proximity as a relevant factor.

(2) Markey (HMIT) v Sanders – not one test but two?

After their defeat in *Batey (HMIT) v Wakefield* (1981) 55 TC 550 it appears that the Revenue, mindful of Browne-Wilkinson J's references to proximity, searched for a case where there was a much greater distance between the two houses in the hope of establishing some kind of rule of thumb for exemption. Such a case seemed to present itself in *Markey (HMIT) v Sanders* [1987] BTC 176. The taxpayer, Miss Sanders, owned a three bedroomed house, built in the seventeenth century but later extended, in 12.75 acres of land. In 1965 she built a three bedroomed bungalow, not very much smaller overall than the main house, and some 420 feet away from it, for domestic staff, near the main entrance but screened from the main house by a belt of trees and separated from it by a ha-ha and a large paddock. This was rated together with the main house, and eventually the whole estate was sold but exemption claimed on the bungalow along with the main house.

In the High Court Walton J found in *Batey* what he regarded as two separate tests, both of which had to be passed – neither was sufficient on its own. He stated these as:

(a) did the occupation of the subsidiary house increase the taxpayer's enjoyment of the main house? and

(b) in the words of the *Batey* judgment, was the subsidiary dwelling 'very closely adjacent' to the main house?

But he found this second test insufficiently precise. He preferred to restate it thus: 'Looking at the group of buildings as a whole, is it fairly possible to regard them as a single dwelling-house used as the taxpayer's main residence?' (*Markey (HMIT) v Sanders* at p. 184). Furthermore, in applying this restated test, it was necessary to consider the scale of the whole estate – and what would be 'very closely adjacent' in looking at the sale of No. 7 Paradise Avenue, Hoxton, would not be applicable to the sale of Blenheim Palace.

In the present case, having regard to the facts that the two houses were not greatly different in size, and that the bungalow was so sited as to take it away from the main house and assure privacy for that house, as well as to the distance factor, Walton J felt that although the first test in *Batey*, the 'enjoyment' test, was clearly passed, the restated second test was failed and the bungalow was not part of the

¶320

main residence. The test was an elastic one but on this occasion, as the judge put it, the elastic had snapped. The taxpayer did not appeal against this decision.

While *Markey* was in transit from the commissioners to the High Court, the third 'servant's house' case, *Williams (HMIT) v Merrylees* [1987] BTC 393, was being heard by the commissioners. This case was to produce a further restatement of the 'entity' test, and a clear refusal to follow the 'dual test' approach in *Markey*.

(3) Williams (HMIT) v Merrylees – the 'entity' test reinstated and developed

The taxpayer purchased, in 1956, an estate in Sussex comprising a four bedroomed house built in 1850 with three reception rooms, a study, bathroom, stabling and outbuildings; four acres of land; and a small bungalow (built about the same time as the main house) with two bedrooms, two reception rooms and a bathroom and kitchen. The distance from the main house to the bungalow was about 650 feet. The bungalow was occupied by a resident gardener/caretaker. At all material times the bungalow and the main house were rated together.

In 1976 the taxpayer sold the main house and about 3.4 acres of land and moved to Cornwall. He retained the bungalow and about 0.6 acres of land, allowing the gardener to stay there rent free in return for looking after the remaining property. A right of first refusal was granted to the purchaser of the main house to buy the bungalow if and when the taxpayer wished to sell it. In 1979 the gardener died, and the taxpayer duly sold the bungalow to the purchaser of the main house.

The general commissioners found for the taxpayer, finding as a matter of fact that the bungalow had been part of the main residence and within its curtilage and appurtenant thereto right up to the 1976 sale, and thus the gain was exempt for the period up to that sale.

Vinelott J thought that Walton J's approach in *Markey* was incorrect. In his view, *Batey* laid down only one test: what had to be found, to secure exemption for a servant's house, was that it was, together with the main house, so appurtenant to that house that they could sensibly be described as a single entity. In deciding whether that test was satisfied, all the circumstances had to be considered: proximity was not a separate test, but only one such circumstance to be weighed along with others, such as the scale of the property and the relative sizes of the two houses. Factors which were crucial in one case might be less so in another and it was wrong to isolate any one in particular.

Attention had to be paid, in this case, to the contemporary construction of the two houses, their relative sizes, and the geographical layout of the whole estate. It was not simply a question of a measuring exercise. He found the question difficult, and was not certain that sitting as a judge of the facts, he would have agreed with the commissioners, but he could not say that the facts contradicted the commissioners' decision.

¶320

However, it has subsequently transpired, in the light of the decision of the Court of Appeal in *Lewis (HMIT) v Lady Rook* [1990] BTC 9, that *Williams (HMIT) v Merrylees* [1987] BTC 393 can no longer be relied on – see ¶321(3).

(4) Lewis (HMIT) v Lady Rook – the emergence of the 'curtilage' test

Lady Rook, the taxpayer in this case, was an elderly lady, who lived alone. In 1968 she bought a property in Kent, Newlands, consisting of a total of 10.5 acres of land and including a substantial house, Newlands House, built in 1804, which had four reception rooms, eight bedrooms, a large hall, an 'imposing' landing, a pantry, a scullery, a silver room, a kitchen and (presumably, although the report does not mention them) at least one bathroom and lavatory, together with an attached former coach house, latterly used for storage and garaging. Also included in the estate were two cottages, No. 1 and 2 Hop Cottages, each having two reception rooms, two bedrooms, a kitchen and bathroom.

The cottages had been created from a former oast house which was built in about 1730. They had a separate road access from that of Newlands House, and had not always been in the same ownership as that house, though it is unclear at what point they came into the same ownership or when they were converted from their former use. No. 1 had previously been occupied by Mr and Mrs F, respectively the gardener and domestic help to the former owner, but Mr F died just before Lady Rook's purchase. Mrs F never worked for Lady Rook, but continued to live at No. 1 until early 1973, paying a small weekly contribution (£1.12) to the rates. She then moved into No. 2 (the previous occupation of which is unclear), continuing to pay the same amount.

Early in 1974, Mr F's successor as gardener, who had apparently 'lived out' until then, moved into No. 1 where he remained until 1978. Later, he moved into the former coach house which had by now been converted to residential use. In 1979, No. 1 was sold, and this gave rise to the appeal. No. 1 was about 570 feet from the nearest point of the main house. Between these two dwellings lay the greenhouses and garden sheds, but there were no natural or man-made barriers, and each was fully visible from the other. Lady Rook gave evidence to the commissioners that she depended for assistance on the gardener, and while he lived at No. 1, she could (and sometimes did) signal to him when in need by a flashing light and a ship's bell.

Before the commissioners, the Crown explicitly accepted the 'entity' test and did not try to resurrect the 'single dwelling-house' argument which had failed in *Batey*. It also accepted Vinelott J's 'composite' view of the 'entity' test (*Lewis (HMIT) v Lady Rook* [1990] BTC 9 at p. 11D–E.) But it argued that, having regard to all the circumstances including distance and lay-out, No. 1 was not appurtenant to Newlands House or part of the 'complex of buildings' which was Newlands, on the grounds that it was historically distinct, predating that house as it did by some 75 years and having previously been in agricultural use, and that it had its own road

¶320

access; it had not been consistently in the same ownership (though the absence of factual detail on this point suggests that the historical background was uncertain).

By contrast, ran the Crown's argument, the coach house was clearly part of the Newlands House 'entity'.

The commissioners found for the taxpayer, in principle, though they gave no explicit reasons; and they also restricted PRR to the period of the gardener's occupation of No. 1 (plus the final balance of the last 24 months [now 36 months]), thus denying relief for the period during which Mrs F had lived there. The latter point was not challenged by the taxpayer in the High Court, and reflects the fact that Mrs F was never Lady Rook's employee.

In the High Court the Crown argued that the 'entity' concept involved considering the curtilage of the main dwelling, and only ancillary buildings within that curtilage could be regarded as part of that house (*Lewis (HMIT) v Lady Rook* at p. 16F). Mervyn Davies J rejected that submission in the light of *Batey* and *Merrylees*; the 'entity' was to be equated with 'the totality of the parts of the place where the taxpayer lives which pertain to a whole and so are integral to his or her style of life' (*Lewis* at p. 16H). The whole 10.5 acres could not be so characterised, yet at the other extreme the main house, coach house and garden clearly could.

In order to ascertain whether No. 1 could also be included the judge took into account:

(a) the distance of some 570 feet between the two houses;

(b) the fact that they had been separately rated;

(c) the occupation of No. 1 by the taxpayer's servant;

(d) the fact that a path led from the cottage to the garden where he worked; and

(e) the taxpayer's age and her reliance on help being close at hand when needed.

On that basis he concluded that '[Lady Rook's] way of living embraced use not only of Newlands House itself with its gardens but also of the cottage ....' and that the entity which was her residence therefore included No. 1. Distance was not of paramount importance in the context of the Newlands set-up' (*Lewis* at p. 17).

The case went on to the Court of Appeal (*Lewis (HMIT) v Lady Rook* [1992] BTC 102), where Balcombe LJ gave the only reasoned judgement. He found the current state of the authorities unsatisfactory and returned to the words of the statute to consider the meaning of the word 'dwelling-house'. Following the Court of Appeal in *Batey* (see ¶320(1)), he accepted that a dwelling-house could consist of more than one building, even if that other building was itself a dwelling-house. He agreed that it was necessary to find an 'entity', but this 'entity' was not 'the entity which is the residence', but the entity which is the dwelling-house. As the judge put it:

¶320

'To seek to identify the taxpayer's residence may lead to confusion because where, as here, the dwelling-house forms part of a small estate, it is all too easy to consider the estate as his residence and from that conclude that all the buildings on the estate are part of his residence. In so far as some of the statements made in *Batey v Wakefield* suggest that one must first identify the residence they must, in my judgment, be considered to have been made per incuriam.' (p. 108E–F).

Balcombe LJ went on to accept the contention of the Crown that in deciding what was included in 'the entity which is the dwelling-house' in cases where there is a main house and other houses, only buildings which were appurtenant to, and within the curtilage of, the main house could be considered for inclusion. He found this approach helpful because it involved 'application of well recognised legal concepts' (p. 108G). The judge then referred to earlier decisions of the Court of Appeal involving a consideration of the 'curtilage' in other legislation and concluded that the emphasis had always been on 'the smallness of the area comprised in the curtilage' (p. 109B). He found that this 'coincided' with the proximity test adopted in *Batey*.

Thus, Balcombe LJ found that the commissioners had adopted the wrong test; they should have asked whether the cottage was within the curtilage of and appurtenant to Newlands, so as to be part of the entity which, together with Newlands, constituted the dwelling-house occupied by Lady Rook as her residence. If they had asked that question the judge did not see how they could have reached the conclusion which they did; they would, in his opinion, have reached the opposite conclusion in the light of the facts that:

(1) Newlands was some 570 feet from the cottage;

(2) the properties were on opposite boundaries of a 10.5 acre estate;

(3) they were separated by a large garden with no intervening buildings other than the greenhouse and toolshed.

All these factors led the judge to the 'inescapable conclusion' that No. 1 Hop Cottages 'was not appurtenant to Newlands, and so was not part of the entity which, together with Newlands, constituted the taxpayer's dwelling-house' (p. 109F). The other members of the court agreed, and the taxpayer did not take the case further.

The 'curtilage' test and its implications are considered in more detail at ¶321.

(5) Integral staff accommodation and the decision in Green v IR Commrs
In the light of the general acceptance, in all the cases just considered, that an integral staff flat in the main house would qualify for PRR, a few words are needed about the decision in *Green v IR Commrs* [1982] BTC 378, (see ¶318(2)) which

was heard by the Court of Session in Scotland in 1982, after the decision of the English Court of Appeal in *Batey*.

The first point in *Green*, concerning the extent of the taxpayer's residence, was discussed at ¶318(2). A separate point in that case concerned the two wings of the mansion house, which were found by the commissioners not to be part of the dwelling-house. Each wing had its own external entrance, but each physically abutted the central block and could be reached from it by internal passages at basement level; the west wing, in addition, seems to have had another passageway to the central block at ground level. The east wing was occupied by the gardener/handyman and his family although the west wing seems to have been physically occupied, if at all, only by the taxpayer and his family.

The commissioners found merely that 'the service wings' did not attract PRR, without giving reasons, and it is not clear whether they accepted the Crown's argument that 'each of the two pavilions [wings] constituted an individual dwelling-house'.

For the taxpayer it was argued in the Court of Session that this conclusion was unreasonable in the light of *Batey*, where the decision had gone in the taxpayer's favour on much less favourable facts; the only reasonable conclusion, it was submitted, was that in *Green* there was a single entity consisting of the whole mansion house plus the two wings. The court accepted that *Batey* propounded the correct test (the 'entity' test – though, following the Court of Appeal's decision in *Lewis v Rook*, that test now seems to be incorrect – see ¶321), but declined to upset the commissioners' finding: it confined itself to asking whether the commissioners' conclusion was perverse and decided that it was not (see ¶316(4) and the discussion of the courts' function and powers on appeal).

On its own showing, it is particularly difficult to reconcile this aspect of *Green* with the English decisions, even though none of those cases involved such a large house or such complex facts (many of the details of which have been omitted here). The decision is perhaps best seen as a particularly clear instance of judicial reluctance to interfere with a finding of fact by commissioners. This may well explain why, in practice, the Revenue appears not to seek to use the case as any kind of authority for denying PRR on an integral staff flat, even if it is in a distinct wing or annex. In none of the English cases which were heard after 1982 does *Green* seem to have been seriously used by the Crown in argument, although in *Markey* Walton J mentioned it briefly as showing that proximity is not a sufficient condition for PRR (*Markey (HMIT) v Sanders* [1987] BTC 176 at p. 184).

(6) Physically distinct buildings separated by properties in different ownership – Honour (HMIT) v Norris

A different variation on the general theme of distinct dwelling-houses came before the High Court in *Honour (HMIT) v Norris* [1992] BTC 153. Here, the question was whether a number of physically distinct dwelling units in the same immediate

¶320

locality, owned by the same taxpayer and occupied by himself and his family and servants, but separated from each other by dwellings owned by unconnected third parties, could be said to be part of the same dwelling-house, such that PRR would be due on the disposal of one of the units. The facts of the case are complicated but need to be set out in full if the case is to be understood.

All of the properties were long leasehold flats in the same square in London. Five flats were involved, numbers 21a, 4a, 10, 19a and 21c. In the period under review flats 19a and 21a, which were adjacent basement flats but originally physically distinct, were joined together to make a single flat. Flat 21a was 95 yards from flat 4a, and 80 yards from flat 10, which in turn was 60 yards from flat 4a; flats 19a, 21a and 21c were on the western side of the square and flats 4a and 10 on the eastern side. The sequence of events was as follows:

(1) The lady who was later to become the wife of the taxpayer, Mr Norris, acquired flat 21a in June 1979 and lived there.

(2) She married Mr Norris in May 1982 and they later had a child.

(3) In July 1982 Mr Norris acquired flat 4a.

(4) In September 1982 the taxpayer's mother-in-law acquired flat 10 and following her death in January 1983 and a subsequent deed of family arrangement, this flat passed to Mrs Norris in January 1984.

(5) In April 1985 Mrs Norris acquired flat 19a and, as noted earlier, this was subsequently physically connected to flat 21a.

(6) In May 1987 Mrs Norris sold flat 10 and acquired yet another flat, 21c, which was on the first floor of the same house as flat 21a. It was the disposal of flat 10 which gave rise to the appeal.

The general commissioners found that flat 4a had been acquired to ease the accommodation shortage at flat 21a following the birth of the child. The two flats were linked by an intercom system. Flat 4a was used as study space by Mr and Mrs Norris, as bedroom accommodation for the nanny employed after the birth of their child, and for Mr Norris's children from an earlier marriage and guests. Flat 10 was similarly used and also accommodated Mr and Mrs Norris while flats 19a and 21a were being connected between September 1985 and April 1986. There were short periods when flat 10 had been used by friends and guests, one of whom made a contribution to running costs.

The taxpayer successfully argued before the commissioners that a dwelling-house could be regarded for PRR purposes as including physically separate buildings and that any condition requiring these buildings to be on the same site or within the same curtilage was not of universal application and in particular was inapplicable in an urban location, and/or where the buildings were all used by a taxpayer and his family as part of the main residence where the taxpayer ordinarily

¶320

resided. It was necessary to look for the entity which constituted the residence of the taxpayer which, in turn, depended on what were the true constituents of the residence in question. All the flats had been acquired for the purpose of, and were in fact used continuously for, ordinary residence and as constituent parts of the family's main residence. The commissioners found that PRR was due on flat 10 since it, together with the other flats, constituted one dwelling-house which was the taxpayer's main residence.

The case arrived in the High Court shortly before the Court of Appeal was due to hear *Lewis (HMIT) v Lady Rook* (see ¶320(4)), and Vinelott J adjourned it until that decision was known. When the hearing was re-convened the taxpayer had, therefore, to contend with the 'curtilage' argument and the revised 'entity' test based on that argument. Again, he argued that the earlier cases, all dealing with country houses, had produced a test which could not be applied without qualification to flats. For example, he argued, a flat on the top floor of a block which was let with storage or garage space in the basement would be a single entity with that space, even though the garage/store might not be within the same curtilage as the flat. If that was so, the same would apply to cases such as his own and other possible permutations of flats in the same occupation but situated on different floors, so long as they were adopted as a single residential unit.

Vinelott J said that in order to decide the case it was unnecessary to resolve the taxpayer's analogies or to formulate any principle of general application. He merely found the proposition that flat 10 and the other flats formed part of a single entity which could sensibly be described as a multi-building and multi-function dwelling-house to be 'an affront to common sense'. Flat 10 had been acquired as a conveniently close separate dwelling-house with a view to its being used as occasional bedroom accommodation for the taxpayers' older children and guests and occasionally for themselves; he compared it with a guest house acquired by a country house owner in a nearby village to provide additional accommodation when the house was full. Accordingly the taxpayer's appeal failed.

Honour (HMIT) v Norris appears, at first reading, to be a decision of limited importance and to be confined to its own highly unusual facts. However, the analogies suggested by the taxpayer are rather less unusual than his own case; there are many flats whose lessees also have the occupation and use of garages or storerooms which are physically quite distinct from their living accommodation, and the writer has encountered at least one instance of the same lessee occupying several physically separate flats in the same block. Vinelott J did not need to decide such cases, but his rejection of Mr Norris's arguments seems to lack any strong reasoning and to owe something to the very oddity of the facts. Yet the commissioners accepted the taxpayer's submissions (supported by evidence from his wife and older children) about the use of the accommodation. In a large country house all the accommodation used by the Norris family and their guests could have been located under one roof and much of it might have been seldom used (see

¶320

¶318(2)), yet it would be startling if a court were to decide that, on a sale of such a house, part of the gain did not rank for PRR. One cannot quite avoid the feeling that this decision lacks any firm rational basis and that a less unusual set of facts might lead to a different result. It is certainly difficult to apply Balcombe LJ's revised 'entity' test from *Lewis v Rook* to facts such as those in *Honour v Norris* with any confidence that it is appropriate – another matter which the judgment in that case does not really address. The Revenue's views on this point are considered below (see ¶321(4)).

¶321 Current state of the law on subsidiary dwellings

(1) Which is the right 'entity'?

With the exception of *Markey (HMIT) v Sanders* [1987] BTC 176, where Walton J's approach has not been followed in later cases, the trend of the cases reviewed above was in favour of the taxpayer until the Court of Appeal's decision in *Lewis (HMIT) v Lady Rook* [1990] BTC 9. Until then, the search was for the 'entity which is the residence of the taxpayer'. If that concept had become a little loose, as Balcombe LJ observed in the Court of Appeal, this was partly because the language of both courts in *Batey (HMIT) v Wakefield* (1981) 55 TC 550 had encouraged the idea that a taxpayer 'resided' not just in the main house but also in those other appurtenant buildings which were occupied for the purpose of that residence (see the quotations at ¶320(l) above).

(2) The Revenue's arguments – only one physical dwelling

It is now clear from the arguments advanced by the Crown in the Court of Appeal in *Lewis v Rook* that the Revenue had never abandoned two lines of argument which appear to date back to the earliest case, *Batey*. The first argument was that there could only be one physical dwelling-house for each application of the relief; this was its only argument in *Batey* and was rejected both in the High Court and the Court of Appeal. In *Lewis v Rook* it was mentioned in argument in the Court of Appeal, but it was accepted by Counsel for the Crown that it could not be used in view of its rejection by the same court in *Batey*; however, Counsel specifically reserved the argument for use if such a case ever reaches the House of Lords (see *Lewis (HMIT) v Lady Rook* [1992] BTC 102 at p. 105F). If this view were to be upheld by the Lords, no PRR would ever be due on servants' accommodation unless it was in an integral staff flat or wing.

(3) The Revenue's arguments – curtilage

The second of these arguments is the argument which succeeded in the Court of Appeal in *Lewis v Rook*, to the effect that in order to decide whether a secondary building is part of the dwelling-house one must consider the curtilage of that house.

The Revenue was probably attracted to this argument by references to the curtilage concept in other legislation, where a narrow physical scope was assigned to the term. Particular emphasis was placed, both by the Revenue's technical specialist division in its advice to inspectors, and by Counsel for the Crown in *Lewis v Rook*, on a case under the *Leasehold Reform Act* 1967, *Methuen-Campbell v Walters* [1979] 1 All ER 606. Under that Act a lessee's right to acquire the freehold of his house extended only to the dwelling-house, garage, outhouse, garden, yard and appurtenances which were occupied with and used for the purposes of the house (*Leasehold Reform Act* 1967, s. 2(3)).

In *Methuen-Campbell*, in the Court of Appeal, Buckley LJ had to construe the word 'appurtenances' in that subsection. He regarded it as denoting whatever would pass under a conveyance without specific mention, i.e. land and buildings within the curtilage (see ¶316(1)). He rejected the view that the mere fact that two properties had passed under a single conveyance necessarily brought them within the same curtilage; the same was true of the fact that they were occupied together, or, most crucially for the Revenue's purpose, that the enjoyment of one was advantageous, convenient or necessary for the full enjoyment of the other. The judge went on: 'In my judgment, for one corporeal hereditament to fall within the curtilage of another, the former must be so intimately associated with the latter as to lead to the conclusion that the former in truth forms part and parcel of the latter.' (*Methuen-Campbell v Walters* at p. 621).

Since the curtilage argument's earlier appearances in PRR cases, another case in the wider legal field had been heard which the Revenue found helpful in the Court of Appeal in *Lewis v Rook*. This was *Dyer v Dorset County Council* [1989] QB 346. This case arose under the *Housing Act* 1980, part of what was popularly known as the 'Right to Buy' legislation introduced by the Thatcher administration.

The plaintiff was employed by the defendant authority as a lecturer at an agricultural college. He occupied a house owned by the authority on the edge of the college grounds, some 450 yards from the college buildings and fenced off from the rest of the grounds but with pedestrian access from them. The plaintiff claimed the right to buy the house, which the authority resisted on the grounds that it came within one of the exceptions to that right contained in para. 1(1) and (2) of Sch. 1 to the 1980 Act. Paragraph 1(1) excluded a dwelling-house which 'either forms part of, or is within the curtilage of, a building to which [para. 1(2)] applies and [satisfies a further condition not relevant to present purposes]'. Paragraph 1(2), broadly, applied to a building held mainly for purposes other than housing purposes and consisting mainly of accommodation other than housing. The issue was therefore whether the plaintiff's house was within the curtilage of another college building, the college buildings being accepted as within para. 1(2).

The authority, of course, seeking to avoid being deprived of its property, argued that the plaintiff's house was within the relevant curtilage, and that the word 'curtilage' in the 1980 Act should be taken to refer to a much larger area than

¶321

would otherwise be the case. The plaintiff argued, naturally, for a narrow construction of the expression and *Methuen-Campbell* was cited in support of this view. The Court of Appeal unanimously upheld the narrow view. On that view the house was not part of the curtilage of any college building and the plaintiff's case succeeded.

'Curtilage', said Lord Donaldson MR (*Dyer v Dorset County Council* at p. 357G) 'seems always to involve some small and necessary extension to that to which the word is attached'. Nourse LJ explored the historical roots of the word in the old French *courtil*, a little court or yard, with the diminutive suffix '-age' further emphasising its smallness. He also quoted with approval the *Oxford English Dictionary* definition referring to 'a small court, yard, garth or piece of ground attached to a dwelling-house and forming one enclosure with it'. He noted that the authorities showed that 'an area of land cannot properly be described as a curtilage unless it forms part and parcel of the house or building which it contains or to which it is attached' (p. 358D). He went on to say:

> 'While making every allowance for the fact that the size of a curtilage may vary somewhat with the size of the house or building, I am in no doubt that the 100 acre park on the edge of which Mr. Dyer's house now stands cannot possibly be said to form part and parcel of Kingston Maurward House [where the main college buildings were situated], far less any of the other college buildings. Indeed, a park of this size is altogether in excess of anything which could properly be described as the curtilage of a mansion house, an area which no conveyancer would extend beyond that occupied by the house, the stables and other outbuildings, the gardens and the rough grass up to the ha-ha, if there was one. Nor do I myself think that Mr. Dyer's house could properly be described as being within the curtilage of the college. It does not form part and parcel of the college buildings. Not only is it entirely separate; it is removed from them at some considerable distance.'

It seems clear, therefore, that the approval of the curtilage argument in *Lewis v Rook* is likely to result in the Revenue maintaining a strict line in future 'servants' house' cases and similar cases involving secondary dwellings. Indeed, this line is stressed in CGT 64245 and 64250. It can be expected that dicta such as those quoted above, which stress the 'smallness' which seems to be at the root of the expression, will frequently be cited by inspectors. In practice this is likely to make it very difficult to argue for PRR on a secondary house which is as far away from the main house as the dwelling in *Williams (HMIT) v Merrylees* [1987] BTC 393 (a decision which is, presumably, now to be regarded as incorrect) and *Lewis v Rook*. It may also lessen the chances of obtaining relief where there is some clearly defined boundary to the main house such as a wall around a yard, a ring of trees or hedgerow, or a moat, and the secondary dwelling is outside that boundary (see CGT 64247). Certainly Nourse LJ's depiction of what he regarded as a typical

¶321

curtilage, in *Dyer*, closely echoes the kind of arguments used, in the writer's experience, by district valuers in PRR cases.

(4) Advisers' approach following the Court of Appeal decision in Lewis (HMIT) v Lady Rook

Few advisers will have clients who are prepared to take a case to the House of Lords in the hope of having *Lewis v Rook* disapproved. However, in the writer's view advisers should not necessarily despair of mounting PRR claims on secondary houses which are outside the immediate environs of a main house. The following points should, it is suggested, be borne in mind:

(1) It may be possible to regard the curtilage of a large main house as more flexible than Balcombe LJ suggested. Nourse LJ, in the passage from *Dyer* quoted above, accepted that it might be possible for the size of a curtilage to vary with that of a house. However, the Revenue will certainly resist the argument that it is legitimate to see a whole estate as a single curtilage (see CGT 64249) – the argument which failed in *Dyer*. They do, however, accept that the question is one of fact and degree and that the 'necessary degree of proximity' will vary from case to case (CGT 64250).

(2) The possibility of such a flexible approach would seem to be consistent with the view expressed by Buckley LJ in *Methuen-Campbell* that it is the 'intimate association' of one property with another which leads them to be regarded as being part and parcel one with another, and therefore in the same curtilage. He was prepared to admit that the concept can, depending on the character and circumstances of the items under consideration, extend to 'ancillary buildings, structures or areas such as outhouses, a garage, a driveway, a garden and so forth'. A boundary line drawn to include such areas might well contain secondary dwellings. This suggests that there may still be considerable scope for negotiation in the light of the facts of each case.

(3) Too much stress should not be laid on any physical boundary around the main house where this is dictated by the circumstances and architectural traditions of the area concerned. For example, moated farm and manor houses are relatively common in East Anglia because the region has little stone of its own and in former times few landowners could afford to build boundary walls with costly imported stone. To take another example, in the Fens it is common to find farmhouses ringed with poplar trees to act as a windbreak. If the owner of a property wished to build, say, a gardener's or housekeeper's bungalow today it might have to be constructed outside such ancient boundaries simply for reasons of space. That should not of itself mean that it is not part and parcel of, and appurtenant to, the main house. The nature and perhaps the age of any physical boundaries may also be relevant;

¶321

a brick wall which has been in place for 100 years is clearly a more significant boundary, when determining the curtilage, than a recently erected barbed-wire fence, and a footpath is a less 'solid' boundary than a public road, a river or a railway line.

(4) Finally, as *Honour (HMIT) v Norris* [1992] BTC 153 (see ¶320(6)) illustrates, the test seems ill-adapted to certain urban properties and to situations where the dwellings in question are separated from each other by property owned by third parties. The Revenue seem to have adapted their stance somewhat here since that case, accepting that a garage which is separated from a house or flat by buildings in different ownership should be seen as 'part of' that dwelling even though not in the same curtilage (CGT 64292). There is also some flexibility in their views of adjoining flats in the same building which are occupied by the same family, even, apparently, if they have not been 'knocked through' to form a single unit (see CGT 64306).

There can be important implications for the 'permitted area' of garden and grounds when identifying the extent of the dwelling house (see Chapter 4).

¶322 Specific problem areas

(1) Occupation by employees of the owner

When the disposal of a subsidiary dwelling-house is in issue it is unlikely to qualify for PRR (assuming that it can pass the now re-stated 'entity' test based on the curtilage concept) except in so far as it is occupied by the taxpayer's domestic employees. This is a consequence of the requirement that it is the residence of the taxpayer whose occupation has to be served. Thus, there was no doubt in *Lewis (HMIT) v Lady Rook* [1990] BTC 9 that the gardener's tenure of the cottage was essential to the taxpayer's well-being, and in the other cases there was no serious attempt to dispute that the employees needed to live where they did to perform their duties.

A curious argument appears in the Valuation Office Manual (VOM 8.21) about gardeners' cottages, to the effect that they are occupied to enhance the enjoyment of the garden rather than the house and should thus not attract PRR. There seems to be no counterpart to this view in the CGT Manual and in the writer's view it is misconceived. The better view is surely that the garden and grounds are themselves maintained to enhance the enjoyment of the house, and those employed in that work are therefore serving the same object.

Following the principles established in rating cases such as *Northern Ireland Commissioner of Valuation v Fermanagh Protestant Board of Education* [1969] 3 All ER 352, the legal occupier of the subsidiary houses in the decided cases is likely to have been the employer, though it is doubtful whether this point in itself would always be conclusive. If, however, the legal occupier is the same person as the physical occupier – as will normally be the case where the house is let on a normal arm's length tenancy to a non-employee – it can hardly be said that the taxpayer is occupying the house as well, which naturally leads to the conclusion that it is not part of his residence.

Cases may arise, however, which are less clear cut even though they still involve employees of the owner. If the occupant's duties are not directly connected with the main dwelling-house or its garden and grounds, the subsidiary house may not attract PRR. In the decided cases the employees were all gardeners, caretakers, handymen, domestics or some combination of these. Where the occupant is employed away from the main house and grounds in some business of the owner, the same analysis cannot be made; the employment will not serve the occupation of the employer's residence. Marginal cases which may prove difficult could, for example, involve employees who perform a few domestic duties in addition to a main employment elsewhere, either with the owner or with a third party.

Example

Lord Colossus is chairman of Colossal Enterprises plc. His home, Colossal Park, includes a former stable block, which is now a garage, adjoining the main house, and a home farm. Over the garage are some former grooms' quarters which are now divided into four self-contained flats, occupied as follows: (1) by Bultitude, butler to Lord Colossus; (2) by Grimbling, his personal chauffeur who is actually employed by the company but also drives Lord and Lady Colossus on private journeys, the benefit of which is taxed under Sch. E; (3) by Jethro Muckspreader, who works for about half his time on the home farm but also helps in the gardens; and (4) by Rita Goodbody, Lord Colossus's business secretary who is also employed by the company and works mainly at its offices in London. (He personally employs a private secretary to deal with his personal correspondence, but she lives in the nearby town.)

Assuming that the stable block can pass the re-stated 'entity' test based on the curtilage, there would be little doubt that flat (1) would attract PRR on disposal of the block, since the butler is purely a domestic employee and probably needs to live on hand. Flats (2) and (3) are occupied by employees who are partly 'domestic', and unless their domestic duties are minimal – clearly not the case with Jethro at least – it should be possible to claim full PRR since the dominant reason for their being housed on the estate is that their domestic duties require this; the inspector might suggest an apportionment of the gains but this, it is thought, should be resisted in principle though possibly conceded if tactical reasons are paramount. Flat (4), however, is provided, apparently, purely as a

¶322

matter of convenience and the secretary has no duties other than those of her employment with the company, so that PRR would not be due.

It may sometimes be the case that even though one of the occupants performs no domestic duties, his or her spouse does; many domestic posts for cooks or housekeepers, for example, are advertised with the rider 'Accommodation provided, husband to follow own occupation'. In such cases PRR ought to be available by reference to the 'domestic' spouse's employment, that of the other being irrelevant.

(2) Occupation by non-employees

Where the occupant of a subsidiary dwelling-house has no employment with the owner in any capacity the prospects for PRR are not bright; though if there was a period when TCGA 1992, s. 222(1)(a) did apply, either because the owner himself was in residence or there was genuine representative occupation by a domestic employee, some relief could still be due under s. 223(4) (see ¶708).

Occupation by non-employees raises other problems. Gratuitous licences, or licences at a nominal rent, to relatives or friends of the owner, or to retired domestic employees or their surviving spouses, will almost certainly mean that the physical occupier is not serving the owner's occupation of the main house. So in *Rook*, again, the former gardener's widow, Mrs F, was not the employee of the owner and paid something, albeit very little, towards her occupation of the house. On this footing there was no PRR for that period (see ¶320(4)). Nevertheless, many domestic employees may retire only very gradually and may still be performing some useful duties at very advanced ages; while they are still receiving some kind of wage and providing a measurable service in return, it is considered that PRR is not prejudiced.

(3) Dower-houses

The position of dower-houses on large landed estates is interesting in this respect. It may be that such a house is physically very close to the main house and has a well documented history of use by the widowed mother of the head of the family. An architect or an historian might regard such a house as, in every sense, 'part of' the main house, but the case law test suggests that even if the re-stated 'entity' test, based on the curtilage, can be satisfied, PRR will not be due since the occupant will not be an employee and will not serve the occupation of the main house in any practical respect. Yet if the 'dowager' instead occupied a wing of the main house and lived there as part of the landowner's household the position might well be different (see ¶1106).

The problem of such houses is likely to become particularly awkward with the phasing out of the former relief for dependent relatives' houses in s. 226 (see ¶1021). That relief would in the past usually have covered this situation, but it will

¶322

not be available, for disposals after 5 April 1988, unless the relative was in occupation at or before that date (see ¶1024).

(4) Garages, stables and other outbuildings
Garages, equipment stores, fuel stores, boilerhouses and similar outbuildings are likely always to have been used by the owner to serve his occupation of the main house; even if they happen to be disused at the time of sale, that should not prevent PRR any more than would the disuse of rooms in the house (see ¶318), provided that they fall within the curtilage of the house.

Even though they may pass the 'curtilage' test, stables which are still in use for keeping horses may sometimes attract Revenue attention on the grounds that they do not serve the occupation of the house, but that of adjacent land, such as paddocks (though see ¶407 for alternative views here). However, it can be forcefully argued that a substantial country house, especially one built before about 1914, would have stabling as a matter of course just as a modern house would have a garage, and for precisely the same reason – to serve the daily transport needs of the owner. The fact that the motor car has since replaced the horse in this respect, and that the horses are now kept simply for recreation, should not, in the writer's view, separate the stables from the domestic 'entity'. There is perhaps a tendency for some inspectors to argue that stables (and, for that matter, other substantial outbuildings such as detached childrens' playrooms converted from former stables or barns) are 'luxury' or 'amenity' items which are not part of the 'entity'.

Such arguments should be firmly resisted, since they represent an attempt to set up some kind of subjective minimum standard of housing beyond which PRR is not to extend. Such an approach is quite absent from s. 222(1)(a), though it is a different matter when we turn to associated land (see ¶410). See also the comments at (6) below.

(5) Redundant former agricultural buildings
Similar problems may arise where the issue concerns a former working farmhouse which has been severed from most of its land and sold to its current owner as a private home. The sale may have included substantial former farm buildings close to the house and within its curtilage, such as hay barns and cowsheds. (Much the same goes for former mill houses, tanneries, forges, etc.) The new residential owner may convert these for domestic use, e.g. as garages, playrooms, etc. or use them as stabling if he has horses for recreation. If so, the considerations at ¶322(4) should apply.

Some such buildings, however, may be of no use to him and may be sold on, perhaps with planning permission for conversion into dwellings or for some light industrial or commercial use. If such buildings were never used by the residential owner and are sold on by him within a relatively short time – say up to two years after acquisition – it is unlikely that any PRR would be due, since they would never

¶322

have been integrated into the domestic 'entity'; historically, they never served any domestic purpose and their subsequent disuse cannot alter that. It may be possible, however, for them to be put to some domestic use in the interim in an attempt to preserve PRR, perhaps as additional garage or storage space or even as venues for dances and parties, and to document this use as far as possible by photographs or memoranda.

However, where planning permission is obtained by the owner for alternative uses, and particularly where the permission was already in existence prior to acquisition, it may be difficult to resist a Revenue claim under s. 224(3) (see ¶307); certainly any expenditure with a view to facilitating a sale, such as the cost of planning applications and architects' fees and, of course, physical conversion work, is likely to entail a restriction of any PRR under that subsection as 'tainted' expenditure (see ¶308).

(6) Garden buildings

In *Batey (HMIT) v Wakefield* (1981) 55 TC 550 at p. 556D–E) Browne-Wilkinson J remarked that garden buildings such as potting sheds and summer houses should logically fall under the dwelling house 'entity' and attract PRR under s. 222(1)(a), because although the draftsman had dealt with the garden and grounds separately under s. 222(1)(b), the garden buildings were not so dealt with. Thus, if they could not be subsumed under s. 222(1)(a), they would fall outside PRR altogether. In the light of the revised 'entity' test as propounded in the Court of Appeal in *Lewis v Rook* (see ¶320(4)), these remarks may have diminished relevance, and were obiter even in *Batey*. They do, however, raise an interesting point. Garden buildings do not naturally seem to fit within s. 222(1)(b), since that subsection confers PRR only on 'land which [the taxpayer has] ... as garden and grounds'; and although s. 288(1) provides that for CGT purposes 'land' includes buildings, this is only the case 'unless the context otherwise requires', and in this context it is difficult to see how a building can be held 'as' a garden or 'as' grounds.

The Revenue set out its approach to this matter in a note in its *Tax Bulletin*, February 1992, pp. 10–11. Briefly, this statement says that inspectors try to distinguish between:

(1) outbuildings forming part of the dwelling-house;

(2) those ancillary to the garden or grounds; and

(3) buildings in neither of these categories.

The statement added that garages and fuel stores, serving the house in its residential function, fell into category (1) and could qualify for PRR under s. 222(1)(a) if they were part of the dwelling-house. Category (2), in the Revenue's view, included 'non-commercial greenhouses, gazebos, garden sheds etc.', and if these were 'merely ancillary to the garden or grounds', their title to PRR would depend on whether they stood in the 'permitted area' (see ¶408ff.). Buildings in category (3) were not considered eligible for any PRR. This statement now appears to have been echoed in CGT 64203 and 64365, which treat buildings in the 'permitted area' as part of the garden unless used for a business or let.

Advisers might, however, consider exploring whether this is strictly correct where it would be advantageous to argue that a garden building and its associated land falls outside either s. 222(1)(a) or (b); this would, of course, be where there is an overall loss which it would be possible to use against other gains if it could be shown to be an allowable loss (see the discussion at ¶1001ff.).

¶323 Servants' houses – practical application of case law principles

In this section an attempt is made to summarise the tax planning and negotiating considerations which arise when dealing with subsidiary dwelling-houses.

(1) Tax planning during ownership

First, one must ask whether any useful planning can be done when a sale of a servant's house, or an estate involving such a house, is contemplated. Arguably, such planning ought to begin when the estate is first acquired, because by the time the sale is contemplated it will be too late to alter the past. Thus, every effort should be made to ensure that there are no lengthy 'gaps' in occupation of servants' houses when employees leave or die: such gaps might prejudice any later claim that the occupation of the servant's house was necessary for the 'reasonable enjoyment' of the main house, especially if there were to be any prolonged occupation by relatives or friends, and lettings otherwise than on service tenancies should obviously be avoided.

Furthermore, the duties performed by the occupants should be real and measurable (see ¶322(2)): mere 'grace and favour' occupation by aged former employees who have completely retired, or their widowed spouses, may prejudice the exemption. This may, of course, pose ethical dilemmas for the conscientious owner.

It may assist in later arguments with the Revenue if the servant's house is treated as one with the main house for council tax purposes, and shared main services may also be important. If the occupant is a caretaker it may help to convince the inspector of the genuiness of his or her job to keep papers relating to any actual burglaries previously suffered, such as insurance claims, and newspaper cuttings about local crime waves. Expensive exercises in landscape gardening, such as the ha-ha and shelter belt which featured in *Markey (HMIT) v Sanders* [1987] BTC 176, may be counterproductive if they tend to take the servant's house outside the curtilage of the main house.

(2) Pre-sale tax planning

Assuming that matters such as those just mentioned have been adequately covered during the period of ownership, what of the period when a sale is contemplated? The cases suggest that from a tax viewpoint there is little to choose between a total sale of the estate or a separate sale of the servant's cottage: it is true that *Batey (HMIT) v Wakefield* (1981) 55 TC 550, *Williams (HMIT) v Merrylees* [1987] BTC 393 and *Lewis (HMIT) v Lady Rook* [1990] BTC 9, where the taxpayers won, involved separate sales, but there is nothing in the judgements to suggest that this was a deciding factor, and in any event Mr Merrylees' sale took place after the sale of the bulk of the estate and not before it. Other factors, notably the need to use losses, may suggest a separate sale. On the other hand, the Revenue might well argue that a separate sale, made with no intention to sell the rest of the estate, suggested that the servant's house was ipso facto functionally severable from that estate and not part and parcel of it.

Where the entire estate is being sold, it will be useful to ensure that estate agent's particulars refer to the 'service' status of a servant's house, and emphasise its attractions as such to potential purchasers. Finally, of course, all such particulars should be carefully kept for use in evidence should a dispute later arise.

(3) Contentious cases – a question of fact

As the decisions make clear – especially the result in *Green v IR Commrs* [1982] BTC 378 (see ¶320(5)) – the array of relevant factors must be considered fully in each case in order to determine whether the subsidiary dwelling is 'part and parcel' of the main house. As such, it is inevitable that each case will turn on its own facts, and generalisations have limited use. Although the previous sections have attempted to delineate the principles involved as fully as possible, there will be no substitute for the skilful assembly and use of all the facts if the matter is disputed by the inspector or before the commissioners. Time spent in research and in the collation of data will rarely be wasted, and practitioners may be surprised how much it is possible for a client to discover about the history of a particular property.

The courts, following the well established rule in *Edwards (HMIT) v Bairstow & Harrison* (1955) 36 TC 207 (see ¶316(4)) will be slow to overturn a decision of fact by Commissioners which is not clearly at odds with the evidence and contains no clear error of law. *Green* indicates the lengths to which they will go before taking the opposite view. It follows that if a taxpayer can succeed before the commissioners the chances of Revenue success in the courts are greatly reduced.

(4) Contentious cases – negotiations with the Revenue

A successful outcome for the taxpayer in such a case will often be largely dependent on the negotiating and presentational skills of his advisers assuming that the case is not entirely hopeless at the outset.

¶323

The vital feature of such cases is likely to be the assembly and use of all the facts. The inspector should be given a complete picture of the estate and it is suggested that he be invited to visit it (any necessary permission being obtained from the new owner) to see it for himself as well as being provided with photographs.

Other vital elements will be as follows:

(a) a clear plan of what was sold (and ground plans of houses);
(b) accurate measurements of the distance between the main and subsidiary dwelling – it is perfectly legitimate, incidentally, to take measurements from the nearest point of the main house;
(c) estate agent's particulars relating to all sales;
(d) as much as can be discovered about the history of the estate, especially the previous status and use of any property which was sold as a servant's cottage – previous owners may be able to help; and
(e) if possible, evidence, written or oral, from resident employees. It may be vital to establish that they were actively engaged on the estate and needed to live there to perform their duties. It will be particularly helpful to have agreed previously with the Revenue that the resident employee is a 'representative occupier' for Sch. E purposes (see ICTA 1988, s. 145(4)(a) or (b)) and that no taxable benefit arises in respect of their accommodation.

Some inspectors may argue that it is not 'necessary' to employ resident staff, and thus seek to trip up the client at the 'reasonable enjoyment' hurdle. This approach should be vigorously resisted, and reliance placed on the words used by Browne-Wilkinson J in *Batey*: 'the taxpayer's reasonable enjoyment of his own residence'. If the particular taxpayer in question had good reason, in his particular circumstances, to employ resident staff, it should not matter that a different owner in different circumstances might make different arrangements.

Inspectors may sometimes involve the district valuer in PRR negotiations in order to obtain an opinion on the extent of the dwelling-house. District valuers now seem to be fully conversant with the principles derived from the case law, and if they become involved it is often more convenient for the taxpayer and his advisers to negotiate directly with them (see VOM 8.21). However, it should be remembered that the district valuer's role is itself advisory, his 'client' being the inspector, and that the inspector, under the guidance of his head office, retains responsibility for all decisions. Copies of correspondence with the district valuer should, therefore, be sent to the inspector.

The district valuer will certainly be involved if, as is often the case, there is also a dispute over the 'permitted area' (see ¶408ff. and VOM 8.4). In such cases he will usually deal with the detailed negotiations over the extent of the dwelling house at the same time. If the matter goes before the commissioners, the practical

¶323

points suggested at ¶412(6)–(7), in connection with 'permitted area' cases, will be equally applicable to 'servants' houses' cases.

A useful practical point is that when there is both an 'ancillary dwelling' issue and a 'permitted area' issue in relation to the same disposal, district valuers are instructed that buildings which form part of the dwelling house must be included in the 'permitted area' (see VOM 8.53). It follows that if the Revenue can be convinced that an ancillary dwelling is properly seen as part of the main house, the land between the two will itself also qualify for PRR (see CGT 64244). The negotiations on both issues must therefore be seen as a single process.

4 The House and its Surroundings

THE SCOPE OF THE EXEMPTION FOR GARDEN AND GROUNDS

¶401 Definition of 'permitted area' within s. 222(1)(b)

TCGA 1992, s. 222(1)(b) extends PRR to land which the individual has with his residence, for his own occupation and enjoyment, as garden or grounds, up to the 'permitted area'.

It is necessary to examine each of the components of this phrase separately.

¶402 Land

Land must be held 'as garden or grounds' (or for occupation and enjoyment as such: see ¶322(6)), as to which see ¶406ff. Although for CGT generally, 'land' includes a building on land (see TCGA 1992, s. 288(1)), this is only the case 'unless the context otherwise requires'. The separate mention of the dwelling-house in s. 222(1)(a), and the qualifying phrase 'garden or grounds' in s. 222(1)(b), indicate that 'land' must be construed more narrowly here. As regards garden buildings such as greenhouses and summer houses, see ¶322(6).

¶403 'Which the individual has'

This phrase must be read with the phrase which follows (see ¶404), but the word 'has' is significant. It draws attention to the fact that PRR can extend to grounds enjoyed with the main residence, even if they are held on a lease or tenancy. The present tense of the verb 'has' is also important where the owner has ceased to own the house at the time when he sells the land, a topic considered in detail later (see ¶417).

¶404 'For his own occupation ...'

The reference to 'own occupation' implies that the individual in question must be in physical possession of the land. If the land is let by him, then he does not hold it for his own occupation, even though he would be 'enjoying" the income from letting it.

¶405   '... and enjoyment'

'Enjoyment' seems to add little at first sight to the 'occupation' requirement. The expression 'occupied and enjoyed with' is used by legal draftsmen to describe property rights, such as rights of way or light, which may pass with land which is being conveyed, although it is difficult to derive any assistance from this here. It may be that the draftsman added the word to make it quite clear that occupation of, and the ability to use, the land must be present, and not merely the legal right to recover possession at will. Thus, a man might let land, such as a paddock, year after year on a succession of informal licences to the local pony club. He would not himself be occupying the land, for his own enjoyment – he would be enjoying the income from it instead. Such land would fall outside TCGA 1992, s. 222(1)(b). It is also likely that 'enjoyment' takes its colour from 'garden and grounds', denoting amenity land as distinct from land held for financial profit, such as a smallholding or agricultural pasture, or land which has simply been abandoned and become waste ground.

GARDEN OR GROUNDS

¶406   The everyday sense of the phrase

Whether land is held as garden or grounds often presents little difficulty: a 'garden' in the *Concise Oxford Dictionary* is 'A piece of ground devoted to growing flowers, fruit or vegetables', and 'grounds' denotes 'Enclosed land for ornament or recreation attached to a house'. On that basis the Act would naturally be contemplating an area containing flower beds, vegetable plots, lawns or trees, and perhaps other ornamental features such as ponds or rockeries.

¶407   Grounds, paddocks and 'wild' land

The addition of 'grounds' is perhaps intended to extend the concept beyond land which is specially cultivated or regularly tended, to areas of 'wild' land or woodland, or paddocks or meadow land, which may perhaps be mown only once or twice a year.

Another reason for the separate mention of 'grounds' may be that part of the land has been physically transformed, e.g. into tennis courts or swimming pools, or simply concreted or gravelled over (perhaps by an owner who dislikes gardening). Such land could not strictly be described as 'garden' land but it would seem indisputably to be 'grounds'.

The Revenue may dispute the inclusion of the paddocks or meadow land within the phrase, since they may sometimes merge imperceptibly into the concept of agricultural land. It is considered that this view is incorrect, since the statutory phrase is 'Land which the individual has ... as garden or grounds'. If a man decides that he prefers the sight of wild flowers, herbs and butterflies in summer to the weekly chore of mowing grass, so that what may once have been a neat lawn becomes a wild and rough paddock, he is nevertheless still holding the land as 'grounds'. The result should be no different if he uses that land to graze his daughter's pony or even a small flock of sheep or goats, so long as he is not actually trading as a farmer or smallholder.

It is true that in *Methuen-Campbell v Walters* [1979] 1 All ER 606, a case already considered in a different context (see ¶321(3)), Goff LJ held that a paddock could not be a 'garden' for the purposes of the *Leasehold Reform Act* 1967, s. 2(3) but for the purposes of that Act it was only necessary to consider whether a paddock was a 'garage, outhouse, garden, yard or appurtenances', and not whether it was 'grounds'. Similarly, in a case under the *Common Land (Rectification of Registers) Act* 1989, 'pasture land' was held not to be 'garden', but in that context it was only necessary to decide if it was 'land ancillary to a dwelling-house' which was defined as a 'garden, private garage or outbuildings ...' and not whether it was 'grounds' (s. 1(3) of the *Common Land (Rectification of Registers) Act* 1989 as construed in *Re Land at Freshfields* (*The Times*, 1 February 1993)). Neither case would seem to be authority for denying paddocks or pasture, held for the owner's own occupation or enjoyment (and not, of course, farmed commercially or let at a rent), the status of 'grounds' for PRR purposes.

In fact, in another Commons Registration case, the High Court held that a plot of more than one acre of woodland and shrubbery, part of which was described as 'impenetrable', largely it seems due to trees which had fallen in the great gale of October 1987, and the remainder as 'largely a wilderness', was nonetheless still a 'garden' for the purpose of that Act (*Cresstock Investments Ltd v Commons Commissioner* [1992] 1 WLR 1088). Since there is no definition of 'garden' in that Act it seems that this case can support a construction of the everyday meaning of the word which would encompass wild land for PRR purposes, provided always that it could still be said that at the time of disposal, it was held for the owner's occupation and enjoyment. Land which had been totally abandoned might fail the latter test, of course.

A quite separate problem will be whether such land is within the permitted area – see ¶408ff.

In its *Tax Bulletin*, February 1992, p. 10, the Revenue comments briefly on the meaning of the phrase 'garden or grounds' and says: 'In general, land is treated as garden or grounds if it is *enclosed land* serving chiefly for ornament or recreation, surrounding or attached to a dwelling-house or other building' [emphasis added]. In the writer's view paddocks or wild areas and woodland will often, on the facts, fit this description, although it is not clear why the Revenue believes that enclosure is relevant. The Revenue's instructions broadly follow the lines indicated above (see CGT 64360–64364) although CGT 64361 still attaches importance to the fact that land should be 'enclosed'. The front gardens of many modern 'estate'-type houses are unenclosed and, indeed, their enclosure is often forbidden by restrictive covenants. It would seem impossible to argue that they are not gardens.

THE PERMITTED AREA

¶408 The basic rule – 0.5 hectares

Land which fulfils the various conditions just described attracts PRR only up to the permitted area (TCGA 1992, 222(1)(b)). This means, in the first place, an area of land, inclusive of the site of the dwelling-house, of 0.5 hectares (s. 222(2)). In the following discussion, the expression 'total plot' is used for convenience to denote the whole area of land, including the house, whose entitlement to PRR is in question.

For disposals before 19 March 1991, the basic permitted area was one acre. The substitution of 0.5 hectares in relation to later disposals (by FA 1991, s. 93) was introduced to conform with European Community drafting practice. It represents a very slight increase, since 0.5 hectares is equivalent to about 1.23 acres.

The following discussion assumes that the taxpayer, with realised or latent gains, is concerned to establish as large a permitted area as possible. However, where losses are involved, the opposite may apply, and possibilities here are discussed at ¶1003(1).

On page 71 is a flow chart to illustrate the way in which the legislation operates.

The House and its Surroundings

GARDEN OR GROUNDS

In relation to a disposal of land held with a residence:

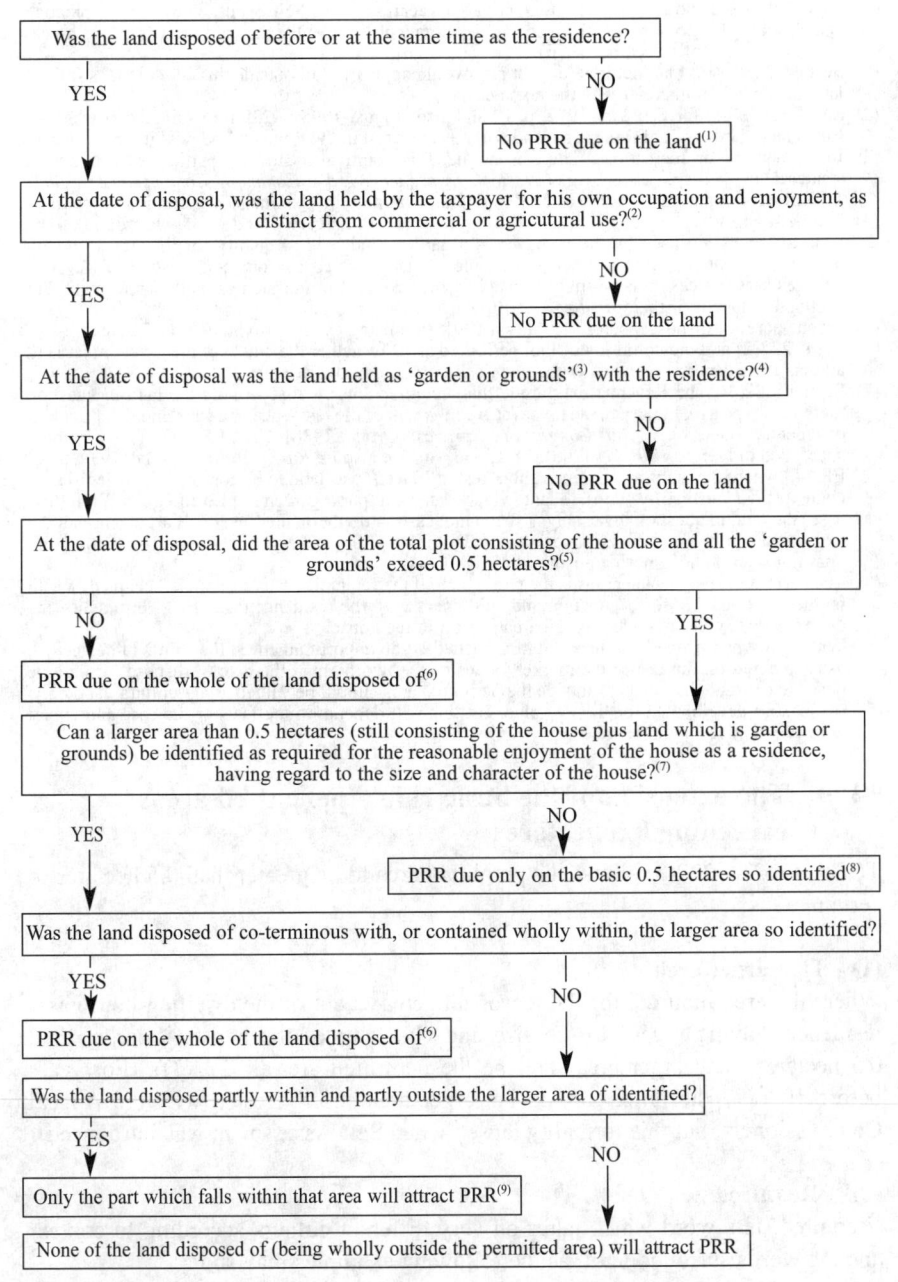

- Was the land disposed of before or at the same time as the residence?
  - NO → No PRR due on the land[1]
  - YES ↓
- At the date of disposal, was the land held by the taxpayer for his own occupation and enjoyment, as distinct from commercial or agricutural use?[2]
  - NO → No PRR due on the land
  - YES ↓
- At the date of disposal was the land held as 'garden or grounds'[3] with the residence?[4]
  - NO → No PRR due on the land
  - YES ↓
- At the date of disposal, did the area of the total plot consisting of the house and all the 'garden or grounds' exceed 0.5 hectares?[5]
  - NO → PRR due on the whole of the land disposed of[6]
  - YES ↓
- Can a larger area than 0.5 hectares (still consisting of the house plus land which is garden or grounds) be identified as required for the reasonable enjoyment of the house as a residence, having regard to the size and character of the house?[7]
  - NO → PRR due only on the basic 0.5 hectares so identified[8]
  - YES ↓
- Was the land disposed of co-terminous with, or contained wholly within, the larger area so identified?
  - YES → PRR due on the whole of the land disposed of[6]
  - NO ↓
- Was the land disposed partly within and partly outside the larger area of identified?
  - YES → Only the part which falls within that area will attract PRR[9]
  - NO → None of the land disposed of (being wholly outside the permitted area) will attract PRR

¶408

NOTES

(1) See *Varty v Lynes* [1976] 1 WLR 1091 and the present tense verb 'has' in s. 222(1)(b). Strictly also applies if house and land are sold together after vacation of the house, but the Revenue's practice is not to take this point unless the land had development value at the date of sale (CCAB Technical Release No. 211 of December 1976).
(2) Section 222(1)(b). Land let in return for rent would appear to fall outside this condition, as well as land occupied commercially by the taxpayer.
(3) See *Tax Bulletin* for February 1992, p. 10 and also August 1995 p. 239 for examples of what the Revenue regards as qualifying. The land will meet this test in the Revenue's view if it serves chiefly for 'ornament or recreation'. There is no need for cultivation to any particular horticultural standard, or, perhaps, at all, e.g. *Cresstock Investments Ltd v Commons Commissioner* [1992] 1 WLR 1088 where wild land was held to remain a garden for Commons Registration purposes.
(4) See *Wakeling v Pearce* (1995) Sp C 32 for an instance of a piece of land which was found on the facts to have been used by the taxpayer as a garden, and held to qualify for PRR even though physically separated from her house by a plot of land owned by somebody else. The Revenue believes that this case was wrongly decided by the Special Commissioners on the latter point, but declined to take it further (see *Tax Bulletin,* August 1995 p. 239).
(5) Or one acre for disposals before 19 March 1991. (0.5 hectares = approximately 1.23 acres).
(6) See s. 222(2) and the definition of the 'permitted area'. Whether the whole of the *gain* on that land attracts PRR depends on whether the other statutory conditions are met.
(7) Section 222(3). The Revenue may argue that 'required' means that without the land in question there would be a real injury to the taxpayer's enjoyment of the residence or a substantial deprivation of amenity – see *Re Newhill Compulsory Purchase Order* [1938] 2 All ER 163. This argument succeeded in *Longson v Baker* [2001] BTC 356. But see also *Re Ripon Housing Order* [1939] 3 All ER 548 where the 'substantial deprivation' test in *Newhill* was held to be confined, in its legislative context (the *Housing Act* 1936), to land which was *not* a 'park, garden or pleasure ground'. In PRR cases the land in question invariably *is* such land, casting doubt on the Revenue's argument, but the Commissioner rejected the taxpayer's argument to that effect in *Longson v Baker.* The *Ripon* point does not seem to have been argued in the High Court.
(8) The permitted area in such cases is the part which, if the remainder was separately occupied, would be the most suitable for occupation and enjoyment with the residence (s. 222(4)). In practice the district valuer will often identify the area nearest to the house.
(9) Where only part of the land disposed of attracts PRR an apportionment of the gain will be needed, usually based on the respective market values of the two parts at the date of disposal. It may be possible to argue that the part outside the permitted area should be valued as agricultural land only, if it has no development or 'hope' value, but this will depend on the facts of the case and expert valuation advice should be taken.

¶409 The extension of the basic rule – permitted areas exceeding 0.5 hectares

TCGA 1992, s. 222(3) allows the permitted area to be greater than 0.5 hectares in certain cases.

(1) The larger area

Where the area required for the reasonable enjoyment of the dwelling-house as a residence, having regard to the size and character of the house, is larger than 0.5 hectares, that larger area shall be the permitted area (s. 222(3)). (For years before 1996/97 the power to fix the larger area strictly rested with the Appeal Commissioners, but this formality lapsed when Self Assessment was introduced).

(2) 'Required …'

'Required' is a word which takes on very different colours according to context and the words surrounding it, as the following examples may show.

(1) An employee may say to his employer 'I require a 20 per cent salary increase'. (2) The rubric to an examination paper may say 'Candidates are required to answer three questions'. (3) A contract may specify that one party is to afford the other all such assistance 'as he may reasonably require'. In (1), 'require' expresses merely a desire: in (2) it expresses an indispensable condition: in (3) the sense is somewhere between these two extremes and indicates scope for argument, because it is coloured by the word 'reasonably'.

It is the last sense which operates in s. 222(3), and this colour is taken from the next words 'reasonable enjoyment' (see ¶409(4)–(5)). What a reasonable person would require denotes something between the extremes of 'ideally desirable' and 'absolutely essential' (see *Acme Flooring and Paving Co (1904) Ltd v IR Commrs* [1948] 1 All ER 546). It is necessary to ignore the circumstances and peculiarities of the individual, and ask 'What would a reasonable man require for his reasonable enjoyment?'

(3) Compulsory purchase cases on 'required'

Since similar wording has appeared in successive compulsory purchase legislation, cases on that topic tend to be cited in negotiations over PRR. The Revenue particularly tends to refer to *Re Newhill Compulsory Purchase Order* [1938] All ER 163. The Revenue published its views on the matters discussed below in its *Tax Bulletin*, February 1992, pp. 10–11, and also in VOM 8.42. Advisers should, as a matter of prudence, read what is said there about *Newhill*, though it will be clear from what follows that the writer disagrees with the Revenue's position. Unfortunately, the High Court was persuaded, in *Longson v Baker (HMIT)* [2001] BTC 356 to adopt the Revenue's view, as discussed below (see (4) below).

Newhill arose under the *Housing Act* 1936, s. 75, which excluded from the operation of the provisions of that Act authorising compulsory purchase 'any land ... which at the date of the compulsory purchase forms part of any park, garden or pleasure ground, or is otherwise required for the amenity or convenience of any house'.

Du Parcq J, discussing the phrase 'required for the amenity or convenience of any house', observed:

> '"Required", I think, in this section does not mean merely that the occupiers of the house would like to have it, or that they would miss it if they lost it, or that anyone proposing to buy the house would think less of the house without it than he would if it was preserved to it. "Required" means, I suppose, that without it there will be such a substantial deprivation of amenities or convenience that a real injury will be done to the property owner' (p. 167C.)

In its *Tax Bulletin* article the Revenue takes the view that 'the corresponding legislative context' of *Newhill* makes that case 'useful guidance' for PRR purposes. The writer greatly doubts this.

In a later case under the same Act, *Re Ripon Housing Order* [1939] 3 All ER 548, Luxmoore LJ pointed out that in *Newhill*, the judge was speaking only of land which was not a 'park, garden or pleasure ground', since the 1936 Act specifically disapplied compulsory purchase powers over land which was such land. Thus, for those purposes, it was not necessary to show that such land was 'reasonably required' in order to defeat an attempted compulsory purchase. The PRR legislation in s. 222(1)(b) deals with land which is held as 'garden or grounds', and this seems very close in meaning to the 'park, garden or pleasure ground' concept which was in point in these two compulsory purchase cases. In the writer's view, Du Parcq J's dictum on 'required' in *Newhill* should not carry much weight as a guide to interpreting s. 222(1)(b), since the judge was dealing only with land which fell outside the 'pleasure ground' concept, whereas PRR cases normally deal with land within it.

Under the *Town and Country Planning Act* 1971, s. 112(1), (now re-enacted in the *Town and Country Planning Act* 1990, s. 226(1)) a local authority can be given powers to acquire compulsorily land which is 'required' to secure the carrying out of development, or for some other purpose necessary in the interests of proper planning.

'Required,' in that context, has been given a narrower meaning than 'desirable'; the local authority has to demonstrate a need for the land in question, and for the powers it was seeking over it, in order to carry out the purposes set out in that Act. On the other hand, the word 'required' has not been equated with 'indispensable', in the sense that the authority need not show that it has exhausted all its other powers; it must merely conclude that without compulsory purchase it is unlikely to achieve its purposes. (See *R v Secretary of State for the Environment, ex parte Sharkey* [1990] 45 EG 113, following *R v Secretary of State for the Environment, ex parte Leicester City Council* [1978] JPL 787.)

In compulsory purchase cases a strict construction of 'required' is to be expected since the statute gives the state confiscatory powers over the citizen's property. Section 222(3), in contrast, is a relieving provision in a taxing statute, and might be thought likely to be interpreted more liberally with the courts tending towards the 'desirable' end of the spectrum of meaning rather than the 'essential' end. However, the *Ripon* case is not mentioned in the Revenue instructions at all, and does not appear to have been cited in the only decided case on this point, *Longson v Baker*, which was decided against the taxpayer, although the facts were somewhat special and the case needs to be examined in some detail.

(4) Longson v Baker and the meaning of 'required'

Mr Longson bought a house in Hampshire, Velmead Farm, in 1979 as his private residence. The house dated back to the sixteenth century and had eight downstairs rooms, five bedrooms and three bathrooms. The outbuildings comprised a garage, hay loft, two hay barns and several stable blocks with 17 loose boxes for horses.

There was also a barn (erected in the taxpayer's ownership period) used as an indoor riding school. The total area of the property was 18.68 acres (7.56 hectares). [The inference is that there were some paddocks or fields although this is not stated]. The taxpayer and his family occupied the property as their main residence until he split up with his wife in 1990, but his wife continued to live there until it was sold in 1998. In 1995 the taxpayer had disposed of his interest to his wife as part of the divorce proceedings and it was agreed that by ESC D6 (see ¶904 below), the property could be treated as his main residence up to that date although he had moved out several years earlier. The 1998 sale by the ex-wife was to a developer and most of the land had subsequently been built over and some of the outbuildings demolished, though the house remained.

The issue was the extent of the permitted area of exempt land under TCGA 1992, s. 222(3) on the 1995 transfer to the ex-wife. The taxpayer argued that the whole 18.68 acres qualified. The district valuer advised the inspector that the permitted area was only 2.61 acres [the case report does not include the plans which were used at the hearing, so it is not possible to see exactly how this area was arrived at, although it is stated that it excluded the indoor school but included at least some of the stables]. The special commissioner had rejected the taxpayer's argument and his case was not helped by the fact that on his own acquisition in 1979, the previous owner had accepted a permitted area of only 2.31 acres for his own CGT purposes.

In the High Court the taxpayer used a different argument. He said that since it was agreed that the stables were part of the dwelling house, the commissioner should have concluded that whole of the grazing land was needed to accompany the stabling and was therefore an area required for the reasonable enjoyment of the residence. This was also rejected by Evans-Lombe J, who said that it was clear from the wording of s. 222(3) that the test was an objective one. Objectively, there was no requirement to keep horses at the property in order to enjoy it as a residence. The test was not whether a particular individual wished to do so; the size of the permitted area could not vary according to the individual wishes and requirements of the taxpayer. If the taxpayer's interest in horses had changed and the stables had been adapted, e.g. to garages for cars, the need for the additional land would immediately disappear. If his argument was right, one might expect there to be a substantial demand for horses by owners of houses which had significant development land as part of their plots. This could not have been the purpose of the legislation. Mr Longson accordingly lost his appeal.

Although the court was referred to the *Newhill* decision, as noted earlier it appears that *Ripon* was not cited. Evans-Lombe J quoted at length from Du Parcq J's judgement in *Newhill* and regarded it as helpful because there was 'a sufficient analogy' between the statute in question in *Newhill* and s. 222(3) for the commissioner to have legitimately relied on it. It is possible that the judge might have taken a different view if *Ripon* had been examined; it was cited to the special commissioner, but he concluded that the case was 'of little assistance as it was concerned principally with whether or not some land included in the compulsory purchase order...was or was not part of the park of Highfield, a large house' ([2000] SCD at p. 249e). This comment, with respect, is not easy to follow unless the Commissioner intended a distinction between a 'park' and 'garden or grounds'. As matters stood, the court held that the commissioner's finding of fact about Mr Longson's permitted area was reasonable.

It must be said that this was not an ideal test case on the meaning of s. 222(3). The very big difference – some 16 acres – between the taxpayer's claim and what the immediately previous owner had accepted as the permitted area, and the fact that the Longson family had previously coped with housing their horses from a much smaller property, must have made the taxpayer's task difficult from the outset even if those facts were arguably irrelevant. It may not have helped his case, either, to have argued exclusively that the whole of the land was required to serve the occupation of the stabling. It was perhaps not surprising that the court rejected an argument in those absolute terms; it seems too vulnerable to the judge's comments about what might have been the conclusion, on that reasoning, if Mr Longson had switched his interests to motor cars (indeed, if he had switched to an interest in elephants, he might on his reasoning have argued for an even larger permitted area to cope with larger animals).

Thus the case represents a lost opportunity to test the relevance of *Newhill* against the *Ripon* case, leaving that issue to be tested by another taxpayer in the future. Perhaps more important, however, are the dicta about the objective nature of the 'required for reasonable enjoyment' test. The judgement emphasises that advisers should, in negotiations, concentrate on what the *dwelling house* can reasonably be said to require, rather than on the supposed subjective requirements of the *taxpayer* in question.

(5) 'Reasonable enjoyment' – the concept of moderation

Longson is a reminder that the argument for the taxpayer must be anchored in the objective requirements of the particular property, and that attention is needed to the whole of the phrase which runs 'for the reasonable enjoyment ....' of the dwelling-house as a residence. This adds the further notions of (1) moderation and (2) objectivity. The reasonable man whose 'enjoyment' is postulated cannot be assumed to be, at one extreme, a wildlife fanatic who 'requires' a large tract of land because he intends to open a big game sanctuary, or at the other extreme, an agoraphobic recluse who will never leave the four walls of his house or look out of a window, and will therefore 'require' no land at all, apart from what is needed for access.

We must assume that a reasonable man would be influenced by any amenity land and that he would take it into account in selecting that particular property as a residence. It will be irrelevant that a particular owner chose it for idiosyncratic

¶409

reasons, such as the particular needs of his personal interests – as in *Longson*. He must be assumed to have taken account of the plot as one of the factors in his decision, neither being completely indifferent to it nor dominated by it to the exclusion of other factors. Mr Longson might be said to have been immoderately influenced by the need for grazing land for a large number of horses.

(6) 'Reasonable enjoyment' – the concept of objectivity

The objective language of s. 222(3) directs attention to the reasonable enjoyment, by this hypothetical occupier, of the dwelling-house as a residence. The key word is 'reasonable'. It directs attention away from any idiosyncrasies of the individual taxpayer in question. The fact that he may hate gardening, or lack the necessary time for it, or be too old and infirm to do the work, may have resulted in a large garden falling into decay; this may affect sale values and the time taken to achieve a sale, but a new owner may still be attracted by the plot, and it does not follow that the garden has ceased to be required for the reasonable enjoyment of the house. Such factors are to be ignored. *Longson* merely confirms this.

However, what cannot be ignored is any action taken by the individual in question which may permanently affect the amenity of the plot, so as to prevent a purchaser from enjoying it as garden or grounds at all, or only at such great expense and inconvenience that few would contemplate the task. This might be the case if he has turned part of the grounds into a gravel pit or quarry, or constructed workshops or aircraft hangars on it. Anyone buying a property thus encumbered cannot expect to 'enjoy' it himself, and the inference may well be that it is not required for the reasonable enjoyment of the dwelling-house. Even more fundamentally, such adaptations may mean that the land in question is no longer 'garden or grounds' (see ¶406ff.).

However, other substantial modifications may not have this adverse effect; e.g. the owner might have made a walled kitchen-garden to serve the house, or have created a lake for ornamental fish, in areas which were previously conventional gardens. This may mean merely that in future the garden and grounds will be enjoyed in a different way, and perhaps appeal to a different, though no less reasonable, type of purchaser.

Substantial difficulties may, however, arise where part of a plot has been sold for building while the balance is retained (see ¶412).

(7) Physically separated garden land

The Revenue may argue that land which is physically separated from the main plot, either by a road or by land in third party ownership, cannot be part of the permitted area, because it is not part of the owner's garden or grounds (CGT 64367). The writer would suggest that this is too sweeping a generalisation. What matters is whether in fact it is held 'as' part of the garden or grounds at the date of the disposal; if so, its separation is not in itself a reason for excluding it from the permitted area. Proximity is important here simply because it is unnatural to speak of two very widely separated tracts of land as a single piece of garden. However, for historical reasons each property in a row of houses may, for example, have a piece of land on the opposite side of the street, or of a stream, which is used in the fullest sense as a garden by its owner. The Revenue in practice may accept this (see CGT 64369) if a prospective purchaser would expect to acquire such land with the house. In *Wakeling v Pearce (HMIT)* (1995) Sp C 32, however, they attempted to argue that some land which was separated by a property owned by a third party could not be part of the taxpayer's garden, even though the special commissioner accepted the taxpayer's evidence that she had used the land as such for many years. The Revenue's argument was rejected, and although they indicated in the *Tax Bulletin* for August 1995 that they thought the decision was wrong in law, the case was not taken further. The distance between the taxpayer's house and the nearest point of the separated 'garden' in that case was only 25–30 feet. The case is, perhaps significantly, not mentioned in the Revenue Manuals.

(8) 'Size' of the dwelling-house
This is the first factor to which the commissioners must have regard in determining whether the permitted area may exceed 0.5 hectares. The natural implication of its inclusion is that the bigger the house, the bigger the plot size it will require. This accords with the common sense proposition that a substantial house may be devalued by an inadequate curtilage; valuers would generally agree that a house with a large 'footprint', or total ground floor area, needs bigger grounds, and a greater degree of privacy, than a more modest house in order to achieve its proper value. An assumed purchaser of a larger house may also be assumed to have a larger than average family which will require more extensive grounds.

(9) 'Character' of the dwelling-house
The second factor to which the commissioners must have regard, its character, introduces a further element of subjectivity. It is suggested that three points in particular need to be considered here: (1) the period and style of the house, (2) its other amenities, and (3) its locality. Taken together, these features may combine to make the house what it is, and impart its distinctive character.

(1) An historic country house may well have been designed for its physical setting and (to quote Du Parcq J's dictum in *Newhill*, see ¶409(3)) would suffer 'a real injury' if severed from a significant part of that setting. Houses such as Blenheim or Castle Howard would simply not be the same houses without their parklands. As with servants' houses (see ¶323(3)) historical research may help to illuminate the interrelationship between buildings and landscape.

On the other hand, a less distinctive house may nevertheless have acquired a sizeable plot through a variety of accidental factors, such as the inheritance, by a previous owner, of land which was turned into a nature reserve; and there may be no indispensable link between the house and the plot.

However, even in a relatively ordinary house, its design may be a clue to a close relationship with its plot. A house with a small front garden but substantial land to the rear or sides may well have been designed with its principal rooms overlooking the latter areas rather than the front, suggesting that the design of the gardens played a large part in determining the design of the house. Severance of that land would materially alter the character of the house, and this may lead to the conclusion that a large area was required for its reasonable enjoyment as a residence.

(2) Some amenities, or the position of the house itself, may justify additional land. Thus, the presence of stables suggests a requirement for paddocks or an exercise yard (see ¶407), although as the decision in *Longson* shows (see (4) above), this point should not be pressed too far. An historic landscape feature such as a ha-ha naturally suggests an intention, on the part of the designer, that the owner should enjoy the land which stretches beyond it in order to benefit from the perspective. A large house close to a busy main road is likely to be significantly devalued if it lacks a substantial garden or other secluded land to the rear or sides; the presence of such land is likely to be a 'reasonable' requirement for a house in that position.

(3) The locality of a house may well influence its materials and design, thus affecting its character, but it is also relevant in relation to plot size. What is 'required' in that respect in Belgravia will be much less than what is 'required' in rural Gloucestershire. London mews houses or Chelsea cottages may 'require' no land at all. In urban areas the reasonable purchaser cannot expect to enjoy uninterrupted views of the horizon and freedom from traffic noise. In the Cotswolds or the Surrey stockbroker belt, on the other hand, a house with five or six bedrooms is much more likely to have a swimming pool and tennis court as well as substantial cultivated areas.

Even in areas where plots in excess of 0.5 hectares are not common, a particular house may still be said to 'require' a large plot, but in such cases there may need to be something exceptional about it as a house; examples might include a house which is very much bigger than its neighbours, or, on a modern development, a corner house which was significantly more expensive when new than identical houses built at the same time. (See ¶412(4) regarding 'comparables'.)

Perhaps the crucial test is 'Would the house sell as readily, for the *same*

¶409

price, if the land in question were excluded?' If the answer to this question is 'yes', then prima facie the 'excluded' land is not 'required'.

(10) The objective test in changing times

One of the main difficulties in practice over 'permitted area' cases concerns older houses, often on the fringes of urban areas, around which there has been substantial development since they were first built.

It would be difficult to deny that what was 'reasonably required' in the way of plot size in, say, 1900 might not always be so regarded today. Most modern householders must do their own gardening or manage with, at best, occasional help. This factor, together with escalating land values, inevitably imposes constraints on plot sizes, especially in towns. But change can operate in both directions; a village which has become fashionable with the well-to-do may see a gradual expansion of plot sizes as owners of what may once have been labourers' cottages with small gardens persuade farmers and large landowners to sell them neighbouring land to extend their plots, particularly where a strong 'Green Belt' planning policy prevents large scale housing development.

It is also possible that a large house in an urban area may command a significant premium precisely because it has always enjoyed an unusually large plot for the area. This very feature then becomes part of its 'character' and may justify the conclusion that the land is 'required'.

Since the verbs in s. 222(3) are in the present tense, it seems that the commissioners may legitimately consider only what is 'required' at the time of disposal, in the light of current circumstances. This may operate to the disadvantage of someone who has occupied his home for a long period during which the character of the neighbourhood has radically changed, e.g. on the fringes of conurbations, or of new towns such as Milton Keynes or Telford. However, this is merely a consequence of the fact that the 'reasonable enjoyment' test has to be applied at the time of disposal: the reasonable man cannot expect to live in a time capsule, insulated from major changes in the locality around him.

¶410 Establishing the permitted area in practice

Having examined the meaning of the tests for the permitted area, we must now look at the way in which the legislation provides for that area to be identified and for the exempt gains to be computed. The flow chart in ¶409 may assist in understanding the logical steps needed here. *In reading the flow chart it should be noted that it is assumed that the 'alternative [Revenue] view', as described in (4) below, is correct.* See (5) below for a discussion of the merits of this view.

(1) Determining the size of the permitted area

As we have seen (cf. ¶401), PRR applies to gains on the disposal of the dwelling-house (TCGA 1992, s. 222(1)(a)), or of land which the owner has for his own occupation and enjoyment with the house, 'up to the permitted area' (s. 222(1)(b)). That area, by s. 222(2), is an area of at least 0.5 hectares, and where the total plot exceeds 0.5 hectares, if the commissioners so determine or the parties agree, it may be larger (s. 222(3)).

It is then necessary to consider s. 222(4). This provides that where part of the land occupied with the residence is not within s. 222(1), i.e. where it exceeds the permitted area in size, the permitted area shall be that part which, if the remainder were separately occupied, would be the most suitable for occupation and enjoyment with the residence.

Pausing there, it appears to follow that if the total plot is less than 0.5 hectares, any disposal, of any or all of the land concerned, must qualify for PRR, unless the land sold cannot be described as 'garden or grounds' at all (see ¶406); or, if it was 'garden or grounds', it was not occupied for the taxpayer's own enjoyment with this residence at the date of disposal (e.g. if it was let).

Although s. 222(3) enables the permitted area to be more than 0.5 hectares in appropriate cases, there is no provision for it to be less than this amount. Occasionally, inspectors may argue to the contrary, perhaps in cases where a very small house occupies a plot of only slightly less than 0.5 hectares. This argument would seem to be impossible to sustain unless the inspector can identify all or part of the disposal as land which is neither garden nor grounds nor occupied for the taxpayer's own enjoyment.

(2) Plot exceeding 0.5 hectares but less than 0.5 hectares sold

This leads on to the question of whether there can be any restriction of relief if the area sold is less than 0.5 hectares but the total plot exceeds that size. In what follows it is assumed that the entire plot is garden or grounds and that no restrictions are required for periods of non-occupation, business use or other reasons.

(3) Is the disposal of an area of less than 0.5 hectares automatically exempt?

Here, the reasoning in ¶410(1) can, arguably, lead to the conclusion that if the area sold is less than 0.5 hectares, it will be 'up to' – i.e. will not exceed in size – the minimum permitted area under s. 222(2). On this analysis, s. 222(3) would only become relevant where the sale is of more than 0.5 hectares. In such cases it would then be necessary to apply the tests in ¶409. In support of this view it can be said that s. 222(1)(b) confers PRR on disposals of land which is occupied with the residence as garden or grounds 'up to' the permitted area; and that the most natural sense of that phrase in this context is not spacial (equating it with 'physically

¶410

located within') but quantitative, equating it with 'not exceeding in size'. On this view, there would never be a need to consider s. 222(3), which provides for a permitted area larger than 0.5 hectares (see ¶409(1)) where the land sold was less than that amount.

(4) The alternative [Revenue] view – no automatic exemption?
The alternative view, which the Revenue in fact adopts (see CGT 64800-64859) is that the correct procedure would be, where the total plot exceeds 0.5 hectares, to first locate the permitted area on the plans using s. 222(3) if necessary – which may result in a permitted area of more than 0.5 hectares – and then to compare this with the land sold. It would then be a matter of simple observation to decide whether the land sold fell within the larger area already identified. On this view, because the identification of the permitted area is the first step, it would follow that when reading that phrase in s. 222(1)(b) one would already have discovered its physical boundaries. The phrase 'up to' in s. 222(1)(b) would then be read in its spatial sense; it would mean merely that PRR was only due on land sold which fell within the area already identified. If the land sold fell outside that area, no PRR would be due even if it measured less than 0.5 hectares.

(5) Comment
In the writer's view, the drafting of the relevant legislation as we now have it is less than crystal clear. If the view outlined at ¶410(4) is correct it seems that the phrase 'up to' is being used in two different senses within the same section, since although that view requires a spatial sense in s. 222(1)(b), as explained above, it is clear that in s. 222(4), the words are used in their quantitative sense; the whole point of subs. (4) is to assist in defining the location of the permitted area, and if they are to be read spatially the subsection arguably becomes circular.

That, however, may not be an adequate reason for rejecting the view in ¶410(4). It must be said that the view in ¶410(3) can produce strange results. For instance, if in year one the total plot of a private residence measures five hectares, including 0.05 hectares being the site of the house, and it is all garden or grounds, what is to prevent the owner selling 0.499 hectares every year for nine years, with each of those sales attracting PRR? If the total garden area is substantially larger than the amount of land which, on the facts, can be justified as the permitted area, there seems, if the view in ¶410(3) is correct, to be nothing to prevent PRR being due on an area of land very distant from the house, so long as it measures less than 0.5 hectares; this view may be considered to give insufficient weight to s. 222(4), which becomes redundant, for the purposes of that disposal.

That said, the Revenue's view (see (4) above) can also produce some odd results, for it will mean that on each disposal of garden and grounds in a sequence, the permitted area has to be determined afresh on the then facts and the whole of the newly identified area becomes available on each occasion. As the Revenue acknowledge (CGT 64831), it is thus possible for more PRR in total to be obtained in a sequence of disposals than would have been due if the same total area of land had been sold on a single occasion. Those tempted to take advantage of this point may, however, need to be warned of the risk that their transactions could be viewed as trading if the intervals between sales are very short or if a single sale is artificially split into separate disposals (see ¶307).

No light, unfortunately, appears to be shed on this question by the Finance Bill debates either in 1962 (when similar wording first appeared in the original short-term gains legislation (FA 1962, s. 11(3))) or 1965.

Thus, it appears that even if the courts were to find the statute ambiguous or to lead to absurdities, reference to *Hansard*, under the rule in *Pepper (HMIT) v Hart and related appeals* [19921 BTC 591, would not assist.

Though the point is not, in the writer's view, free from doubt, on balance the view in ¶410(4) may be the better view, and in view of the Revenue's stance it will be adopted henceforth here for the purposes of discussion.

(6) Identifying the physical area

Adopting the view outlined at ¶410(4), therefore, irrespective of the amount of land sold by the disposal in question, the correct procedure, where the total plot exceeds 0.5 hectares, will be to:

(a) determine the size of the permitted area, either by agreement or, failing that, by a decision of the commissioners;

(b) decide, using s. 222(4) to assist, which area of land on the plans, of the size thus determined, is the 'most suitable' area;

(c) ascertain by inspection, where there is a part disposal, the extent to which the land sold falls within the boundaries identified in (b); and

(d) calculate the taxable gain – this is considered at ¶410(7).

It follows from this that at step (c), the land sold may be wholly within the permitted area, in which case it attracts PRR in full; wholly outside it, in which case it attracts no PRR; or partly within and partly outside it, in which case an apportionment is needed (see (7) below).

The following example may illustrate how this procedure operates:

Example 1

Cuthbert has owned The Grange for many years as his only residence. The whole of the plot has now been sold. The total plot consists of two hectares (about 4.94 acres). There is a small front garden, including the driveway giving the only access to the plot, measuring about 0.1 hectares. The house occupies about 0.05 hectares and there are narrow strips of land at either side of the house in total comprising another 0.05 hectares, so that the bulk of the plot,

1.8 hectares, lies behind the house. After negotiations it is agreed with the Revenue that the permitted area, applying s. 222(3), is 0.8 hectares including the house. This means that a further 0.75 hectares of land must be identified, to make up that 0.8 hectares.

The application of s. 222(4) now in effect requires the inspector to ask: 'If Cuthbert had only possessed 0.75 hectares out of this land, and the balance had been occupied by another person, which 0.75 hectares would have been most suitable for his occupation and enjoyment with the house?' Common sense suggests that any occupier of The Grange would have insisted on having the front garden and the two side strips – otherwise there would have been no access to the house or to the land at the rear. This accounts for 0.15 hectares, leaving another 0.6 hectares to be found at the rear.

The identification of this remaining land must depend on the physical characteristics and layout of the plot (see (8) below). If the 1.8 hectares is all cultivated gardens it is likely that the remaining part of the permitted area will be simply the 0.6 hectares nearest to the house, since no owner of the house would be likely to regard the most distant 0.6 hectares as more 'suitable'. However, if there was a formal garden immediately behind the house, measuring, say, 0.2 hectares, beyond which lay 1.2 hectares of low lying marshy ground unsuitable for cultivation, and beyond that again, perhaps on higher ground, lay a further 0.4 hectares of cultivated gardens, the sensible conclusion might well be that the most 'suitable' 0.6 hectares, if the remainder were separately occupied, would consist of the 0.2 hectares of formal garden plus the most distant cultivated 0.4 hectares.

This example illustrates the effect of the procedure suggested above in a total disposal. If Cuthbert had sold only, say, 0.4 hectares of land behind the house and retained the remainder (including the house), on the view adopted here (see ¶410(4)) PRR would not be automatic, and the site plan would need to be inspected to ascertain the extent to which the land sold fell within the permitted area in order to decide the extent, if any, to which it fell within the 'permitted' 0.6 hectares. To the extent to which it fell outside that area no PRR would be due to Cuthbert.

(7) Calculating the taxable gain

Having identified the physical area, or areas, which form the permitted area, the final step is to calculate the taxable gain, if any. Clearly, if the permitted area includes the entire land sold, there will be no taxable gain unless a restriction is necessary for non-occupation under s. 223(2) or business use under s. 224(1) or (2). In other cases, it is suggested that the land outside the permitted area should be valued on its own facts in order to calculate the taxable gain (ultimately, there is a computation under TCGA 1992, Pt. II, Ch. III so that a just and reasonable apportionment is prescribed: s. 52(4)). Here, of course, the advice of a professional valuer should always be taken.

This exercise will not necessarily produce the same arithmetical result as a straight apportionment of the whole gain based on size. It is necessary to consider the attributes of the 'non-permitted' land and to ask whether it has development or 'hope' value, or whether it should be valued merely as garden or (in rural areas) agricultural land, and if the latter, to consider its quality as agricultural land.

Example 2
Sunil sells his house and two hectares (about 4.94 acres) of land for £1m, producing a total gain of £750,000. It is eventually agreed that the permitted area is an area of 1.2 hectares including the house and the land closest to it, but the 0.8 hectares furthest from the house are outside that area.

It is unlikely that Sunil's taxable gain will be simply (0.8/2) × £750,000 = £300,000. If the non-permitted land has development value it might well be worth, say, £600,000, in which case the taxable gain would be calculated as follows:

Total gain as above £750,000

Apportioned to non-permitted area:

$$£750,000 \times \frac{£600,000}{£1,000,000}$$

Taxable gain £450,000, rather than £300,000, with the balance of £300,000 being exempt.

This example assumes that none of the allowable expenditure which was deducted in computing the total gain of £750,000 could be attributed directly either to the permitted land or the non-permitted land. In practice, this point should always be considered and any necessary allocations made.

Conversely, if the non-permitted land has no more than agricultural value the gain apportioned to it will be very much less; it might be worth as little as £10,000 in all, leading to a taxable gain of £7,500. It is irrelevant that the house and the remaining land, valued without the non-permitted land, might be devalued by much more than £10,000.

In the above example, the apportionment has been made by reference to valuations on the footing that this produces a 'just and reasonable' result as directed by s. 52(4). However, an apportionment by area might, depending on the facts, give a closer approximation to such a result. If there is a dispute as to which is the right method and it cannot be resolved by negotiation, the question of the right method must be decided by the commissioners, as is clear from the wording of s. 52(4). However, if the commissioners decide that the apportionment should

¶410

be based on valuations, and the parties cannot agree on what the valuations should be, this aspect must be resolved by the Lands Tribunal (TMA 1970, s. 46D, and see also the Revenue's *Tax Bulletin*, February 1992, p. 11).

It is suggested that the valuation of non-permitted land should recognise development value only where there is an actual planning consent which includes that land and adequate access to the whole plot sold. Otherwise, some 'hope' value (the amount dependent on local planning policies), is the most which can be recognised.

In the absence of any such development or 'hope' value, it is unlikely that any more than agricultural value should be taken into account. There can sometimes be an issue over whether an identified area of 'non-permitted' land which, taken in isolation, has no road access, should be assumed to have a right of way to the 'permitted' land; for the Revenue's views, see VOM 8.44. In that paragraph of their instructions, district valuers are advised to assume the existence of an easement giving access to non-permitted land even when there is in fact none. In the writer's view that is probably sensible; when deciding which area of land is to be the permitted area, s. 222(4) requires an assumption that the balance of the land is owned by a third party, but there is nothing to suggest that this assumption also has to be made when *valuing* the identified non-permitted land, or that, even if such an assumption could be made for that purpose, the taxpayer would be unwilling to grant an easement over the permitted land to the notional third party. Without access, of course, the non-permitted land might arguably be almost valueless, but such an argument is unlikely to be accepted and is probably unrealistic.

(8) Identifying the physical area in practice

Example 1 above indicated a possible approach to the process of identifying the boundaries of the permitted area. In practice the procedure may be simplified by obvious physical boundaries such as the edge of a cultivated area and the beginning of a 'wild' area, or by streams, hedges, fences, walls, ditches, or an abrupt change in ground level. Land which is near to the house is generally more likely to be 'suitable' than remoter land or land which is out of sight of the house, unless the lie or character of the land is unusual; or unless a large estate is involved, where, for example, a kitchen garden (which clearly contributes to the enjoyment of the house if the occupants eat its produce) may be separated from the house by other land. Even then, it would be unusual to find that the intervening land was not 'required' in the sense necessary for s. 222(3), and thus not within the permitted area.

Again, it will often be appropriate here to seek the views of a valuer or surveyor who knows the area and its properties well.

¶410

¶411   Part disposals of land

Some of the most contentious PRR cases in practice concern the disposal of part of the land while the house is retained, especially when the disposal is of building land. Perhaps surprisingly, however, no case on this point has yet reached the courts.

(1)   The Revenue's argument

Often in such cases the Revenue will argue that the land sold cannot have fallen within the permitted area, since the very fact of its separate sale proves that it could not have been 'required' for the reasonable enjoyment of the residence. This argument has considerable force in many cases but it is by no means the only possible interpretation of a set of facts.

(2)   Factors supporting the Revenue's argument

Inspectors and district valuers are likely to argue that the continuing demand for residential building land since the Second World War has caused a progressive shrinkage of plot sites and increased the attractions of a sale of part of a previously large garden, especially one exceeding 0.5 hectares.

In these conditions, the argument runs, it is not 'unreasonable' for an owner to diminish his holding of land or impossible for him to 'enjoy' the resulting reduced plot. District valuers will be quick to adduce 'comparables' in the form of details of other formerly large plots in the vicinity which have since been split up, and of the numerous modern housing estates which occupy what were once the grounds of very large houses. The data produced will also, no doubt, include evidence of the subsequent sale, perhaps several times over, of such large houses with their reduced grounds, as private residences.

Where the vendor of building land has remained in occupation of the house and has no plans to move elsewhere, these arguments may be very difficult to rebut. The vendor has, of course, reduced the value of his property but in economic terms he has merely replaced one asset, land, with another, cash. Indeed, his total wealth has probably increased considerably as a result, and this will go a long way to redress any loss of amenity. The chances of success for the taxpayer in such a case are probably slim, especially if he took positive steps to enhance the value of his property before marketing it, e.g. by seeking planning permission. (See ¶412(4) for other instances of likely Revenue success and ¶412(5) for planning possibilities if PRR seems a forlorn hope.)

(3)   Circumstances in the taxpayer's favour

Nevertheless, it is important to remember the objective language of TCGA 1992, s. 222(3) (see ¶410(8)). The vendor in question may have sold part of his land and increased his total wealth, but it must still be asked whether he has deprived the dwelling-house as a whole of land which, objectively, is required for its reasonable enjoyment as a residence. It is perhaps easier to illustrate this point with an example than to generalise about it.

Example
Lady Counterblast is in her 90s and in poor health. Her home, Counterblast Manor, which has ten reception rooms and eight bedrooms, now stands in 10 hectares (nearly 25 acres) of land, but when she came there as a young bride in 1930, the estate extended to over 40 hectares. Death duties forced her late husband, the last Lord Counterblast, to sell off much of the land in the 1940s, and on his own death in 1970 all but the present 10 hectares had to be sold for the same reason. Lady Counterblast's investments have performed badly and she can no longer afford to retain the staff of gardeners who once tended the nationally famous rose gardens and terraces. The nearby village, Counterblast Magna, has been chosen as the site for a new development of 4,000 houses. Her advisers tell her that she could obtain several million pounds for the remaining land.

Eventually and reluctantly she sells all except the house, which she cannot bear to leave, and about one hectare of gardens; these include the remaining 300 metres of a famous avenue of lime trees planted in 1750 by the first Lord Counterblast and which once stretched for three miles. Shortly afterwards, she dies. Her executors try to sell the house as a family home, but it is now surrounded by cheap and rather unpleasant modern houses and fails to attract a reasonable offer. Eventually, a major bank buys it and turns it into a residential training centre.

This example illustrates the point that a substantial sale of adjacent land, especially where the house is very large and part of an historic landscape, can devalue the house to such an extent that it is no longer marketable at all as a private home; it may be suitable for other purposes (including perhaps residential flats) but as a *residence* it is no longer viable. Objectively, the larger holding, or at least some of it, was required for the reasonable enjoyment of *that particular* house as a *residence*; the sale which occurred was dictated by the particular circumstances of one owner. It is not practicable to delineate all the permutations of facts which might arise, but it is considered that some PRR should be due, even on a part disposal of building land, where substantial violence is done to the setting and value of a large house through circumstances outside the vendor's direct control. Where exactly the permitted area would fall would, of course, depend on all the facts (see ¶410(8)).

A different owner (perhaps younger and less impoverished than Lady Counterblast) might have decided that she no longer wished to remain in the house, and might have sold slightly less land for development (to minimise the devaluation of the house) while selling the house separately to a single residential purchaser. If the two sales were planned concurrently and actually took place within a few months of each other, it is considered that some of the building land might still qualify for PRR (though it would be essential to sell the land before the house – see ¶417).

(4) Changes to plot boundaries

The part disposal of land which was acquired by the owner *after* the purchase of the house is a situation where resistance to CGT liability may be very difficult, especially where that land was retained for a relatively short time. Such a disposal may argue against any contention that the total plot was objectively required for the reasonable enjoyment of the residence; and if the period of retention is very short there is even a risk of a Revenue attack under s. 224(3) or on 'trading' lines (see ¶307).

If such additional land is retained but a part disposal is made from the *original* holding, the prospects for PRR may be brighter, on the basis that the land sold can credibly be brought within the permitted area (see ¶409). This may, in fact, be a preferable strategy if part of the total plot has development value.

If the land subsequently acquired is retained until the sale of the main holding (the total plot exceeding 0.5 hectares) the case for the taxpayer must be stronger, especially where he has fully integrated the additional land into his garden and grounds, e.g. by removing any old fences or walls and bringing any previously 'wild' land under cultivation. If he has not done so, the true inference may be that the additional land was never, for him, garden or grounds (cf. ¶406).

(5) Planning strategies if relief unlikely to be due

If PRR is unlikely to be obtained on a part disposal of land, perhaps where the Revenue arguments outlined at ¶412(2) seem strong, can anything be done to reduce the tax bill?

As with most forms of tax planning, the answer is 'Quite possibly, but only if matters are planned well in advance'.

In the present context, this means well in advance of any planning application or other steps to enhance the value of the property or market it, and while real uncertainty exists as to any sale taking place (see *Craven (HMIT) v White* [1988] BTC 268).

Possibilities may include:

(a) a simple gift of the relevant land (or the owner's share of it) to a spouse liable to CGT at only 20 per cent instead of 40 per cent, and perhaps with annual exemptions or losses available (which will have no IHT costs – unless, possibly, the donee, but not the donor, is domiciled outside the UK – IHTA 1984, s. 18(2)): or

(b) a gift to a UK resident discretionary trust for a beneficiary other than the owner or his spouse, which will attract hold-over relief (see s. 260(1)), and reduce the rate of CGT on a subsequent sale by the trustees to 34 per cent – although this may involve IHT liability.

A third possibility, before the changes introduced in FA 1991 and if the tax at stake justified the costs, would have been a transfer of the relevant land, while it still commanded a relatively low value, to an offshore trust.

However, if the settlor is 'interested' in the settlement as defined at Sch. 5, para. 2, e.g. if he, his spouse, children or grandchildren (or their spouses) have a life interest, gains made by the trustees will normally now be taxed as the settlor's. This strategy is now, therefore, only feasible if the owner genuinely wishes to give the fruits of his gains to remoter beneficiaries, such as nephews, nieces or friends. Even then, unless there are likely to be non-resident or non-domiciled beneficiaries, this only defers the tax bill, since gains made by offshore trustees may be subject to a ten per cent surcharge when distributed to UK resident beneficiaries (s. 91). All such strategies require full professional advice throughout and should not be attempted without such advice.

Finally, where substantial sales of what is likely to be part of the non-permitted area are contemplated over several years, some form of trading venture may be worthy of consideration – at least so long as income tax and CGT rates remain the same (cf. ¶307(5)) and subject to taper relief considerations. This could perhaps be operated as a joint venture with a developer (a *partnership* has substantial commercial risks, although a limited liability partnership could be considered). This strategy could appeal to some farmers or members of Lloyd's who have income tax losses on a substantial scale, against which income tax profits could be used. The Sch. D commencement and cessation basis of assessment may be exploited with advantage. It will be important to elect, under s. 161(3), to bring the land into trading stock at historical cost (assuming this to be less than current market value) in order to avoid a deemed disposal under s. 161(1) when the venture starts.

¶412 Negotiations and contentious cases in practice

(1) How big can the permitted area be?

The first question asked by taxpayers contemplating the sale of houses with large plots is usually 'How much land will be exempt?'

As the foregoing discussion illustrates, every case turns on its own facts and no two properties are alike in all respects. The most helpful generalisations which can be offered are:

(a) that a disposal of the total plot often greatly enhances the chances of negotiating a substantial permitted area when compared to a part disposal; and

(b) that the larger the house and the more intimate and long established the relationships, visual and practical, between it and its surroundings, the better the prospects of a large permitted area are likely to be.

The best advice which can be offered is to examine all the evidence and submit as large a claim as this will support; the process of argument with the Revenue is essentially one of negotiation and compromise, and the negotiator simply has to start with the highest figure which he can justify without destroying his own credibility at the outset.

Throughout negotiations, it will be helpful to bear in mind that the identification of the permitted area involves (1) asking *how much* land is required for the reasonable enjoyment of the dwelling-house as a residence, and (2) where the area thus found is located using the 'most suitable' test in TCGA 1992, s. 222(4) (see ¶410(2) and (6)).

(2) Assembling the evidence

Much of what was said about the 'servants' houses' type of case at ¶323(3) applies equally to 'permitted area' cases. Research and careful preparation are equally essential; again, a commissioners' determination of fact is unlikely to be overturned by the courts (which doubtless explains why no such cases have reached that stage).

A careful examination of the physical site is advisable; advisers should beware of relying on plans alone, especially plans which lack topographical detail, if they are not familiar with the property. Pre-sale planning is important here, since after a sale it may be difficult to gain access and later owners may make significant alterations (see ¶323(2)). The vendor should be encouraged to take numerous photographs which will be of a high enough quality to give a stranger an appreciation of the whole plot and its relationship to the house; views of the garden from the house are particularly important, but also useful are views of the relevant elevations of the house, especially where the principal rooms face the garden (see ¶409(7)). Internal photographs may be valuable to give the necessary idea of the 'size and character' of the property (see ¶409(6)), and of the views available from various rooms. Finally, good aerial photographs help to give an overall impression of the total plot.

Pre-sale gathering of this kind of evidence is essential if there is to be a part disposal for building; it is too late to accumulate evidence about the garden and grounds when they have disappeared beneath an estate of new houses.

If all else fails, the taxpayer must be asked to ransack his attic and family albums, and those of his relatives; most people who have lived in a large house for many years have accumulated some photographs which may at least be better than nothing.

Historical research may also pay dividends if the grounds are of high landscape value and were originally laid out by professionals. Where a property has passed down several generations of the same family it is possible that the original plans and specifications for the garden may survive; alternatively they may have been the subject of specialised academic study and details may be held in the local County Record Office.

Good plans are essential; they should show enough detail to supplement the photographic record (to which they should be cross-referenced) and should also highlight natural and man-made features of importance. Contour lines should be clearly shown, as well as a scale to assist in calculations of area.

Another source of useful information and evidence may be the local authority's Planning Department. Especially where a listed building is involved, planning officers may be prepared to give a view as to what they regard as the curtilage of the building for planning purposes; since listed buildings consent is normally required for development within the curtilage, planners have a special interest in determining its extent. It may be possible to argue that if listed buildings consent is regarded as covering particular land, that land is part of the 'most suitable' land for occupation with the residence.

(3) Drawing the line

Negotiations on behalf of the Revenue will invariably be conducted by the district valuer; the inspector is expressly forbidden by his instructions to offer any opinion on the extent of the permitted area or on matters of valuation, and once he has identified the issues involved, including the extent of the dwelling house, the extent to which it has been used as a residence and the extent of the garden or grounds (CGT 64821) and collected any other relevant information, he will act merely as a post-box (see CGT 64803). The district valuer will usually conduct any 'servants' house' negotiations at the same time (see ¶323(4)).

The district valuer often starts by looking for the nearest obvious boundary to the house, and basing his opening offer on this. For example, if a country house stands in open parkland to the front, with a gravel forecourt, and to the rear there are formal gardens to a depth of (say) 200 yards, after which the parkland resumes, he may simply draw a line which encloses only the forecourt, the house itself and the formal gardens plus a little land to either side of the house. If there are walls, hedges, ha-has or drives near the house he may well base his line on these. With a smaller property he may draw his line along the edge of the lawn where it meets a shrubbery or kitchen garden.

These proposals should sometimes be treated as opening skirmishes rather than conclusive thrusts. The district valuer's initial proposal will sometimes be found to leave a substantial country house absurdly short of adjacent land and with a garden

¶412

whose length is little more than the 80 to 100 feet commonly found in modern suburban properties.

An interesting example of the need to examine such proposals very critically was revealed by the Parliamentary Commissioner for Administration (the 'Ombudsman') in his report for 1987/88 (*Sixth Report*, House of Commons Papers 1987/88 No. 672 pp. 52ff.). This case involved the sale of a house and grounds together comprising 2.75 acres (1.11 hectares), and including a tennis court, a swimming pool, a croquet lawn, a rose bed and a spinney. The district valuer's initial proposal was for a permitted area of 1.15 acres (0.465 hectares). This bisected the tennis court, croquet lawn and rose bed, and excluded the swimming pool, yet included its filtration plant. Eventually the case was settled on the basis of a larger area (two acres (0.8 hectares) including the swimming pool and the whole of the tennis court).

The Ombudsman's investigation found that the taxpayer 'had good reason to feel aggrieved … what should have been a reasonably straightforward case had turned into a frustrating saga for him'. The Revenue was censured for 'persisting in the view that the presence of the swimming pool and tennis court had to be regarded as irrelevant to the issue of the permitted area', and also, incidentally, for taking more than 32 months to resolve a case in which the final tax bill was a mere £327.

Doubtless this case is an extreme instance, but it illustrates the importance of visualising the appearance of the property if the district valuer's suggestion were to represent the actual holding of land. It is most unlikely that anyone would regard half of a tennis court, and a filtration plant severed from the pool for which it was built, as 'most suitable' land within s. 222(4) (see ¶410(2)).

If it is not possible to argue with any conviction for the total plot as the permitted area (perhaps because not all of it is 'garden or grounds' or some of it represents very recent additions to the historic curtilage), it may be possible to identify a more distant natural or artificial boundary. This might result, for example, in the exclusion of broad-leaved woodlands (as distinct from ornamental shrubberies), large paddocks (especially if let for grazing) or areas which are only doubtfully suitable for the owner's own enjoyment, such as abandoned barns, chalk pits or other derelict parts.

(4) 'Comparables'
An important element in the district valuer's negotiations will be the use of so-called 'comparables', especially in relation to the 'size and character' test (see ¶410ff.). He should always be asked for full details of any allegedly comparable properties, and should not be allowed to offer merely vague generalisations about properties in the same locality. For all kinds of good reasons these may not be truly comparable: they may have completely different outlooks or grounds of no particular landscape or horticultural value; they may have been sold in 'forced

¶412

sale' conditions (see ¶411(3)) or in a significantly different market. He should be asked to disclose in advance details of any 'comparables' on which he intends to rely before the commissioners; but it should be remembered that what is said here applies equally to any 'comparables' which the taxpayer intends to use.

(5) Valuation aspects

If it is not possible to regard the entire area sold as within the permitted area, the valuation of the excluded portion of land will clearly become a matter of considerable practical importance. See ¶410(6) for problems regarding access and 'hope' value. This must be part of the professional valuer's province, but if a defendable low value can be placed on the excluded land, it may be much more cost-effective to reach agreement with the district valuer on that basis than to pursue a possibly costly and long-drawn out dispute about the boundaries of the permitted area. It is worth doing sample computations in such cases to establish the additional tax saved by, say, each additional 0.1 hectares which might theoretically be brought within the permitted area. Such an exercise may lead to the conclusion that further argument is not worthwhile. In any event it will enable the client to make an informed decision as to how much further he wishes to press the matter. It is also worth noting that the district valuer cannot agree a permitted area of more than two hectares without reference to his regional manager (VOM 8.78); if there is little more land than this at stake a tactical compromise which avoids such a reference may have attractions for him.

There is some helpful guidance about the district valuer's role in these matters in the Revenue's *Tax Bulletin*, February 1992, p. 11.

(6) If negotiations fail – hearings before the commissioners

The comments below are applicable both to disputes about the 'permitted area' and, in many cases, 'servants' houses' issues (see ¶323).

If deadlock has apparently been reached in negotiations it may be in the taxpayer's interests to seek a hearing from the commissioners.

The client must be advised at this point of the likely professional costs of a contested hearing, and that the commissioners have no power to award costs to a successful party.

The inspector may be stimulated, by the prospect of having to prepare for such a hearing, into reappraising the merits of his case, and if it is not strong, it is possible that he may concede the point without the need for a hearing. He may, alternatively offer some kind of compromise: for instance, he may propose a somewhat enlarged 'permitted area'. However, a request for a hearing should never be treated as an exercise in bluffing, and should only be made if the client is prepared to go through with it. He can, however, be advised that a favourable result before commissioners is unlikely to be overturned in the courts (see ¶323(3)).

A procedural point of some importance concerns the body of commissioners who should hear the case. Detailed jurisdictional rules are set out in TMA 1970, Sch. 3. Under these rules the taxpayer may elect for the hearing to be before the general commissioners for the area where he usually resides at the time of the election, or (if different) for the area where he has his place of business if self-employed, or his place of employment if a director or employee. The election must be made at the time of lodging the appeal, although the Board has discretion to accept a later election; but failing any election, the Board can nominate a division of commissioners for any of the three areas mentioned above.

In PRR cases there may be some tactical advantage in electing for the 'residential' division if that is the same as the division where the property in question is situated; local knowledge can be influential in such matters, and a taxpayer may feel that he stands a better chance of a sympathetic hearing before commissioners familiar with the locality and its properties (perhaps even with the particular property in question) than before a distant tribunal, especially if he is a Sch. E taxpayer whose 'employment' commissioners may sit hundreds of miles away from the area. (Sometimes the circumstances make this impossible, e.g. if, when the appeal is lodged, the taxpayer no longer resides in the area where the property was situated – which was the case in *Williams (HMIT) v Merrylees* [1987] BTC 393.)

Although it is possible to elect for a hearing before the special commissioners (see TMA 1970, s. 46), the writer would rarely, if ever, advise this course. It can take longer to arrange for a hearing by the 'Specials', who are professional lawyers and sit mainly in London, than the local 'Generals', who are usually laypeople. Also, the Revenue's line in PRR cases, both in relation to 'permitted area' and 'servants' houses' cases, is often a highly legalistic one, much less likely to commend itself to a lay than to a specialist tribunal. Also, of course, any benefits of 'local knowledge' mentioned above would be forfeited.

It should be noted that in so far as the point at issue concerns the valuation of land, the appeal must be heard by the appropriate lands tribunal (see TMA 1970, s. 46D(1)(b)). Thus, if as well as the issue of the 'permitted area' or whether a subsidiary dwelling is part of the main house, there is also a dispute about the apportionment of gains between the exempt and non-exempt areas, the latter point (involving valuation) may have to be argued before a separate tribunal.

(7) Contentious cases – at the commissioners' hearing

The practical conduct of contentious hearings is not within the scope of this book. However, a few points peculiar to PRR appeals may be mentioned.

It cannot be stressed too heavily that the key to success will often be the correct marshalling and presentation of all the facts favourable to the taxpayer (see ¶323(3)). A method which is frequently adopted, and appreciated by many commissioners, is to prepare a dossier containing all the relevant plans,

¶412

photographs (whose quality should obviously be good) and other documents such as sale particulars, together with a summary of the agreed facts, in chronological order, and an outline of the arguments for the taxpayer. The final part of the dossier might contain brief extracts from any cases to which the taxpayer's representative will be referring. Copies of the dossier can then be handed to each commissioner, the clerk and the Revenue's representative. Such a dossier should avoid the need for the commissioners and the clerk to take detailed notes.

If distance is not an obstacle and any necessary permission can be obtained, there is no reason why the commissioners should not be invited to visit the property to see it for themselves if this is thought likely to be favourable to the case, or perhaps if the physical layout is especially complex. Alternatively the commissioners may be prepared to accept videotaped evidence.

Finally, thought should be given to the use of witnesses. Four categories may be considered:

(1) In permitted area cases it will often be vital to establish the way in which the land in question was used, or perhaps altered, during the taxpayer's ownership. In 'subsidiary dwelling' or 'servants' houses' cases, it is equally vital to bring out the extent to which the property in question served the occupation of the taxpayer's residence, and the reasons for his employment of any domestic staff. The only person who can convincingly speak on such issues is the taxpayer himself. Only he knows the real facts in this regard. Unless he would make a bad witness, perhaps because of old age, illness or incorrigible garrulity, he should always be called in his own cause.

(2) In 'servants' houses' cases, the employees themselves, if available and willing to appear, may also be called to explain the nature of their duties and, it is to be hoped, the necessity for them to 'live in' in order to perform them; they may be able to state convincingly that they would not have accepted the position in question if no accommodation had been available.

(3) Some witnesses may be able to speak from personal knowledge of the history of the house before the taxpayer owned it, in order to show that any associated land claimed to be within the 'permitted area' has always been used as garden and grounds of the house, or, in 'servants' houses' cases, that the subsidiary dwelling has been historically part of the main residence. These may include previous owners, professional valuers with extensive local experience, and (possibly) reputable local historians who have researched the topic. The two last named types should be regarded as 'experts' so that expressions of opinion, rather than fact, will be admissible in evidence.

(4) Finally, if there is a valuation issue which is being heard by the Lands

¶412

Tribunal, the taxpayer would normally be advised to retain his own expert valuation witness.

The inspector may well call the district valuer as his own witness (again as an 'expert') and he should, of course, be cross-examined.

If the decision goes against the taxpayer consideration should be given to requesting a stated case. The way in which the commissioners formulate the stated case is often vital to the outcome if the case goes on to the High Court, and only by examining it carefully can advisers form a view about the prospects of overturning the finding in the courts on the grounds that it contradicts the facts or contains an error of law. Expert legal advice should always be taken at this stage even if it was not taken earlier.

(8) Co-operation between professionals

In the writer's opinion, the sale of associated land is best viewed as an exercise in which all a client's professional advisers – accountants, tax advisers, solicitors and valuers – should pool their skills at the preparatory stage. This is particularly true where deals with developers are contemplated. Not only should such co-operation produce the best financial result for the client; it is also the best way to minimise any taxation problems after the event.

LAND ACQUIRED BEFORE THE HOUSE OR RETAINED AFTER ITS SALE

¶413 Land acquired before the house

PRR extends only to a dwelling-house itself (TCGA 1992, s. 222(1)(a)) and land which is held as garden and grounds with it up to the permitted area (s. 222(1)(b)). The latter provision, however, does not require the land to be held concurrently with the house throughout the owner's period of ownership, if full PRR is to be obtained.

If the land is held as garden or grounds at the time of its disposal (as to which see ¶417), the only effect of its initially having been held as bare land is that part of the total gains may not qualify for PRR because the land will not have been the owner's residence in that initial period (see s. 223(2)). If that period is relatively short, an extra-statutory concession may assist (see ¶414).

¶414 The terms of the ESC

ESC D49 applies where an individual acquires land and has a house built on it which he then uses as his only or main residence; it also applies where there is a delay in occupying the new house because of the need for alterations or redecorations to it, or the process of selling a previous home. In either case, if the period between the acquisition of the land and the occupation of the house does not exceed one year, the Revenue will regard that period as part of the occupation period, thus avoiding any loss of PRR in respect of the initial period. The year's grace may be increased to two years if there are good reasons outside the taxpayer's control.

¶415 Where the ESC may assist

Clearly the year's grace in ESC D49 can be invoked where the delay does not exceed one year; but it should be noted that the text refers to the owner 'then' going into residential occupation. Its predecessor until 1994, Statement of Practice D4, used 'thereupon', which seemed likely to mean 'immediately after completion of the house'; 'then' seems less strong, and may imply that there may be a gap between completion of the building or alterations and the occupation of the new home, so long as the total period between acquisition of the land or house and its occupation falls within the concession. The old SP D4 did not cover delay due to the protracted sale of the previous home.

'Good' reasons for an extension of the year's grace would naturally include delays in building caused by bad weather or unforeseen structural problems, but they do need to be outside the taxpayer's control; so shortage of funds, or of time if the owner is doing the work himself, might not qualify. Delays caused by planning difficulties might qualify if they were not reasonably foreseeable at the outset. Local Revenue officers in charge can authorise the additional year (see CGT 65010).

If there may be difficulty in coming within the ESC, it is possible that a judicious use of the 'final 36 months' rule may help someone who already has a residence elsewhere.

Example

Andrew, a jobbing builder, has owned Greenacre for some years and occupied it as his only residence. In September 2001 he bought a plot of land with outline planning permission for a bungalow. He obtains full planning permission in December 2001 and starts work on the bungalow in January 2002. He has considerable other work on hand and progress is slow, but by the end of the Summer of 2002 he has finished the walls and roof and connected the essential services to his new bungalow, including the installation of central heating. He decides to leave the erection of the garage and the internal carpentry and decoration work until he has more time, but the house is (just about) habitable. He therefore moves some belongings in and spends several nights a week there. He elects to treat the new bungalow as his main residence under TCGA 1992, s. 222(5)(a) (see ¶506) on 1 September 2002.

So long as Andrew sells Greenacre no later than 31 August 2005, he should suffer no loss of PRR either on it or on the bungalow. The last three years (maximum) of ownership of Greenacre are protected by s. 223(1) (as amended). The first year of ownership of the bungalow plot is protected by ESC D49, since he occupies it as his (deemed) main residence as soon as he can; thereafter his election protects him until Greenacre is sold, and after that he has only one residence in any event. He can therefore finish the bungalow off at his leisure.

Andrew would not need to make an election in favour of the bungalow plot for the 12 months in which it is protected by the ESC because of the specific words to that effect at the end of the text.

¶416 Land retained and sold after the sale of the house

(1) The problem
The converse situation to that just discussed – land retained after the sale of the house but later sold separately at a gain – is also fraught with problems. These were frankly acknowledged by the High Court in *Varty (HMIT) v Lynes* (1976) 51 TC 419. However, where losses are involved, the decision in this case could be used to advantage to throw up an allowable CGT loss – see ¶1003(2).

(2) The decision in Varty v Lynes
Here the taxpayer, Mr Lynes, acquired a house in a total plot of less than one acre in 1968, and lived there until June 1971. He sold the house and 'part' of the garden (the measurements are not stated in the report) for £10,000, and in May 1972 he sold the remaining land, also for £10,000. He had been given some comfort by the local authority, at the time of the first sale, that planning permission would be granted on the remainder, and indeed outline permission was granted between the two sales. He claimed that what is now TCGA 1992, s. 223(1) applied to exempt the gain on the second sale (there was, of course, no doubt about its application to the first) on the basis that it should cover any part of the land occupied with the house as garden or grounds: and that the words 'land which he has ....' in s. 222(1)(b) should be interpreted as meaning 'Land which he has while owning the residence' (see *Varty (HMIT) v Lynes* at p. 420E).

The Revenue relied on the contrasting tenses of the verbs in s. 222(1)(a) and (b): the former referred to a dwelling-house 'which is, or has at any time ... been, his only or main residence', whereas the latter referred only to 'land which he *has*' as garden or grounds with his residence, and confined relief to land which was so held at the point of its *own* disposal.

Brightman J preferred the latter view, while accepting that they both produced anomalies. On the Revenue's view, he said, 'It must follow ... that if the taxpayer goes out of occupation of the dwelling-house a month before he sells it, the exemption will be lost in respect of the garden' (see *Varty (HMIT) v Lynes* p. 424F). By this he meant that the *whole* of the gain on the garden since the acquisition of the property would be taxable, having apparently accepted the Revenue's submission that there was no provision for apportionment so as to tax only the gain applicable to that final month (though see the comment at (5) below). In the case before him the facts were different, not only in that the time between the two sales was some 11 months, but also in that there were two separate sales.

However, as Brightman J observed, equally odd results could follow on the taxpayer's view. He instanced the purchase of a house and garden in 1960, with the house sold in 1970 and the garden retained until 1990 when it was sold 'as a desirable and extremely valuable building site' (see *Varty (HMIT) v Lynes* at p. 424H). On the taxpayer's argument a substantial development gain could be sheltered behind PRR.

The judge decided against the taxpayer, adopting the robust view that 'It is no good counting up anomalies on one side and the other and twisting the language in order to produce what may seem to be, on balance, the most sensible result, and the one which perhaps Parliament might have preferred if all the various combinations of circumstances had been fully debated' (see *Varty (HMIT) v Lynes* at p. 424I).

(3) The effect of the decision

This decision produced what may be considered an unjust result, which can be best seen in the actual figures involved. The gain on the assessment which was upheld was £6,930, and although there is no computation in the stated case this must have been arrived at as follows:

	£	£
Net proceeds of site in May 1972		9,895
Net cost of whole property in 1968	6,920	
Apportioned to first sale in June 1971:		
$£6{,}920 \times \dfrac{£10{,}000}{£10{,}000 + £7{,}500}$		
	3,955	(2,965)
Taxable gain on sale of remaining land		6,930

¶416

(The fraction used above must have been based on the fact that the first sale was for £10,000 and the value of the remainder at that point was agreed at £7,500 – see *Varty (HMIT) v Lynes* at p. 420B.)

There was no suggestion that the remaining land sold in May 1972 had been used for any other purpose except as garden land between 1968 and 1971; the gain on a time basis for the final 11 months was £2,395 (£9,895–£7,500). However, Mr Lynes was taxed on a gain of £6,930 when his true 'development gain' cannot have been much more than £2,500. (The difference of £4,430 in 1972 represented approximately four times the present writer's salary in his first job which he started in the same year).

(4) The Revenue's practice – sale of garden land after sale of house

The Revenue still takes this point, apparently regardless of whether the land remaining after the sale of the house has development value. The CGT Manual says that land which is disposed of separately after the disposal of the residence 'cannot qualify' for PRR (see CGT 64380). The trap into which Mr Lynes fell is therefore still a real danger.

(5) Brightman J's illustration – vendor going out of occupation before completion of sale of house plus garden

The Revenue does, however, view Brightman J's illustration in *Varty (HMIT) v Lynes*, about the sale of the house and garden (together) after vacation of the house (see ¶416(2)) as only obiter, and inspectors are instructed not to argue for liability here (see CGT 64386-64387). In the writer's view this is correct. It could even, in the writer's view, be argued that if a man vacates his home and then sells the house and garden a short while later, at the date of disposal, he still holds the garden 'for his own occupation and enjoyment with that residence as garden or grounds' (see s. 222(1)(b)), since that is the purpose 'for' which it is still held at the date of disposal and until completion of the sale the owner may resume occupation and use of the garden at any time. However, since *Varty v Lynes* has never been overturned by a higher court and in the light of the Revenue's clearly stated view (see ¶416(4) above), it must be prudent to keep within the terms of the decision and to avoid a 'dangling' sale of the associated land after that of the house if possible.

¶417 Crystallising an exempt gain on 'retained' land

There may be an alternative approach to the problem identified in *Varty (HMIT) v Lynes* (1976) 51 TC 419. If it is unavoidable that some garden land has to be retained following the disposal of the dwelling-house, it may be possible to crystallise a gain which ranks for PRR by disposing of this land, at the same time as the sale of the dwelling-house, to a trust of which the owner is the life tenant.

¶417

Subject to any 'permitted area' problems, it is considered that this disposal should rank for PRR. It will have no IHT implications because the land will simply remain in the owner's estate (IHTA 1984, s. 49(1)). Any subsequent gain on the garden land will not, of course, attract PRR (following *Varty (HMIT) v Lynes*) and will be taxable on the settlor as his own gain (s. 77); but if the land is sold quite quickly this gain should be minimal (possibly covered by the settlor's annual exemption), and the aim of the exercise, to secure PRR for the period during which the land was held with the house, will have been achieved. The trust would require wide powers so that the cash from the sale could eventually be appointed back to the settlor.

¶418 Bringing land within the garden

Finally, what is the position where the garden or grounds were, on the facts, not within the test in TCGA 1992, s. 222(1)(b) at some earlier time in the taxpayer's ownership? If they can be brought within that test *at the time of disposal*, PRR should be available, subject to the 'permitted area' problem (see ¶409).

Example

In 1989 Hazel acquired The Gables, a small cottage in a plot of just less than 0.5 hectares, about half of which was rough pasture. Until 1992 she let this part, fenced off, to a neighbouring farmer as grazing land. In 1992 she terminated his tenancy and paid a landscape gardener to remove the fences, rotovate the land, lay down turf and plant shrubs, so that the whole plot became garden. She sells up completely in 2004.

When Hazel sells up, there can be no doubt that the whole plot is 'garden or grounds' which she occupies and enjoys with her residence. Exemption appears to be due on the whole gain, on the whole plot, (both cottage and enlarged garden), from 1989 to 2004. In effect, Hazel has applied the reasoning in *Varty (HMIT) v Lynes* in reverse to her advantage.

A different result could follow if Hazel's incorporation of the rough pasture into the garden was done with a view to sale, and only shortly before sale; that would involve the application of the 'tainted expenditure' rule in s. 224(3) (see ¶308) and some PRR would probably be lost.

¶419 Conclusion

The whole question of land retained after the disposal of the house is beset with problems. *Varty (HMIT) v Lynes* (1976) 51 TC 419, though it was, on the wording of the Act, rightly decided, highlights an unfortunate defect in the legislation.

To remedy that defect, further legislation would be required. This could perhaps require an apportionment of the total gain on 'retained' land between the period of its use with the dwelling-house (which would be exempt to the same extent as the gain on the house) and the period after the sale of the house (which would be taxable).

Meanwhile, clients who encounter this aspect of PRR may need very careful advice particularly where substantial sums are involved.

¶419

5 The Multiple Owner

RESIDENCES AND MAIN RESIDENCES

¶501 The need for a distinction

Private residence relief is available only for a property which is, in fact or by election, the owner's main residence, so that it is necessary to distinguish between the two concepts. A prior question, however, is whether the subject property is a 'residence' of the owner at all: without this a PRR claim will fall from the outset.

¶502 Lack of definition of 'residence'

Section 222 of TCGA 1992 does not define a 'residence', in common with the rest of the taxing statutes. We therefore need to consider the everyday meaning of the word in its context, which is a provision giving relief from CGT on the disposal of a capital asset. In everyday English, someone could be said to 'reside' in a building, in certain contexts, even if he stayed there only for one night: compare the hotel bar which describes itself as 'open to non-residents'. Clearly a more substantial degree of attachment is required here, as it was, for example, in the context of the now abolished mortgage interest relief (see ¶1101). In *Frost (HMIT) v Feltham* (1980) 55 TC 10, a case on the latter relief, at p. 131, Nourse J put it simply thus: 'A residence is a place where somebody lives'.

It is probably impossible to improve on this. If a man is staying in a seaside hotel on holiday but occupies a house in London when he is not on holiday, he would not ordinarily answer the question 'Where do you live?' with 'In this hotel' (even if he was speaking in the 'residents' lounge'). A residence for tax purposes thus denotes permanence of abode, a place which is a man's home, though not necessarily his only home.

The point at which a dwelling-house becomes a person's residence must be a question of fact and degree in all cases. The description 'dwelling-house' tells us merely what type of property is being described (see ¶301ff.) whereas to discover whether it is a person's residence we need to know how that person spends his time. A house which the person in question never occupies at all, even for a single night, cannot be said to be his residence whatever his intentions on acquiring it: this was the position in another mortgage interest relief case, *Hughes (HMIT) v*

Viner [1985] BTC 156, where the house in question could not be occupied for structural reasons. In *Kirkby v Hughes (HMIT)* [1993] BTC 52 it was held that a builder's occupation of certain properties had not been sufficient to make them residences of his. In *Goodwin v Curtis (HMIT)* [1996] BTC 501, a brief period of occupation of a house clearly intended to be sold as soon as possible lacked the necessary permanence to amount to residence.

In *Frost (HMIT) v Feltham*, however, a taxpayer who merely spent 'some time each month' at a house which he owned in Wales, while clearly spending most of his time at a public house in Essex of which he was the licensee, was able to establish that the Welsh property was a residence of his; it was relevant that this was the only property he had ever owned, and that he had no security of tenure at the public house.

It is the fact of use which appears to be more important in this context than its duration, regularity or legal status: in the latter connection, it is not impossible that someone could be resident in a house which was actually let or licensed to a third party, especially where the tenant or licensee is a connected person. A home provided rent-free to an elderly parent might well be a residence of the child if the latter needed to spend the night there regularly to provide care. An exclusive tenancy granted at arm's length for a full rent, however, probably raises a presumption against residence by the lessor.

A property which the owner occasionally visits, but where he never spends the night, probably lacks the necessary quality of permanence associated with an 'abode': see *Williams (HMIT) v Merrylees* [1987] BTC 393 (see ¶320(3)) where the gardener's cottage was held by the commissioners not to be a residence of the taxpayer once he had sold the main house since he made only occasional daytime visits (para. 5(9), 7(e) and 9(2) of the stated case at [1987] BTC 395, 396), a finding which the taxpayer did not challenge in the High Court.

In this text the expression 'factual residence' will be used henceforth to indicate a property which, on this approach, can be said to be a residence of the owner, whether or not it is his main residence.

¶503 Main residence (in the absence of an election under s. 222(5))

(1) Residence, not just ownership

Where a person owns only one property, only that property can possibly qualify for PRR. But someone may own more than one property without having more than one residence: if there is only one factual residence (see ¶502) the other properties are irrelevant for PRR.

However, it has long been recognised that someone can have two residences simultaneously. For example, for electoral registration purposes, students have been held to be resident at their university address even though they also have homes elsewhere (*Fox v Stirk and Bristol Electoral Registration Officer, Ricketts v Cambridge City Electoral Registration Officer* [1970] 2 QB 463). Lord Denning's dictum in that case is quoted at CGT 64456 and the Revenue regards Lord Widgery's formulation as applicable to PRR cases:

> 'This conception of residence is of the place where a man is based or where he continues to live, the place where he sleeps and shelters and has his home'.

In such multi-residence cases, it is necessary to ask 'Which is the main residence?' The discussion below considers the position in the absence of an election under TCGA 1992, s. 222(5) – the latter point being separately discussed at ¶505. The expression 'factual MR' will be used for convenience to denote the property which, on the facts, is the main as distinct from a secondary residence.

(2) Time test

In distinguishing a main from a secondary residence the Revenue tends to start by asking where the taxpayer spends the majority of his time. This may take the form, initially, of a simple counting of nights, and the inspector may contend that unless more than 183 nights a year, on average, were spent at a property, that property cannot have been the factual MR. For persons with significant free capital and leisure this may well be the right approach and will usually yield a result in accordance with common sense: someone of independent means who has a London *pied a terre* and a country estate will usually spend more nights at the latter than at the former.

It should be noted here that ownership is quite irrelevant to the issue: the country estate in the previous instance could well be owned by a family trust or by the individual's parents, but that will not prevent its being a factual MR if the facts justify that conclusion.

(3) Complicating factors

In other cases, however, the time test may be too simplistic. The taxpayer's disposition of his time may not represent a free choice. The demands of business or family may force him to spend the majority of his time away from the property he regards as his home. In *Frost (HMIT) v Feltham* (1980) 55 TC 10 (see ¶502) the taxpayer was obliged by his brewery tenancy to spend most of the year in Essex but his 'home' was clearly in Wales: it seems that this was the place to which he retreated whenever he could. Nourse J produced an historical parallel in the person of Lord Eldon, an eighteenth century Lord Chancellor with a town house in London but an estate at Encombe in Dorset:

¶503

'Sometimes [Lord Eldon] was only able to get down [to Encombe] for three weeks or so in the year, for the partridge shooting in September. True it was that Lord Eldon also had a good house in [London], but it could not really have been suggested that he did not use Encombe as his principal or more important residence.' ((1980) 55 TC 10 at p. 14B.)

This question arises for decision less frequently now than it did before the introduction of the special relief for job-related accommodation (see ¶610) which now resolves the issue for many taxpayers whose presence at a particular property for much of the year is a requirement of their jobs. (*Frost (HMIT) v Feltham* concerned periods before the introduction of the analogous (and now itself abolished) mortgage interest relief in ICTA 1988, s. 356(3)). The point may still be relevant, however, in cases where the strict terms of that relief cannot apply, or where other factors are involved.

Example
Mary owns two houses a few miles apart: Briar Cottage, which she bought for her own use some years ago, and Willowdene, which she bought in 2001 for her elderly mother. In 2003 her mother suffers a heart attack and Mary and her brother, Cyril, who also lives nearby, decide to take turns to spend a night sleeping at Willowdene to look after their mother, but as Cyril has a young family whereas Mary is single, she volunteers to be 'on duty' each weekend.

Although Mary may spend more than 183 nights a year at Willowdene, and although that property does not qualify for the old dependent relative relief since it was acquired after 5 April 1988 (see s. 226 and ¶1021), it is likely that reference to the principles in *Frost (HMIT) v Feltham* will lead to the conclusion that Mary's factual MR is still Briar Cottage.

¶504 Planning

The Revenue is normally reluctant to concede that a property can be a factual MR if it fails the time test (see ¶503(2)) and the onus will often be on the taxpayer to demonstrate that a different conclusion is justifiable. If, therefore, it is necessary to rely on the factual position with regard to such a property (usually because the possibility of a TCGA 1992, s. 222(5) election has been overlooked at the correct time – see ¶518), everything possible should be done to maintain links with that property so that it can truly be said to be the client's main base. The importance of taking an all-round view was emphasised in the cases quoted with approval by Nourse J in *Frost (HMIT) v Feltham* (1980) 55 TC 10 where similar issues arose under the *Leasehold Reform Act* 1967, s. 1(2). There was, it was said in one such case (*Byrne v Rowbotham* (1969) 210 EG 823) 'an infinity of variations to take into account in deciding which was a man's home.'

Areas to which attention should be paid may include:

(1) The place of liability for the council tax.

(2) Where applicable, the property on which any mortgage interest relief was claimed up to 5 April 2000 (see ¶1101).

(3) The place of registration for voting purposes (for which the test is simply the 'place of residence').

(4) The place where the owner is registered with a doctor.

(5) The address shown on important personal documents such as passport applications and driving licences.

(6) The place where the majority of the owners' personal possessions are kept – or those of greatest value to him.

(7) The address held for the owner by third parties such as his bankers, insurers, and (most importantly) his inspector of taxes.

(8) The place where his family business associates and friends would naturally expect to find him, when he was not called elsewhere by other commitments.

In summary, then, a man's main residence is to be equated, on the broad line of authority examined, with his 'real home', where his roots are, and where he would choose to be if he had no conflicting demands on his time. This is a test of depth of attachment rather than length, and although a time test may provide a starting point, it will not always be conclusive.

¶505 Main residence by Revenue determination

If there is doubt as to the factual MR and in the absence of an election under TCGA 1992, s. 222(5)(a), until 5 April 1996 the inspector had to determine the issue by a notice under the former s. 222(5)(b), subject to a right of appeal.

This procedure disappeared with the advent of self assessment from 6 April 1996. In the absence of an election under s. 222(5)(a) (see ¶506 below), it is up to the taxpayer to form a view about which residence was the factual MR and make his return accordingly. This is discussed below in ¶1030.

MAIN RESIDENCE BY TAXPAYER'S ELECTION UNDER s. 222(5)(a)

¶506 Is an election necessary?

The election to treat a property as a main residence (called in what follows an 'elected MR') is only competent 'so far as it is necessary' to determine which of two properties is the main residence for any period. There is no possibility of an election where there are single *successive* residences (see the discussion of marital breakdown at ¶904(2)). Nor can one be made where there is more than one owned property but only one of which is a factual residence (see ¶502).

¶507 An election is conclusive

If an election is competent and is validly made, it is conclusive in the taxpayer's favour ('the individual may *conclude* that question ...') and an inspector's determination under TCGA 1992, s. 222(5)(b) (see ¶505) cannot be made. The only matter which the inspector could properly investigate would be the status of the properties concerned as factual residences or otherwise.

¶508 In writing

The legislation is quite clear that written notice must be given, but in practice no form is prescribed and an informal letter will suffice so long as it is unambiguous and includes full details of the property concerned and the effective date. A vague intimation of the possibility of an election or a request for information about the procedure would not seem to suffice (see *Ward-Stemp v Griffin (HMIT)* [1988] BTC 12, a case about the former wife's earnings' election where preliminary steps towards an election fell short of an actual election). Good practice suggests the need for a standardised letter, and this *must* be signed by the client; inspectors are instructed not to accept an election signed by an agent (CGT 64523). Advisers responsible for completing tax returns must, of course, ensure that a copy of the election is kept permanently (see ¶1033).

¶509 The time limit

Before 1993 there was some doubt about the time limit for an election, although in some limited circumstances a concession may assist (see ¶520).

The Revenue view is that the election must be made within two years of the date when the taxpayer first has two factual residences. This rests on the opening words of TCGA 1992, s. 222(5): 'So far as it is necessary for the purposes of [s. 222] which of two or more residences is an individual's main residence for any period ...'. The Revenue takes the view that as soon as there are two or more factual residences, the 'necessity' mentioned above arises; it follows that when the draftsman goes on to say, in subs. (a), 'the individual may conclude that question by notice given ... within two years of the beginning of *that period*' (emphasis added), he means the period beginning when the 'necessity' first arose.

Example
Oswald acquired Redacre on 6 April 1997 as his only residence. On 6 April 2001 he acquired Brownacre which he immediately began to use as an alternative residence. The Revenue view would be that it was 'necessary' to conclude the question of Oswald's main residence on 6 April 2001, so that unless he elects for one or other property as his elected MR by 5 April 2003 his rights under s. 222(5)(a) would be forfeited as regards those properties.

An alternative view advanced by some commentators until the decision of the High Court in *Griffin (HMIT) v Craig-Harvey* [1994] BTC 3 was that the 'necessity' postulated in the subsection does not arise until there is a disposal which would be taxable in the absence of PRR. The 'period' in question, on this view, was any retrospective period which began not more than two years before the election was made, allowing a taxpayer to delay his election if he wished, although a delayed election could not confer any relief for a period prior to its starting date.

(1) The Craig-Harvey case
In *Griffin (HMIT) v Craig-Harvey* three properties were involved. The taxpayer acquired the first, a London property, 48 Stockwell Park Crescent, in November 1981. On 12 August 1985 he acquired a country property, Balldown Farmhouse. On 9 July 1986 he completed the sale of Stockwell Park Crescent and the purchase of the third property, 7 Sibella Road, also in London. He sold the farmhouse on 26 January 1989 and the assessment on the gain on this property gave rise to the appeal. He had submitted an election under what is now s. 225(5)(a) in favour of the farmhouse on 21 January 1988, purporting to backdate this to 22 January 1986 under the view summarised at ¶509(2). The inspector contended that the election could have effect only from 9 July 1986, the date when 7 Sibella Road was acquired. Although the taxpayer succeeded before the special commissioner, he failed in the High Court.

Vinelott J held that the correct construction of what is now s. 222(5)(a) was that although it preceded what he called the 'general rule' in [old] s. 222(5)(b) providing for a determination by the inspector of the 'question' as to which property was the main residence 'for any period' (see ¶505) – it was in substance an exception to that rule. It gave the taxpayer the right to 'conclude that question' by an election made within two years 'from the beginning of that period'. The most natural meaning of 'that period', in the judge's view, was 'the whole or part of any period' during which there were two or more residences. In this case he held that this period began when the taxpayer first had the two residences in question, the farmhouse and 7 Sibella Road, and not, as the taxpayer contended, any period starting not more than two years before the date of the election.

At first blush it might seem that the election was in time even on the Revenue's view since it was made within two years of the acquisition of 7 Sibella Road on

9 July 1986. However, although the judgment is not explicit on the point, it appears that the judge must have reasoned that this interpretation would have extended the period covered by the election back to a period when the taxpayer had a different pair of residences, i.e. the farmhouse and Stockwell Park Crescent. In order to deem the farmhouse to be his main residence before 9 July 1986, it seems that the taxpayer would have needed to make a separate election as between that property and Stockwell Park Crescent, no later than 11 August 1987, and this was not done.

This case was complicated by the fact that three residences were involved, but ignoring that feature, the decision supports the Revenue's long-standing view, summarised at ¶509(1), that the time limit runs from the date when the taxpayer first has two or more residences and cannot simply be backdated by two years from the date when it is made. It also suggests that in any event an election between a particular combination of residences cannot extend back into a period when a different combination existed.

Vinelott J found no ambiguity in the statutory language, but nevertheless considered the Crown's argument that if ambiguity did exist, reference debates in *Hansard*, under the rule in *Pepper v Hart (HMIT) and related appeals* HL [1992] 591; CA [1990] 552; ChD [1989] 595, supported the Revenue's view.

As originally drafted, in the *Finance (No. 2) Bill* 1965, what is now s. 222(5)(a) merely stated that where it was necessary to determine which of two or more residences was an individual's main residence, an election could be made in favour of one of them within two years of the acquisition of the property so elected. A government amendment in Committee then inserted the words 'for any period' at the end of the preamble to what is now s. 222(5), and provided for the time limit to run from the 'beginning of that period', instead of from the acquisition of the elected property. Speaking to this amendment, the Financial Secretary to the Treasury, Mr MacDermot, said:

> 'Under sub-section (7) [the present s. 222(5)] there is no provision for the case of a man who has one house and does not need to make any option but who later buys another house and then wishes to opt to treat the other as his principal residence. The effect of this amendment is to keep open the option so that he can exercise a choice *within two years from the time when he acquires the second house*'. (*Hansard* Vol. 713, col. 1002, emphasis added.)

The amendment was passed without further debate.

Although he did not consider there to be any ambiguity, Vinelott J said that if any ambiguity had existed it would have been resolved in favour of the Revenue by this statement of the intention behind the amendment.

¶509

(2) Subsequent changes in the facts

It is also clear from *Griffin (HMIT) v Craig-Harvey* that where a taxpayer has two factual residences, say, (A) and (B), and he later sells (A), the subsequent acquisition of a further factual residence (C) enables him to elect under s. 222(5)(a), as between (B) and (C), even if he never made such an election as between (A) and (B). The time limit, on the Revenue's view, for this election will be two years from the date when he first used (C) as a factual residence, but it cannot extend back into the period when the residences were (A) and (B).

It seems that if a property which has been a factual residence is retained, but ceases to have that status – e.g. because the owner lets it on an exclusive tenancy – the same reasoning should apply. The effect of any s. 222(5)(a) election ceases, since the 'necessity' for a decision no longer arises (see ¶506). There seems to be no reason why this should not also apply where an elected MR ceases to be a factual residence.

Is the taxpayer able to alter the position by acquiring a further factual residence while retaining those he already has? It seems that he can, since the 'conclusion' reached as a result of an earlier election, or a determination by the inspector, is no longer necessarily valid – for an example see ¶518. This point seemed to be supported by the remarks – albeit obiter – of Vinelott J in *Griffin (HMIT) v Craig-Harvey* at p. 9H.

(3) Interests by way of licence only

The October 1994 *Tax Bulletin* announced a change of practice with implications in this area. From that time the Revenue has argued that a property which is held on a mere licence as distinct from one where there a legal or equitable interest, is not able to figure in an election, because a licence is not an interest which can give rise to a gain on disposal, and not therefore to a gain to which s. 222 could apply. The implication of this view is that the taxpayer's interests in both (or all) the residences between which a valid election is made must be capable of realising a capital gain on disposal, even if they are not freehold or long leasehold interests but some form of shorter lease which could be disposed of for a gain. The implications are noted below (see ¶520).

MARRIED COUPLES AND THE s. 222(5)(a) ELECTION

¶510 Generally

Section 222(6)(a) of TCGA 1992 provides that for a married couple living together (even under independent taxation after 5 April 1990) 'there can only be one residence or main residence for both'; that where an election under s. 222(5)(a) affects both spouses, it must be made by both of them; and that where an inspector's determination under s. 222(5)(b) affects a residence owned by the husband and a residence owned by the wife, it must be given to both, and either may appeal.

Speaking naturally, there can, clearly, be situations where a man and his wife have different main residences, or even where one spouse has a residence in which the other never resides. The effect of the legislation, however, appears to be to treat a couple for PRR purposes, in some respects, *as if they were a single unit*, although this can produce some odd effects as will be demonstrated below. Nevertheless, the requirement for a joint election under s. 222(5)(a) is clearly equitable and prevents one spouse from depriving the other of relief without the other's consent.

In the next few paragraphs 'H' denotes the husband and 'W' the wife.

¶511   Both spouses had a residence before marriage and continue to use both

If when a couple marry they each have a residence and continue to use both of them, the Revenue accepts that marriage can start the 'clock' for an election between one of the properties, and thus they can (jointly) elect within two years of marriage (see CGT 65425). Presumably there is no reason why this should be confined to two properties – H might have two residences and W one (or vice versa) before marriage, and the election could then be made for any one of the three. More commonly, H and W will have one residence each. Neither will have been eligible to make an election before, but after marriage, as a couple, they can do so, and may well need to be advised.

¶512   Both spouses have more than one jointly owned residence before marriage

If the couple already own more than one jointly owned residence before they marry, they might have already each made an election for one of them; or conceivably, H may have elected one house and W may have elected the other house. Can matters just be left there after marriage? Strictly the answer is probably no, because marriage brings with it the requirement that any election must be joint. Separate elections by H and W as two unmarried individuals therefore have no further validity, even if they both elected for the same property. Best advice is therefore that the couple should within two years of marriage make a joint election for one of the available residences. This can give the chance to review matters and perhaps switch an election that may no longer be appropriate. This is also the Revenue view, so it will be advisable to make a joint election (CGT 64527) – a point to include in letters of advice when clients are about to marry. If no election was made, any pre-marital elections would appear to lapse from the date of marriage and thenceforth it would be a question of fact which property was the joint main residence – with the risk that it would be the 'wrong' property in terms of which one is likely to be sold, or sold for the larger potential gain.

¶513 Only one spouse owned 'electable' properties before marriage

What is the position where H owned more than one residence before marriage but W owned none – for example if they lived together and he owned two houses but she owned none? If that continues to be the case after marriage, the Revenue's view is that neither spouse has had a change in what they occupy as a residence and there is no opportunity for a new election (CGT 64526). On that view, if the spouse who had more than one residence before marriage has already made an election, however, there would seem to be a choice – either to leave matters as they are, if that still seems to be appropriate in view of the couple's future plans, or to vary the previous election if it does not. The variation can be made as respects any period starting within the previous two years (TCGA 1992, s. 222(5)(a)) – see ¶519 below. It would seem that only the spouse who made the previous election can make the variation.

The reasoning behind the Revenue's views in CGT 64526 seems hard to follow, in contrast to that in the two previous situations (¶511 and ¶512). If H (solely) owns both Whiteacre and Blackacre, and both H and W used both houses as residences before they were married, *and* they continue to do so afterwards, it is not easy to distinguish this from the situation where H owns one and W the other, but both are used as residences before and after marriage – in effect the situation in ¶512. Yet in that situation the Revenue view is that a new election can be made on marriage.

A summary chart may assist here:

	Situation on marriage	*New elections possible (within two years of marriage)?*
(1)	Each spouse separately owns a residence and couple continue to use both after marriage	Yes
(2)	As (1) but only one home so used	No
(3)	Spouses *jointly* own more than one residence and continue to use both after marriage	Yes

	Situation on marriage	*New elections possible (within two years of marriage)?*
(4)	One spouse owns more than one residence but the other owns none	No (in Revenue's view, see CGT 64528) but also see discussion in ¶513 [Can also vary any existing election]

¶514 End of a marriage

(1) The fiscal unit
The opening words of TCGA 1992, s. 222(6) indicate that the subsection applies only in the case of a man and his wife 'living with him'. It seems to follow that the treatment, for this purpose, of the couple as a fiscal unit applies only so long as they are not separated.

(2) Ending of a marriage preceded by separation
Separation clearly brings to an end the fiscal unit for PRR purposes (see above). Each spouse may thereafter, for CGT purposes, have a separate residence or main residence. Any joint election under s. 222(6)(a) will certainly then cease to have effect as regards the spouse who no longer resides at all in the property concerned. If the other spouse remains in that property as his or her only residence, the election strictly becomes redundant as regards that spouse. If either spouse, now considered as a single person, has more than one factual residence after separation, it seems that a fresh election could be made and would be effective in respect of that property, though in practice the Revenue may regard a joint election as continuing in force as regards a spouse who continues to use the property concerned as a factual residence. To put the matter beyond doubt, however, it would be advisable for that party to make a fresh election in his or her own name.

Example
Richard and Liz own three properties jointly, Holmelea, Lake View and a flat in London. Holmelea is covered by a joint election under s. 222(5)(a). They decide to separate on 1 January 2003. Richard moves into the London flat. Liz stays at Holmelea but it is agreed that she will have the sole use of Lake View which is likely to be transferred to her as part of any divorce settlement.

From 1 January 2003 Richard apparently has only one factual residence, although it is unclear at precisely what point Holmelea ceases to be a factual residence for him, particularly if he spends any nights there after the separation.

In any case, following the separation, he is not bound by the election for Holmelea to be regarded as the couple's main residence.

Liz may if she wishes make a fresh election for either Holmelea or Lake View by 31 December 2004. If she does nothing the Revenue may regard the joint election as continuing in respect of her for Holmelea but it would be prudent to make a fresh election in any event, unless Holmelea is never likely to be sold.

There may, however, be dangers in a s. 222(5)(a) election being made after separation, and these are discussed in more detail at ¶904(2).

(3) Divorce

It follows from the statutory emphasis on 'living together' that divorce has no effect in this context, except in the rare case of a couple who do not separate until the decree absolute, or the even rarer case of a couple who divorce but do not separate. In either case, after decree absolute s. 222(6) has no application and the consequences will be identical to those applicable on separation.

(4) Ending of a marriage by death

Essentially the same consequences follow on death as on separation: the surviving spouse may in strictness need to make a new sole election to retain elected MR status, and in any event may make a fresh election for a different property if desired.

For the position regarding imputed ownership and occupation where a property passes to a surviving spouse on death, see ¶314(3).

(5) 'Living together'

The references to a couple 'living together' in s. 222(6) are to be construed in the light of the income tax definition in ICTA 1988, s. 282 (see s. 288(3)). Thus a defacto permanent separation will operate to end the fiscal unit for this purpose in the same way as a separation by formal agreement or court order (see ICTA 1988, s. 282(b)).

¶515 An anachronistic rule?

It remains to be asked, however, whether the rule that there may be only one joint residence is appropriate in the era of independent taxation of married couples which began in 1990: PRR is now the only area of CGT where a couple are treated less favourably after marriage than they would be if they had lived together unmarried (see FA 1988, s. 104(1)). The continuation of TCGA 1992, s. 222(6) may have political expediency (since couples with more than one home tend to be relatively wealthy and might be regarded as undeserving of any special treatment) but in logical terms it is now an anachronism.

PLANNING WITH THE s. 222(5)(a) ELECTION

¶516 Which property to elect?

First, it may not always be necessary to make an election at all. If the property likely to realise the greatest gain is the factual MR and likely to remain so indefinitely, there may be no need to take any action, since a determination under TCGA 1992, s. 222(5)(b) would favour that property in any event. However, where the future is less easy to foresee, an election should be considered.

In many cases, the choice of which property is to be subject to an election under s. 222(5)(a) will be simple: where one property is always likely to produce a much bigger gain than the other (e.g. a substantial family home in the South East of England compared to a small cottage in the highlands of Scotland) the former should clearly be protected. In cases where potential gains are less divergent or market prospects uncertain, the choice is harder, and may revolve around considering which property is likely to be sold first or whether one is ever likely to be sold. In such cases it might be prudent to choose the property likely to be sold in the foreseeable future: the other property may after all be retained until death, or benefit from a future re-basing of CGT, such as occurred in 1988 (with regard to 31 March 1982).

¶517 The danger of delay

Taxpayers may be tempted to put off a decision if the choice seems difficult, but this could be most unwise: the time limit rule (see ¶509) may operate so that a particular property cannot be chosen if it is allowed to pass by, and the relief would be due on whichever property was the factual MR – which, on the facts, might prove to be the one which was retained until death, thus wasting the relief, or might produce a much smaller gain on sale than the other property.

¶518 Remedial measures if time limit missed

If the time limit has been missed, all may not be quite lost. It could be possible, with careful planning, to start the 'clock' running again by acquiring a third factual residence so that an opportunity to make an election can arise (for the reasoning here, see ¶509(4)). Since factual residence has no necessary connotation of ownership (see ¶520), this third factual residence need not be owned, thus avoiding the need for further capital outlay, and this may salvage some relief where otherwise there would be none.

Example
Ethelred owns two homes, Unready Towers, his family seat in the country, and

Putitoff Mews, a small house in London. He ignored his accountant's advice to make a TCGA 1992, s. 222(5)(a) election for the country house when he bought Putitoff Mews in 1997, thinking that Unready Towers would never be sold (an ancient legend says that ill luck will attend an Unready who sells the Towers). Since 1997 he has spent much more time in London than in the country. In 2002, however, vast oil deposits are found at the Towers beneath the house and grounds, and Ethelred is advised that he could sell the estate for vastly more than he imagined. The gain on the house alone could be over £10m.

Ethelred is out of time (on the view upheld in *Griffin (HMIT) v Craig-Harvey* [1994] BTC 3, see ¶509(3)) for an election between the Towers and Putitoff Mews and a determination under s. 222(5)(b) would almost certainly favour the latter, less valuable house. However, if he now takes a rented flat, other than on a mere licence (see ¶520 below), in London and makes it a factual residence, it seems that he can elect afresh for the Towers from 2002 until its sale. This will at least secure PRR on the Towers for that period though it cannot, of course, undo the gains which will have accrued between 1997 and 2002. With the addition of the exemption for the last 36 months under s. 223(1) as amended, however (see ¶519), Ethelred has salvaged something from the wreckage. So long as his residence at the flat is real and substantial and the sale of the Towers to a specific purchaser is not virtually certain, it seems unlikely that the Revenue could attack this situation following *Craven (HMIT) v White* [1988] BTC 268 and *Shepherd (HMIT) v Lyntress Ltd* [1989] BTC 346.

Ethelred could achieve the same effect, of course, by selling Putitoff Mews (with PRR being due on the factual MR) and acquiring a new residence as owner or tenant, but this may not suit his wishes or the state of the property market.

¶519 Using the 'last 36 months' exemption and the 'variation' facility

The exemption afforded by TCGA 1992, s. 223(1) for gains accruing in the final 36 months of ownership (usually calculated on a straight-line apportionment) is absolute for any property which has at any time in the period of ownership been the factual or elected MR of the disponor, even if factual MR status ceased before 1 April 1982 (as to which see ¶618). This is of some assistance even to those who have never planned for PRR at all, as illustrated in the example at ¶520. When added to the facility to vary an existing s. 222(5)(a) election retrospectively up to two years back, it can be a very useful planning tool for sheltering relatively short-term gains in a period of rising values.

The extent to which the Revenue accepts that a varied election can be used in planning is clear from the example at CGT 64512. This has been reproduced below (with dates brought forward). It illustrates how a variation can be very useful, because the switch can affect a much longer period than that to which it applies.

This is because once a property has acquired main residence status for any period, however short, it automatically qualifies for the relief for the final three years of ownership (s. 223(1)):

> **Example**
> George has had two residences for many years, X and Y. Some years ago he elected for X as his main residence. On 1 January 2003 he sells Y for a large gain. On 1 February 2003 he submits a variation of the original election in favour of Y with effect from 1 February 2001. A week later, on 8 February 2003, he submits a second variation, back to X, from 8 February 2001.
>
> Y has been validly nominated as the main residence for one week in February 2001. That gives George PRR on Y for the whole of the last three years of ownership, from 1 January 2000 to 1 January 2003. The penalty for this is merely a loss of one week's worth of PRR on X, which will probably be completely insignificant when, if ever, he sells X – it will probably be covered by the annual exemption.

This is Revenue-sanctioned planning; there is no official suggestion that such elections are 'artificial'.

¶520 Licences and interests of negligible value

In deciding which of two or more properties is the factual MR for PRR purposes the law is completely indifferent to ownership. Thus, someone may occupy two factual residences but own only one of them freehold and hold the other on a short lease. Since the latter will not normally be assigned at a profit, it will not give rise to a gain on disposal. The taxpayer in such cases may not appreciate the possible need for a TCGA 1992, s. 222(5)(a) election until it is too late (see ¶310).

It may be possible, however, for someone in this position to use ESC D21, which provides that in such situations a s. 222(5)(a) election may be made 'within a reasonable time of the individual first becoming aware of the possibility' of doing so even though it would otherwise be out of time, and will then be regarded as effective from the date when there were first two or more factual residences. It seems that the late election permitted by this concession could be made even after the disposal in question, though the text is not explicit on this point.

> **Example**
> Margaret has worked for a charity caring for the homeless in London for many years. She spends all but two weeks' holiday a year, plus one weekend each month, in London where she rents a flat near the hostel where she works on a weekly basis. Some years ago she inherited a small country cottage from her

parents which she uses when off duty, and where she keeps most of her belongings.

Eventually, Margaret becomes too old and infirm to carry on her work and has to go into a nursing home as a permanent resident. She is forced to sell her cottage to pay the nursing home bills. Almost certainly, in the absence of an election, the inspector would determine that her factual MR was in London although of course she had no valuable interest in her flat. CGT will have to be paid on the sale of the cottage. If properly advised, Margaret could have made a s. 222(5)(a) election within two years of first using the inherited cottage as a factual residence.

In the *Tax Bulletin* for October 1994 the Revenue announced that they had been advised that accommodation occupied under a mere licence – such as much job-related accommodation (see ¶521 below) – could no longer figure in an election under s. 222(5)(a); only a legal or equitable interest in the property, such that a disposal could give rise to a chargeable gain in the absence of PRR, could thenceforth be subject to an election. Elections dated later than 16 October 1994 which rely for their effect on a residence occupied under licence are regarded as invalid. Transitional provisions for earlier elections are described at CGT 64540–64542.

Thus, if Margaret, in the above example, had lived as a guest or companion in a friend's house while working at the hostel, with no security of tenure, the result in the Revenue's view would be different. She would be unable to use ESC D21 because she could not make a valid election (even out of time); an election would inevitably rely for its effect on her occupation of her friend's home on a mere licence, even though it would of course be made in favour of the cottage which she owns.

If, however, she was provided with accommodation by her employer, the result might well be different again, as discussed in ¶523 below.

Perhaps because not many people were affected by this change of view, it has been little discussed. In the writer's opinion it is by no means clear that the Revenue is always right to take the 'new' view. There would appear to be little economic difference between Margaret's situation in the above example whether she has a short let of a flat owned by a third party, lives with a friend, or occupies a flat owned by her employer; in the first case she may be able to assign her lease but is unlikely to be able to make a profit, and in the other situations she has nothing to sell. The distinction which the Revenue draws in many cases is between 'interests' which are all either practically or legally worthless.

Unless they wish to challenge the Revenue on appeal, however, taxpayers should note this 'licence trap' in planning of the type illustrated in ¶518 above. When acquiring an additional residence in order to re-start the two year 'clock', a taxpayer would have to ensure that his entitlement to occupation was based on

¶520

more than a mere licence. The Revenue may well have been prompted to review their thinking in 1994 by elections based on very short term occupation rights.

¶521 Job-related accommodation

The question of TCGA 1992, s. 222(5)(a) elections as applied to job-related accommodation is discussed in detail at ¶610. The view suggested at ¶610 is that the protection of an election is equally necessary in such cases. Whether ESC D21 (see ¶520) is available to assist with time-limits in such cases is not clear, but since its text refers to 'accommodation provided by the employer' as an example of situations where it might apply, the natural inference is that it would be available.

¶522 Losses

Finally, where losses are involved it may be possible to withdraw elections in certain circumstances, as discussed at ¶1003(3).

6 The Absentee Owner

'PERIODS OF ABSENCE'

¶601 The definition

The definition of a 'period of absence' for PRR purposes is contained in the final words of TCGA 1992, s. 223(3) and covers any period during which the property disposed of was not the factual or elected MR (as to which see ¶503). It does not include a period during which a different property was the elected MR. This rule means that if the period in question contains any subsidiary period, of whatever duration, during which a s. 222(5)(a) election was in force on a secondary residence, the extended reliefs afforded by s. 223(3) cannot operate.

¶602 Practical pitfalls

This is a potential pitfall, because even a short overlap with such an 'elected' period seems to blight the entire period of absence. It is therefore important to plan the timing of elections, and variations, carefully. Any election in respect of a secondary residence made before the period of absence begins should therefore be revoked beforehand, unless that property will also cease to be a factual residence (in which case the election becomes redundant); the requirements for preceding and subsequent periods of OMR should also be borne in mind (see ¶606). It must be ensured that the owner has neither a factual residence, nor a factual or elected MR, which is eligible for PRR during the period of absence – other than the property which it is sought to bring within the s. 223(3) rules.

Even a property which is a factual residence abroad may be within the scope of this trap if a taxable gain could arise on its disposal, since it would be a residence on which PRR could be claimed: those who leave UK homes empty while working abroad should therefore, if they are to use the special relief in s. 223(3)(b) (see ¶604), strictly ensure that their accommodation abroad is provided by their employers, or otherwise such as to be incapable of yielding a taxable gain. In deciding whether there is any other residence eligible for relief when applying the absence rules, the Revenue ignores property occupied under a mere licence, consistent with its practice as explained above in ¶520 (see CGT 65047).

THE THREE TYPES OF 'PERMITTED ABSENCE' IN s. 223(3)

¶603   Any three years – s. 223(3)(a)

This exemption is unlimited as to reasons, and may be an aggregate of shorter periods, as shown by the bracketed words in the subsection. The intention seems to be to sweep up any absences which do not fit within the specific categories in TCGA 1992, s. 223(3)(b) and (c). It is doubtful whether s. 223(3)(a) is needed to cover very short absences such as holidays or business trips, which do not deprive the 'main residence' of its status as such, and certainly the Revenue does not take this point in practice.

¶604   Absence from the UK due to employment – s. 223(3)(b)

(1)   'Throughout which the individual worked ...'

These words mean that in strictness the exemption here covers only a continuous period (the bracketed phrase allowing aggregation which appears in subs. (a) and (c) is absent), and that the overseas employment must be exactly co-terminous with it. This is reinforced by the use of the phrase 'worked in an employment', in contrast to the use of 'hold' and cognate words in the Sch. E rules, e.g. ICTA 1988, s. 19(1) and Head 1, and s. 192(3). In practice, however, the Revenue does not normally take this strict view and disregards outward and return journeys together with reasonable leave periods (see CGT 65042). Substantial gaps spent abroad between foreign employments could, however, be dangerous; they would not prejudice the entire period spent abroad, because each period of employment, whatever its duration, would in principle qualify (see ¶604(4)), but the 'gap' periods could only be protected by TCGA 1992, s. 223(3)(a) (see ¶603).

(2)   Employment or office

The subsection provides no help for those who go abroad to pursue a trade or profession: such people may need to create companies by which they can be employed if they are to benefit. Nor is there any assistance for those who are not technically employees, however hard they may be working, e.g. some voluntary aid workers. In both cases, however, it is possible that the absence could be covered by s. 223(3)(a) or (c) (see ¶603 and ¶605) or a combination of the two, if it did not exceed seven years. Section 223(3)(c) refers only to a 'place of work', not a 'place of employment' (see ¶605(2)).

(3) All duties performed outside the UK

In contrast, again, to the Sch. E rules, there is no saving here for 'incidental' duties performed in the UK: contrast ICTA 1988, s. 132(2) which specifically applies only for the purposes of Cases I and II of Sch. E. Taxpayers in this position will often be relying on ibid. s. 335(1) to secure that they are not UK resident for tax purposes and this also includes the 'Incidental duties' saving in subs. (2).

In strictness the performance of even incidental duties of the employment in the UK, although carrying no adverse income tax consequences, could be said to deprive such people of the benefit of s. 223(3)(b) for the entire period of the particular employment; and there is no comfort here in the CGT Manual (see CGT 65042) which specifically mentions this point. This might not be fatal if the absence could be covered by subs. (a) or (c) (see ¶603 and ¶605) which will be the case if it is less than seven years in total, but the maximum benefit available under those subsections would not be available if needed in future for the property concerned.

If this point were tested in the courts and the legislation was found to be ambiguous or to lead to absurdities, it appears that under the so-called '*Hansard* rule', as formulated by the House of Lords in *Pepper v Hart (HMIT) and related appeals* HL [1992] 591; CA [1990] 552; ChD [1989] 595, the relevant debate in Committee on the *Finance (No. 2) Bill* 1965, where the provision originated, might now help to resolve the matter. Earlier in the relevant debates, a member had raised the question of whether PRR was lost when a taxpayer vacated his residence for the purpose of employment abroad. The government tabled, as an amendment, the provisions about 'permitted absences' which now appear in s. 223(2). Speaking to this amendment, the Financial Secretary to the Treasury, Mr MacDermot, said:

> 'With regard to the case of the man who goes overseas ... we are advised that the terms of the new sub-section (4)(b) [the present s. 223(3)(b)] are wide enough to cover any period during which such an individual may visit this country either on leave or for purposes incidental to his employment, and he will still be entitled to the benefit of the exemption even though during those periods he does not occupy the house which he owns.'

A backbencher, Mr Maxwell-Hyslop, then intervened to say:

> 'I am doubtful about the accuracy of what the Rt Hon and learned gentleman [Mr MacDermot] says because of the words: "*all the duties of which* are performed outside the UK". If a man returns to this country on duty for a meeting, by definition all the duties are not being performed outside the UK. Would not paragraph (b) [s. 223(3)(b)] then fall?'

The Minister replied:

'I am assured that the same point arises under the Income Tax Acts under Schedule E where it is necessary to determine whether the duties of an office or employment are performed outside the UK, and it has been determined for that purpose that visits of the kind that I have indicated are not regarded as being the performance of duties within the UK, *and the same construction and interpretation will be applied to the Amendment.*' (*Hansard* Vol. 715, col. 1742, emphasis added.)

This exchange, featuring a clear statement from the promoter of the amendment, may support the view that 'incidental' duties do not interrupt the absences permitted under s. 223(3)(b). In the writer's view, this statement must also override the expression of the Revenue's view in CGT 65042, which may have been written in ignorance of the Parliamentary exchange quoted above.

(4) Continuous period
This exemption is unlimited in length, so that there is no need for the facility to aggregate short periods which appears in subs. (a) and (c).

As regards the concessional extension to the 'before and after' rule, see ¶606(3).

(5) Non-working spouse
Where the property in question is jointly owned by a married couple, but only one spouse fulfils the employment conditions, gains accruing to the other spouse while he or she is abroad, accompanying the working spouse, are not strictly covered by subs. (b). However, ESC D3 assists here by deeming the conditions to be satisfied by the other spouse while they are satisfied by the employee. Unmarried couples are not catered for, but the non-worker could use the alternative route in subs. (a) (but not, in this case, subs. (c) – see ¶604(3)).

¶605 Other work-related absences – s. 223(3)(c)
Section 223(3)(c) of TCGA 1992, confers a further exemption for periods of up to four years, including aggregated shorter periods, but only in rather restricted circumstances.

(1) 'Prevented from residing ...'
This exception only runs where the owner is 'prevented from residing' in his home. These words appear to suggest *force majeure* of some kind rather than mere personal preference. It is unlikely that someone could bring himself within the subsection if he decided that one property was more convenient for his work than another, but was not required to move as a condition of his employment. The word 'residing', used without any qualification, also presumably has to be given due weight.

The circumstances must, apparently, 'prevent' the property in question from being the taxpayer's factual residence at all, even occasionally. If his place of work is located close enough to the property for him to be able to reside in it occasionally, but he chooses not to do so, he could be said not to be 'prevented from residing' in the property, but merely prevented from using it as his main residence. This interpretation would rob the subsection of much of its usefulness, except for those who work at a great distance from the property concerned. As communications improve this could be an increasing nuisance and highlights again the difficulties caused by the draftsman's confusing alternation between the concepts of a residence and a main residence. However, some problems may be avoided by the interpretation of the phrase 'in consequence of' which follows.

(2) **'In consequence of the situation of his place of work'**
This is the first 'leg' of the s. 223(3)(c) exemption. The phrase 'In consequence of' should, it seems, be interpreted slightly differently from phrases such as 'By reason of', where it is possible to become embroiled in linguistic distinctions between immediate and root causes (see in a Sch. E context, *Hochstrasser (HMIT) v Mayes* (1959) 38 TC 673): all that is necessary is to show that, directly or otherwise, the situation of the place of work has resulted in the employee's being prevented from residing in the property concerned.

Example
Martin is an engineer in the oil industry. For some years he has worked at his company's main UK office in London and owns a main residence in Guildford. In 1999 he was appointed project manager for a major new oilfield development in Dorset. The project lasts until 31 December 2002 and Martin is required to move to Dorset where he is provided with a rented house by the company. He lets his Guildford house meanwhile and does not re-occupy it at all until January 2003. His wife and family accompany him to Dorset and his children attend local schools while they are there.

Martin would almost certainly be unable to claim any Sch. E expenses under ICTA 1988, s. 198(1) for the cost of living in Dorset, but he should come within s. 223(3)(c) as regards the Guildford house. He was clearly required to move house by his employer and 'in consequence' of having to work in Dorset, he has let his house in Guildford, thus being 'prevented from residing' there. This should avoid any suggestion that Martin has been 'prevented' from using the Guildford house merely because he has let it.

(See the wide interpretation of 'in consequence of' in what is now ICTA 1988, s. 703(2) in *IR Commrs v Joiner* (1973) 50 TC 449 at p. 466, where Goulding J approved the view that the phrase has to be construed by looking at a chain of causation with an apt analogy: 'A child is commonly thought of as a consequence of its conception, notwithstanding the intervening event of its birth'.)

It is interesting to note that the first 'leg' refers to the situation of the taxpayer's place of *work*, not of his *employment*; this suggests that the first 'leg' might be wide enough to embrace the self-employed and voluntary workers (see ¶604(2)), whereas the second 'leg' seems to be confined to employees. In fact, the Revenue seems to regard both legs as available to the self-employed (see CGT 65044).

(3) 'Or in consequence of any condition …'
This is the second 'leg' of s. 223(3)(c). Its beneficiaries would seem to be only those employees (see ¶605(2)) whose homes may not be a great distance from their work, but who are nevertheless required to live 'on the job', perhaps for security reasons. Examples might be a bank employee who is required to live in a flat over the bank or, possibly, a prison governor who is required to occupy quarters within the prison walls even though his home may be in the same town. The difficulties over the phrase 'prevented from residing' noted in ¶605(l), however, are equally present here; few people in these categories would be required to be 'on call' at the workplace so frequently that they were unable to use their homes for even occasional residence. Fortunately, many such people would now fulfil the 'job-related accommodation' conditions, which do not involve the same difficulty (see ¶610).

(4) 'Being a condition reasonably imposed …'
The draftsman may here be trying to prevent artificial conditions being imposed, perhaps affecting a taxpayer who is a controlling director and can thus 'impose' them on himself. In the absence of this qualification, such a person could, perhaps, vacate his UK home while 'requiring' himself to spend five months of each year in the Bahamas, thus retaining PRR for his UK home. However, given that the exemption does not operate at all if the taxpayer has another residence which ranks for PRR (see ¶601) the scope for avoidance would in any event be limited.

The rule could have bizarre consequences where employer and employee are at arm's length: if Scrooge requires his clerk, Cratchit, to spend 24 hours a day, 365 days a year in the office to act as nightwatchman because he is too mean to buy a burglar alarm, on pain of dismissal if he leaves the premises, this could well be an unreasonably imposed condition, but the loser would be Cratchit if it meant that his own home did not rank for PRR while he was so employed! The logic may, in fact, lie in the common law rule that an employee is bound to obey only reasonable requests from his employer (affirmed, in the context of relocation, in *Jones v Associated Tunnelling Co Ltd* [1981] IRLR 477). An employee who complied with an unreasonable request to move could thus be regarded as undeserving of any special tax privileges.

(5) Removal expenses for employees

Extensive provisions were included in FA 1993 to define the removal expenses and benefits which can, up to a limit of £8,000 per 'move', be paid free of tax to relocated employees. All such expenses and benefits must be reasonably incurred by the employee, or reasonably provided to him, in connection with a change of his residence (see ICTA 1988, Sch. 11A, para. 3(2) and 4(2)). 'Residence' in these rules means that employee's 'sole or main residence' (see ICTA 1988, Sch. 11A, para. 25). The latter expression is undefined, and must therefore be interpreted according to the facts – see ¶503 – where an employee has more than one residence. There is no equivalent to an election under s. 222(5)(a), and any such election has no effect on the position under ICTA 1988, Sch. 11A. Equally, however, there seems to be no reason why an employee who is relocated by his employer, or who moves his sole or main residence to take up a new employment, should not be eligible both for tax-free removal expenses, subject to the £8,000 limit and the detailed rules mentioned above, and for PRR during a period of absence from his previous residence which is protected by s. 223(3)(c): though to qualify for the latter, the 'before and after' rule (see ¶606) will need to be considered.

¶606 The 'before and after' rule

(1) Resuming residence

The last words of the penultimate sentence of TCGA 1992, s. 223(3) deny its benefits unless there is 'a time', both before and after the period concerned, when the property is the taxpayer's only or main residence. (This feature offers an opportunity for those with losses, as discussed at ¶1003(4).)

Where there is more than one factual residence it seems that the rule can be met by a s. 222(5)(a) election in favour of the property concerned, but it should be a factual residence during the 'time' in question.

(2) 'A time'

How long is 'a time'? In the context of a relief for main residences, where factual residence is a requirement with its connotations of permanence (see ¶502) it is hardly likely that the courts would accept that factual residence could be established in a very brief period. A few nights of occupation will not suffice and regard should be had to the tests of factual residence at ¶504. It may assist if a taxpayer who intends to dispose of the property very quickly first establishes his 'residence' there by advising the usual third parties, such as his bank, the local authority, and of course his inspector, of his return.

If reliance is placed on a s. 222(5)(a) election, the length of actual occupancy may be fairly brief, but if there is no other factual residence, six months' occupation is probably the minimum necessary to avoid a Revenue challenge. A shorter period may suffice if unexpected changes, such as a new job, overtake an original intention to stay longer.

The Revenue's views seem broadly in line with this (CGT 65050–65051).

(3) Concessional treatment

There is a useful concession, however, for those who have benefited from s. 223(3)(b) or (c) (but not (a)) in ESC D4, which removes the need to re-occupy if the terms of an employment require the taxpayer to live elsewhere. This does not seem to be restricted to the same employment which conferred title under those subsections.

¶607 Additive conditions

The conditions in TCGA 1992, s. 223(3) are additive, as is clear from the words 'and in addition' at the end of both subs. (a) and (b). A maximum period, or aggregated shorter periods, of seven years can be covered under subs. (a) and (c), plus unlimited further periods under subs. (b): and if one of the latter periods is the final period before disposal the need to re-occupy may be dispensed with if ESC D4 applies (see ¶606(3)).

Where there are multiple absences, it seems that the 'times' required by the 'Before and after' rule can do duty more than once: the condition does not require periods immediately before and immediately after the period of absence.

Example
John buys a house in 1990 and lives there as his only residence until 1991. He then spends (1) five years employed abroad until 1996; (2) a year's extended holiday in the USA during 1997; (3) four years employed on an oil rig in the Orkneys up to the end of 2001. In 2002 he returns to his home and lives there for a year until he sells it in 2003.

The absences are covered as follows: (1) by s. 223(3)(b): (2) by s. 223(3)(a) being less than three years: (3) by s. 223(3)(c). In any event the gains from 2000 to 2003 would be exempt under the 'final three years' relief (s. 222(3)(a)). The first period of factual residence (1990/91) satisfies the 'Before and after' rule even though there were no such periods between the absences: in respect of each head of claim under s. 223(3), 'there was a time' both before and after they occurred during which factual residence existed.

However, if reliance has to be placed on the 'any three years' exemption under s. 223(3)(a), actual re-occupation will be needed at some stage because ESC D4 cannot apply to this situation. There is an example illustrating this at CGT 65067.

¶608 Effect of exceeding the specified periods

The Revenue's practice is to restrict PRR only for the excess over the three years stipulated in TCGA 1992, s. 223(3)(a) or the four years in subs. (b), and not, as might strictly be justified, to deny any PRR for the periods of absence in this event. This was stated in an ICAEW Technical Release TR 500, issued in 1983, and is implied in the example at CGT 65066.

¶609 Sale of home to a relocation agency

A concession may assist where, on a relocation, an employee or director cannot sell his house on the open market and instead sells it to a relocation agency which then allows him to share in any profit on a later sale. This is discussed at ¶1020.

A flow chart which may assist in understanding the 'permitted absences' rules appears on page 131.

JOB-RELATED ACCOMMODATION (JRA)

¶610 Background

Until what is now TCGA 1992, s. 222(8) was inserted into the PRR rules by FA 1978, s. 50 those who were required to occupy accommodation provided by their employers faced difficulties if they owned other houses. The rule in s. 223(3)(c) may have enabled some of them to count their occupancy of JRA as if it was occupation of their own properties, but as has been seen (see ¶605) these rules are potentially very restrictive. The introduction of a special relief to extend PRR to properties owned by such people followed the introduction, from 6 April 1977, of a similar relief for mortgage interest, which was found in ICTA 1988, s. 356(3) until it was abolished along with mortgage interest relief generally, from 6 April 2000. This meant that the definition of JRA, which was previously imported into PRR from the mortgage interest legislation by cross-reference, had to be incorporated directly into the PRR code in s. 222(8A)–(8D), but there is no difference of substance between those subsections and the old definition. There are also areas of interaction with the Sch. E benefits legislation in ICTA 1988, s. 145(4).

The main beneficiaries of the JRA reliefs are probably military personnel, the clergy and teachers in boarding schools. Certain self-employed traders may also qualify, notably publicans – their problems having been highlighted in *Frost (HMIT) v Feltham* (1980) 55 TC 10 (see ¶503(3)).

The Absentee Owner

PERIODS OF ABSENCE

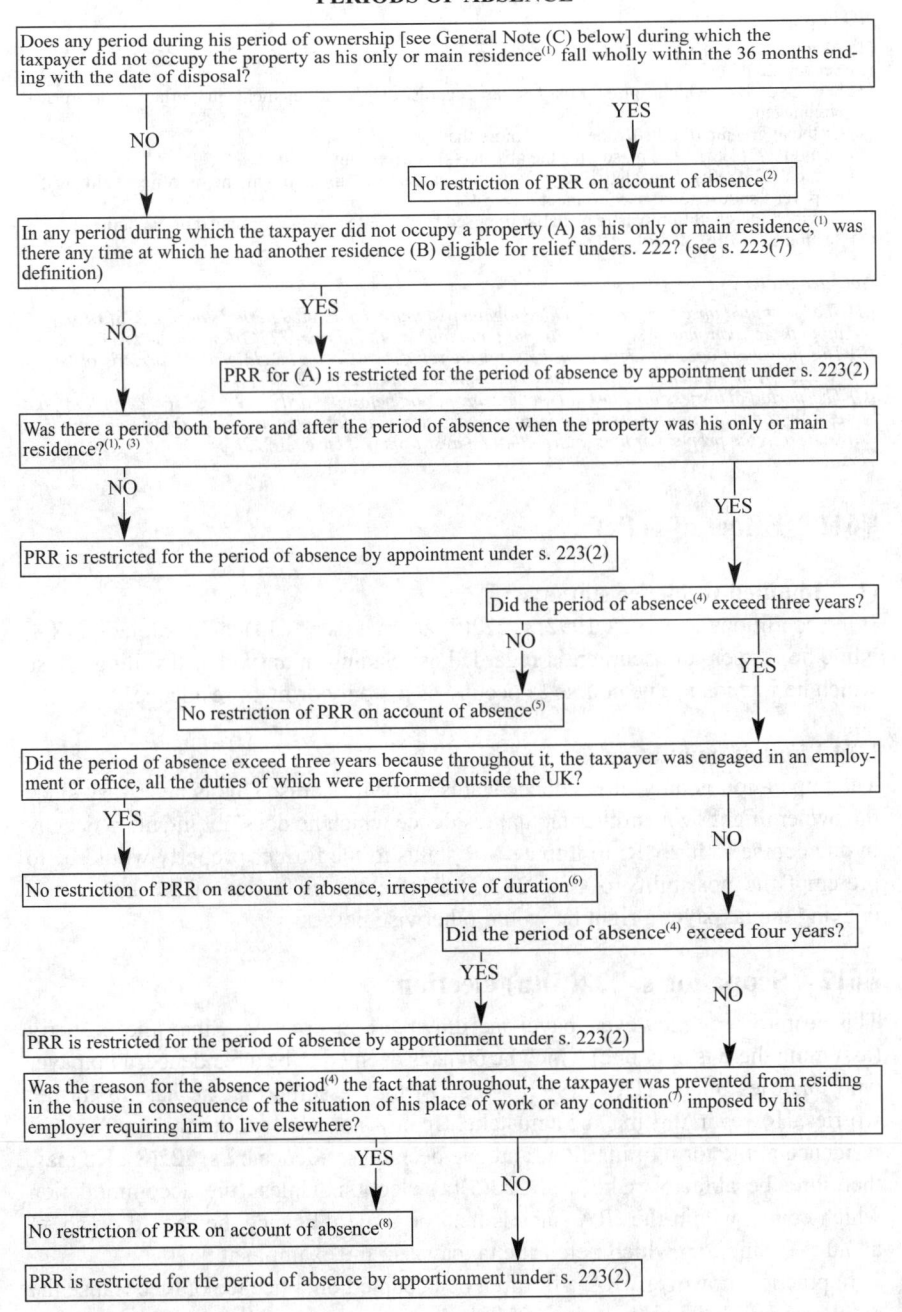

Does any period during his period of ownership [see General Note (C) below] during which the taxpayer did not occupy the property as his only or main residence[1] fall wholly within the 36 months ending with the date of disposal?

- **YES** → No restriction of PRR on account of absence[2]
- **NO** ↓

In any period during which the taxpayer did not occupy a property (A) as his only or main residence,[1] was there any time at which he had another residence (B) eligible for relief under s. 222? (see s. 223(7) definition)

- **YES** → PRR for (A) is restricted for the period of absence by appointment under s. 223(2)
- **NO** ↓

Was there a period both before and after the period of absence when the property was his only or main residence?[1], [3]

- **NO** → PRR is restricted for the period of absence by appointment under s. 223(2)
- **YES** ↓

Did the period of absence[4] exceed three years?

- **NO** → No restriction of PRR on account of absence[5]
- **YES** ↓

Did the period of absence exceed three years because throughout it, the taxpayer was engaged in an employment or office, all the duties of which were performed outside the UK?

- **YES** → No restriction of PRR on account of absence, irrespective of duration[6]
- **NO** ↓

Did the period of absence[4] exceed four years?

- **YES** → PRR is restricted for the period of absence by apportionment under s. 223(2)
- **NO** ↓

Was the reason for the absence period[4] the fact that throughout, the taxpayer was prevented from residing in the house in consequence of the situation of his place of work or any condition[7] imposed by his employer requiring him to live elsewhere?

- **YES** → No restriction of PRR on account of absence[8]
- **NO** → PRR is restricted for the period of absence by apportionment under s. 223(2)

¶610

NOTES

(1) As a matter of fact or by election under s. 222(5)(a).
(2) Section 223(1).
(3) See ESC D4, which omits this test as regards the 'after' element in certain work-related circumstances.
(4) Or the aggregate of all such periods if more than one.
(5) Section 223(3)(a) – the reason for the absence(s) is irrelevant.
(6) Section 223(3)(b). See also ESC D3, which may allow an employment or office held by the taxpayer's spouse to be used to meet this test.
(7) Provided the condition was reasonably imposed for the effective performance of his duties.
(8) Section 223(3)(c).

Note generally:

(A) The 'permitted absences' can be added together so that an unlimited period under s. 223(3)(b), plus up to three years under s. 223(3)(a) and up to four years under s. 223(3)(c), can be protected.
(B) This flowchart does not deal with the separate reliefs which can be claimed for periods of letting (s. 223(4)) or residence in job-related accommodation (s. 222(8)).
(C) The 'period of ownership' does not include any period before 1 April 1982 (s. 223(7) definition), but can in some circumstances include a period (after that date) before the taxpayer acquired an interest in the property if he acquired that interest from a spouse (s. 222(7)).

¶611 Effect of relief

(1) Imputed residence status

If the conditions of TCGA 1992, s. 222(8) are met (see ¶614), an occupier of JRA, while he is such an occupier, is regarded as residing in any other dwelling-house which he intends in due course to occupy as his only or main residence.

(2) Limit of imputation

The imputation is only of residence status, not MR status. This is necessary since the owner might own another factual residence which he does not intend to occupy in due course as his MR; to impute MR status to the former property would be to pre-empt the possibility of a s. 222(5)(a) election in favour of the latter, thus denying the taxpayer a right he would otherwise possess.

¶612 Scope for s. 222(5)(a) elections

This feature may, however, have one drawback in practice. Since the property (assuming there is only one) which he owns is deemed to be a residence, a taxpayer who qualifies under TCGA 1992, s. 222(8) may assume that he has no further worries. However, this may be a mistake. He now has two 'residences': one factual residence in the form of his JRA, and one deemed residence by s. 222(8). He may, therefore, be able to make a s. 222(5)(a) election. Unless the accommodation which comes within the JRA rules is held on a mere licence, he should do so, to avoid the same trap which befell the taxpayer in the example at ¶520.

In practice, however, JRA will often be occupied on a licence only, because the employee will have no security of tenure once the employment ends, and may be required to move the location of his accommodation during the employment – in other words he has no right to occupy any particular house, flat or rooms. Employers will normally be unwilling to grant formal tenancies because they will not want to lose the ability to gain possession when the employee leaves – the accommodation probably being needed for his or her successor.

The Revenue's change of view in 1994 about property occupied under licence has made the issue of elections for many of those occupying JRA largely academic. (For details see ¶520 above). Someone who owns a freehold house in one area while occupying JRA under licence in another area will, in the Revenue's view, be unable to make an election under s. 222(5)(a); but because he is deemed to reside at the former property by s. 222(8) – even if in fact he never does – that property can qualify for PRR (CGT 64558).

In the writer's view this is not without difficulty. The individual mentioned above has only one factual residence, in favour of which he cannot (say the Revenue) elect. His own property is deemed to be *a* residence, but it is very unlikely to be the factual MR. On a strict view, he could be left with no property on which PRR is due. In practice, however, since 1994 the Revenue has apparently viewed s. 222(8) as conferring *main* residence status where the JRA is merely held on licence (see CGT 64557).

Elections will only therefore need to be considered where JRA is occupied under a tenancy. This may be the case with some farm workers and perhaps others; but it is important to take competent legal advice in this area about the nature of the employee's interest in the property. If his interest is more than a mere licence, an election should be considered.

If an election is needed, the normal action would of course be to elect in favour of the property which the employee owns: the imputation of residence overrides the facts, so that he is able to do this even if he has never set foot in that property in his life.

As to time limits, ESC D21 should apply (see ¶520).

¶613 Lettings irrelevant

TCGA 1992, s. 222(8) relief carries on regardless of whether the deemed residence is in fact let. In such cases, if the owner later ceases to occupy JRA but keeps the house for residential letting, the period of relief under s. 222(8) opens the door to relief for part of the remaining gain under s. 223(4) (see ¶711).

¶614 Conditions for JRA relief

(1) Residence in JRA

Section 222(8)(a) of TCGA 1992 requires the taxpayer to reside in what is for him JRA as defined in s. 222(8A)–(8D). The main conditions for an employee here are set out in subs. (8A)(a) (subs. (b) deals with traders). Broadly, they focus on three circumstances where accommodation is provided: (1) out of *necessity* for the proper performance of the duties, (2) by *custom* in the employer's trade, and for the *better performance* of the duties, or (3) because of a *special threat to the security* of the employee.

In the absence, therefore, of any of these three features (the third being highly exceptional), a claim under s. 222(8) will fail. The relief is still on occasions surprisingly restrictive as can be seen from the Sch. E case of *Vertigan v Brady (HMIT)* [1988] BTC 99. This was a case on ICTA 1988, s. 145(4) (the wording of which is in all essentials the same as in s. 222(8A)(a)) where the taxpayer sought to avoid assessment on the benefit of free accommodation. He was employed as a nurseryman and was required to be 'on stand-by' throughout the working week and two weekends out of every three, but failed to show either contractual necessity or trade custom. A CGT appeal by such an employee, on the disposal of a house which he owned elsewhere, would, presumably, meet a similar fate.

If possible, therefore, employees who are provided with free accommodation, and also own property personally, should seek to have a requirement to occupy the JRA incorporated in their contracts.

Contractual terms are less crucial where the employer operates in a business where such provision is customary, and where the provision is for the better performance of the duties (subs (8A)(a)(ii)). A housemaster at a boarding school should be able to bring himself within this requirement especially if he can show that he needs to 'live in' to perform pastoral and extra-curricular duties, but the same may not apply to an employee who is simply offered accommodation by his employer because there is a spare flat available, unless there is some practical linkage between its occupation and the performance of the duties.

(2) Intention to occupy owned property as main residence
The second condition for this relief, in s. 222(8)(b), requires the taxpayer to intend in due course to occupy the property which he owns as a main residence. Strangely perhaps, no evidence of such intention is stipulated in the legislation, but if the facts suggest that at some point the taxpayer's intentions changed, an enquiry into the tax return may follow. Property which continues to be let for a long period after the taxpayer has ceased to occupy JRA may give the Revenue a reason for such an enquiry (see CGT 64560) and there is an example at CGT 64565 where an intention changes. However, there is no reason why relief should not run on a property which, as events turn out, is never the factual MR of the taxpayer – so long as his intention so to use it was genuine.

¶615 The self-employed
Self-employed people may also benefit from the JRA relief, by means of TCGA

1992, s. 222(9) and the definitions in s. 222(8A)(b). However, the conditions are much tighter than those applicable to employees. The conditions involve:

(1) a contract entered into at arm's length requiring the taxpayer or his spouse to carry on a particular trade, profession or vocation;

(2) the taxpayer or his spouse carrying on this activity from premises provided by another person;

(3) contractual occupation of those premises or of others provided by that person.

Publicans with conventional brewery leases will usually qualify, as may some franchise operators (e.g. of 'fast food' shops). A trader who leases a shop together with accommodation for himself and his family, however, is unlikely to qualify if he would be free to sub-let the living space and to live anywhere he chose.

This head of relief applies, by s. 229(9), only from 6 April 1983 (FA 1984, s. 25(2)(b)). Earlier periods could only be protected by election or factual residence (as in *Frost (HMIT) v Feltham* (1980) 55 TC 10): see ¶502. It might be possible to make an out-of-time election even now for such periods if the case could be brought within ESC D21 (see ¶520).

¶616 JRA relief and the permitted absences

What is the position if the taxpayer ceases to reside in JRA but comes within one of the permitted absences in TCGA 1992, s. 223(3)? (see ¶604).

While JRA status continues under s. 222(8), any owned property to which the 'intention' test applies is deemed to be a residence: if there is no other candidate, it will be the only residence, or alternatively it may (by election subject to the point about licences above) be the elected MR. In either event, it will be capable of benefiting from the permitted absences in s. 223(3), if both before and after the absence, there was a time (see ¶606(2)) when s. 222(8) applied. This does not seem to be affected if, on return, the taxpayer occupies *different* JRA.

Example
The Revd Obadiah Slope, a country vicar, decides that he has been called to missionary work. He resigns from his parish and vacates his vicarage – which was accepted by the Revenue as JRA – and leaves for five years abroad. However, he also owns a house in Cornwall where he spends his holidays, which he does not sell because he is afraid that he would not be able to afford to buy a similar house for his eventual retirement if prices rise while he is away. When he returns to the UK, he is appointed to a new parish and moves into a new vicarage, but retains the Cornish house.

The absence is covered by s. 223(3)(b). The 'before and after' rule is satisfied by the existence of qualifying JRA (albeit in different places) both before and after the period abroad. Accordingly, the Cornish house seems to avoid any loss of PRR while its owner is abroad.

¶617 Time limits and JRA

Nothing in the concession about time limits for TCGA 1992, s. 222(5)(a) elections, ESC D21 (see ¶520), seems to preclude its application for JRA cases, even though it pre-dates the latter relief. It may be useful for those who failed to realise in time that they needed to elect, although it remains unclear whether it could still be invoked after disposal of the property concerned. The fact that many JRA properties will be occupied under licence will often make elections impossible in any event.

THE 'PERIOD OF OWNERSHIP'

¶618 The relevant dates

This concept is relevant in computing the gain remaining after 'permitted absence' relief, and for the 'final 36 months' relief.

In the original form of the legislation this period (then the final 12 and later the final 24 months) could not include any period before 6 April 1965. Absences before that date did not restrict PRR: equally, a total absence of factual residence after that date meant that no PRR at all was due, except for the two final years. If there had ever been factual residence, even if it had ceased long before 6 April 1965, the 'final 24 months' exemption was due. This stemmed from the words 'but inclusive of the last 24 months of ownership in any event' in the precursor to s. 223(2)(a). Following re-basing of the tax in 1988, the same principles apply, when considering disposals after 5 April 1988, by reference to 1 (*not* 6) April 1982, the revised base line (see s. 223(7)). But even if factual or elected MR status ceased before 1 April 1982, relief can still run for periods where it was established before that date, and this is equally true of the 'final 36 months' relief established for disposals after 19 March 1991 (see CGT 64943).

The necessity for the rule in s. 223(7) was highlighted by the Court of Appeal's decision in *Richart (HMIT) v J Lyons & Co Ltd* [1989] BTC 337, a case about roll-over relief, where at the time in question, the relevant legislation (CGTA 1979, s. 115(6)) lacked any equivalent provision, so that business use prior to 6 April

1965 was able to contribute to roll-over relief on the sale of premises subsequently disused.

The 'period of ownership' can in some instances be extended to periods before the acquisition of the property by the taxpayer in question (see ¶314).

The advancement of the 'base line' to 1 April 1982 may be important in certain divorce situations (see ¶905).

The 'period of ownership' ends, in the Revenue's view, on the date which is taken as the date of disposal for CGT under s. 28 (see CGT 64927). In the normal case where this takes place under a contract, it will be the contract date (s. 28(1)), unless the contract is conditional, when it will be the date when the condition is fulfilled (s. 28(2)). Events after that date would therefore seem to be irrelevant for PRR purposes. If the disposal takes place by a deed of gift, the period of ownership would appear to end at the date of that document.

This naturally leads to the question of when the ownership period begins. Section 222(7) provides that where the individual has different interests at different times, it begins at the date of the first acquisition taken into account in arriving at deductible expenditure. This clearly applies where, for example, his first interest is as a tenant and he later acquires the freehold (see ¶314); the ownership period would not begin until the acquisition of the freehold, and absences before that date would be irrelevant. In the more straightforward case where the first interest acquired is the freehold under a contract, it appears to follow that the period of ownership begins, strictly, when an unconditional contract is entered into, under the rule in s. 28(1). Typically, however, there will be an interval of at least a few weeks before legal completion, during which the individual will be unable to occupy the property and PRR cannot, therefore, strictly operate. In practice the Revenue does not appear to take this point (CGT 64931 illustrates only the enlargement of a tenanted interest into the freehold), but if completion was artificially delayed for a long period it appears that this might result in a loss of relief.

¶618

7 The Business User

THE HOME AS OFFICE

¶701 Authority for restriction of relief by reference to usage

The only direct authority for excluding part of a gain from PRR on grounds of business usage is TCGA 1992, s. 224(1). This confines apportionment of a gain on these grounds to cases of exclusive use of part of the property for a trade, business, profession or vocation. If s. 224(1) is inapplicable, the Revenue would have to justify a restriction by s. 222(1)(a), which refers to the possibility of part only of a dwelling-house being the main residence – words echoed in s. 223(1).

¶702 PRR contrasted with income tax 'expenses' rules

While TCGA 1992, s. 224(1) is directed at exclusive use, the rules applicable to allowable expenses under Cases I and II of Sch. D, and under Sch. E, are directed at the exclusive purpose of expenditure: see ICTA 1988, s. 74(a) and 198(1). These differences may sometimes work to the taxpayer's advantage.

¶703 Schedule D usage

The case law on Cases I and II of Sch. D, though its detail is beyond the scope of this text, establishes that a taxpayer may only claim a deduction for expenditure which is exclusively related to the business, even though the 'wholly' condition has been held not to preclude apportionment. Thus the cost of heating and lighting a room at the trader's home used exclusively for business can be allowed, and the bills, relating of course to the whole house, can be dissected to arrive at the right fraction. The prohibition on 'dual purpose' expenses applies where an expense cannot, by its nature, be dissected and relates both to business and private matters: see *Mallalieu v Drummond (HMIT)* [1983] BTC 380. This doctrine strictly prevents the deduction of telephone rental costs (*Lucas v Cattell (HMIT)* (1972) 48 TC 353) and mortgage interest (*R v HMIT & Anor, ex parte Kelly* [1991] BTC 50), though partial allowances may be given by concession.

In a CGT context, however, a Sch. D trader merely has to show that he does not use any part of his home exclusively for his business to avoid any restriction of PRR (see CGT 64663–64666).

Example
Herbert is a partner in a firm of accountants. He often needs to work at home and uses his study for this purpose. The study is also, however, used by (1) Herbert himself in his capacity as treasurer of the local golf club, (2) his wife, who is the local co-ordinator of the 'Meals-on-wheels' service: and (3) his children for their homework. There is a telephone extension in the study but no separate line. Part of the total household lighting, heating and telephone costs are claimed in his firm's income tax computations.

Herbert's firm is unlikely to obtain a Sch. D deduction for the telephone rental costs and the inspector may also argue about the lighting and heating costs unless there is a separate heating source in the study: even then any allowance is likely to be concessional because of the non-business use of the study by the family and Herbert himself. But for CGT, Herbert can show that no part of the house is exclusively used for his business, so no restriction of PRR should arise on its sale.

A similar situation to Herbert's often arises in farming cases, where unless there is a dedicated farm office, or other specialised rooms such as a dairy, as part of the farmhouse, the Revenue does not look for any PRR restriction even though some relief has been given for Sch D Case I purposes (see CGT 64680–64681).

¶704 Schedule E usage

A possible difficulty in TCGA 1992, s. 224(1) in this context is that there is no reference to an office or employment. An argument could perhaps be mounted that since the subsection does not refer to a business owned by the taxpayer, a Sch. E taxpayer who sets aside a room exclusively for use in his employer's business would suffer a restriction on PRR. This problem is most likely to occur where the taxpayer is a controlling director but with the increase in 'teleworking' it might nowadays also arise in other cases. The Revenue's attitude is set out at CGT 64690–64691, which indicates that only where a 'large part' of the house has 'clearly' been used for employment purposes would a restriction be sought; inspectors are asked not to take the point over the use of a room as a study even if a Sch. E expense allowance is given. Ordinary 'teleworkers' are thus unlikely to experience problems. The effects of a restriction might, however, be mitigable by roll-over relief under the extended provisions of s. 157, or (to the extent that a market rent is not charged to the company) retirement relief, on disposals before 6 April 2003, under s. 164, subject to the detailed conditions applicable to those reliefs.

¶705 Roll-over relief

If a restriction to PRR is imposed by TCGA 1992, s. 224(1), it seems that roll-over relief under s. 152 would, in principle, be available on a replacement property, enabling gains to be deferred: even if a Sch. E user suffered a restriction (see ¶704) that relief is extended to employees by s. 158(1)(c). For further discussion see ¶1104.

¶706 Retirement relief

In principle, a Sch. D user who suffered a PRR restriction could, on a disposal before 6 April 2003, claim retirement relief under TCGA 1992, s. 163–164 subject to the detailed rules therein. In practice, such a taxpayer might find difficulty unless he sold the whole business at the same time as his house (see *McGregor (HMIT) v Adcock* (1977) 51 TC 692), or could use the 'associated disposal' rules in s. 164(6). Employees, if affected, could in theory use s. 164(1) or (4).

¶707 Computational problems

(1) Apportionment of consideration

Section 224(1) of TCGA 1992, in contrast to s. 224(2) (see ¶707(3)) contains no reference to apportionment of consideration where there is to be a restriction of PRR. The authority for apportionment where there is business use at the date of disposal lies in s. 222(10), applicable where only part of the property is the only or main residence, but also generally 'wherever required' by s. 222–226.

The right approach here must depend on the facts. The Revenue view is that any fractions on which a Sch. D Case I or II expense allowance has been based provide only a 'poor' guide (CGT 64665). The writer would agree where those fractions have not been based on any recently reviewed objective facts, but in other cases they may be as good a guide as any. The district valuer will usually base them on respective values (CGT 64673), but this too will not always be realistic. It will not always be meaningful to ask what an exclusive business portion would fetch if sold separately, because, for example, there would be no market for a single room in a private house used as a study or workroom. This method might be more appropriate, for example, to a self-contained extension used as a doctor's surgery, or residential accommodation over a shop or offices. In the writer's view it is only sensible to apportion by value where there exists a real market for the type of accommodation in question by which value can be gauged. If there is no such market, fractions based on respective floor areas may be more appropriate – assuming the numbers are material.

A valuer should be able to give a professional opinion on this point and to negotiate with the district valuer if necessary. The reduced notional consideration thus found will be the basis for apportioning the allowable base cost in the CGT computation, subject to a total disallowance of any expenditure which related solely to the business portion. (See example at CGT 64674, although it should be noted that the insistence on apportionment by value in that example may not always be appropriate as discussed above).

(2) Single dwelling-house or separate business asset?
It is sometimes difficult to decide whether s. 224(1) is in point, or whether there are two assets, a dwelling-house together with a business property.

Here the references in s. 222 to 'part' of a dwelling-house seem not to assist. As a matter of construction they appear to pick up the words of s. 222(1)(a), which refers to a *part disposal* of a dwelling-house, not to an entire disposal including a business portion.

A possible interpretation of s. 222(10) is that the objective status of the whole property as a dwelling-house is not affected by one owner's exclusive business use of part of it. This seems to accord with common sense in many cases: a new owner of the whole will often be able, with minimal alterations if any, to use the whole as a private house. However, there will be cases where this is less easy to sustain; for example, a property which has been used as a shop, with residential accommodation above or to the rear or side, may be rated as partly business premises (see *Local Government Finance Act* 1988, s. 64(8)), and a new owner may need to make significant alterations in order to use the whole as a dwelling.

If business use has been so extensive that the part so used does not resemble what the average person would call a 'dwelling-house' at all, it appears that PRR cannot apply to that part, and there would be no question of relief for the final 36 months or any other period. In practice, however, the position is often less clear cut, and the facts may indicate that one is dealing with a single asset, a dwelling-house, part of which is used for the business. In such cases s. 224(1) is in point.

At first sight, the distinction seems academic, since s. 224(1) provides that s. 223 will apply to the 'non-business' part, and (by implication) only to that part. However, this may not yield the same result as follows from the previous approach. If the 'business' part is a distinct asset it is necessary to apportion expenditure and consideration separately to it, whereas under s. 224(1) the gain is apportioned, as the last step in the computation, between the private and business proportions, with s. 223 applying only to the former: this may be significant if, for example, there has been substantial expenditure on the business part which could give rise to an allowable loss if the 'separate asset' approach is justifiable.

(3) Change of use
It appears from the present tense verb 'is' in the wording of s. 224(1), that the subsection applies only where there is exclusive business use at the date of disposal. If such use has ceased before that date, s. 224(2) comes into play.

As well as dealing with changes of private occupation and use (as to which see ¶315ff.) s. 224(2) also deals with such changes in a business context.

¶707

No hard and fast rule for apportionment is laid down: s. 224(2) merely requires the relief to be adjusted in a just and reasonable manner. In practice, apportionments by a mixture of time and relative values, assuming straight line growth in the latter, are likely to be used, though see ¶707(4) for an alternative approach. Problems may arise with the interaction between this rule and the 'final 36 months' relief in s. 223(1), which may be illustrated by the following example.

Example
Cecilia is in business as a commercial artist. She bought her house on 6 April 1994 for £120,000. From then to 5 April 1997 she used one room of the house exclusively as a studio. From 6 April 1997 to 5 April 1999, having rented more suitable premises elsewhere, she used the studio for her work only occasionally, when she was very busy, and its main use was as a playroom for her children. From 6 April 1999 she did all her work at the business premises and the studio was converted into a bedroom. She sold the house on 5 April 2002 for £500,000. An estate agent advises that without the former studio the house would have fetched only £450,000 and the Revenue agrees this figure.

Adopting the interpretation in ¶707(2), it is suggested that the whole property was, throughout Cecilia's eight years' ownership, a dwelling-house which was her main residence. The gain relating to the final 36 months is thus exempt under s. 223(1), so that of the total gain of £380,000, 3/8ths, i.e. £142,500, is exempt on this ground.

The other periods are dealt with thus:

(1) 1997–99: no exclusive business use, so s. 224(1) does not apply and a further 2/8ths, i.e. £95,000, is also exempt.

(2) 1994–97: here s. 224(1) does apply because the studio was exclusively used for the business. The fraction of gain apportioned to this period is 3/8ths, i.e. £142,500. Of this, the exempt fraction will be 450/500ths, i.e. £128,250.

In summary, of the total gain of £380,000, only £14,250 (£142,500 – £128,250) will be taxable.

The interpretation in ¶707(2) can be tested by considering what the position would have been if the exclusive business use had taken place in the final three years instead of the first three years. On the interpretation adopted here, s. 224(1) is in point since there was exclusive business use at the date of disposal. Total exemption would be due for the period from 1994 to 1999, covering 5/8ths of the gain, i.e. £237,500. Of the remaining 3/8ths, i.e. £142,500, 450/500ths would remain exempt, leaving £14,250 taxable as before: there could be no question of all gains for the final 36 months being exempt.

This view avoids the otherwise anomalous result that even though residential occupation continued throughout, a larger exemption would follow from exclusive business use in the final period of ownership than at the beginning. However, if all residential use of the house had ceased completely on, say, 5 April 1998, but the workroom had been used for business until disposal, the result would be different: the 'final 36 months' relief would have applied only to 450/500ths of the gain, and the computation would be as follows:

(1) Gain attributable to four years' wholly residential use = 4/8 x £380,000 = £190,000: wholly exempt.

(2) Gain attributable to final four years = balance of £190,000: of which 1/4, i.e. £47,500, is wholly taxable, and of the remaining 3/4, i.e. £142,500, s. 224(1) provides that only 450/500ths i.e. £128,250 is covered by the 'final 36 months' relief.

(3) Thus the taxable gain would be £380,000 − (£190,000 + £128,250) or £61,750.

(4) Alternative methods of apportionment

In the examples at ¶707(3) the apportionment calculations have been performed by time and 'straight line' values, a method which, in the writer's experience, the Revenue normally adopts. However, other approaches might also be considered where they would give a more favourable result for the client. The only statutory requirement is that the relief should be adjusted in a just and reasonable manner (s. 224(2)). The method used in the examples above assumes that the value of the property grew evenly over the period of ownership. If that was indeed the case, the method used would achieve a just and reasonable result.

However, reality is rarely that simple. The possibilities can be illustrated by an adaptation of the example of Cecilia at ¶707(3).

Example

Suppose that Cecilia had indeed used her house exclusively for business in the final three years of ownership, from 1999 to 2002. It might be the case, on the facts, that the property did not increase significantly in value at all between these dates. If credible independent valuation evidence could be produced to this effect and this was accepted by the district valuer, it would, in the writer's view, be manifestly unjust and unreasonable to use straight-line time-apportionment as previously illustrated. If the Revenue could be convinced that the value of the property at 5 April 1999 was no less than £500,000, the whole of the gain actually made would have accrued in the 1994–99 period, when the property was not being used at all for Cecilia's business. PRR would thus be due on the whole gain and there would be no gain on which the restricting rules in s. 224(2) could operate.

The Revenue is thought to have accepted arguments to this effect where the

¶707

injustice of a straight-line apportionment is evident. In practice, Cecilia would greatly strengthen her argument here if she had considered selling in 1999 and obtained a valuation (or better still, a serious offer) in the region of £500,000 and still has written evidence to that effect.

Contrast, however, the type of situation illustrated in Example 2 at ¶305(4), involving complete absence of residential occupation for a period, where the Revenue does not accept that s. 224(2) can be used to avoid a straight-line apportionment. There is an example of this situation, and confirmation of the official view, at CGT 64771.

(5) Relationship between s. 224(1) and s. 224(2)
The foregoing analysis has suggested that s. 224(2) is necessary to deal with exclusive business use which ceases before disposal (as well as the quite separate problem of changes in what is occupied as a residence, discussed at ¶305(4)). This, in the writer's view, is the correct analysis since s. 224(2) authorises an adjustment of 'the relief given by s. 223': that seems to import s. 224(1) as well (which contains the 'exclusivity' condition) since s. 224(1) operates to modify s. 223.

However, it is sometimes argued by inspectors that s. 224(2) has a wider significance; they argue that it can catch cases where there have been frequent changes of use from 'business' to 'private' and vice-versa, even though the accommodation in question is never devoted wholly to one use or the other for any significant period. An example might be a homeowner in a seaside town who occasionally lets surplus bedrooms to paying visitors by the week in summer, but at other times these rooms are vacant or used by family visitors or friends. This is considered to be a question of fact and degree. If the rooms in question can be switched from business to private use, and back again, with no modifications whatsoever to the structure, furniture or fittings, it seems harsh to regard the business use as 'exclusive' in any meaningful sense of that word. After all, it would be only a short step from this argument to the contention that even someone like Herbert, in the example at ¶703, is using his study 'exclusively' for business while he is working there, unless other members of the family are *simultaneously* using it privately! It must be doubtful whether the courts would accept such an extreme view.

(6) Losses
Finally, this discussion has proceeded on the assumption that it is disadvantageous to the taxpayer to use part of his home exclusively for his business. However, that will only be the case where he expects to make a gain on its disposal. If a loss is anticipated, it may, of course, be to his advantage to demonstrate exclusive business use of part of the house, because this will give rise to an allowable loss, available against other gains of that year or succeeding years (see ¶202). (It may

THE LANDLORD

¶708 Residential lettings and s. 223(4)

(1) When s. 223(4) applies
The special relief for lettings, in TCGA 1992, s. 223(4), is only available in computing a gain to which s. 222 applies, by the opening words of s. 223(4). This is similar wording to that in the opening of s. 223(1), and seems to mean that if s. 222 applies to any period of the taxpayer's ownership, s. 223(4) relief is, in principle, available – even, apparently, if s. 222 applied only to periods before 1 April 1982 (see ¶618). Thus if a property has at any time been the taxpayer's factual or elected MR, a s. 223(4) claim may be competent.

For the interaction of s. 225 with s. 223(4), see ¶806.

(2) Pre-1 April 1982 lettings
If all the residential lettings took place before 1 April 1982, it seems that s. 223(4) will still, in principle, apply although this would not appear to be significant since the effect of s. 223(7) is to disregard the absence of the taxpayer from residential occupation before that date, thus removing any restriction which would otherwise apply to his PRR, and avoiding the need for any additional relief via s. 223(4).

(3) Meaning of 'residential accommodation'
Section 223(4) is only available where the property is 'let by [the taxpayer]' as residential accommodation. As a preliminary point, this seems to deny the relief if the taxpayer lets to a third party who then sub-lets in this manner.

More important is the meaning of 'residential accommodation' in this context. In the context of a relief for residences generally one possible construction of this phrase is that the tenant should himself make his home there: not necessarily his only home, but somewhere where his presence is substantial and more than as a mere bird of passage (cf. ¶503).

This view (generally held by the Revenue from 1980 to 1990) was adopted by Millett J in the High Court in *Owen v Elliott (HMIT)* [1989] BTC 19. The case concerned a married couple who owned a seaside hotel; they occupied part of the hotel as their private quarters. The guests usually stayed for one or two weeks in the summer but sometimes for longer, up to three months, in the winter; but there were rarely more than one or two of these 'long stay' guests at any one time. The taxpayers' case was based on the wider sense of 'residential' in contrast to 'business, storage or other accommodation' (see the judge's summary at p. 24D). Millett J upheld the Crown's contention that 'residential' in what is now s. 223(4) had to take its meaning from the context, which in turn took one back to s. 222 itself as the 'parent' provision. It was necessary for the tenants, on this view, to have used the accommodation as their homes 'for short or lengthy periods' (p. 25C).

The judge seems to have been influenced by the transitory nature of the guests, and hinted at a purposive construction when he said:

'It is easy to see a social purpose in encouraging homeowners to make some part or all of their homes available to others to use for short or lengthy periods as their home ... It is difficult to discern any social purpose in providing further tax relief by this means to persons who run hotels or guest houses on a commercial basis for holiday-makers and tourists.' (p. 25B–C).

However, the Court of Appeal ([1990] BTC 323) unanimously rejected this approach and upheld the argument of the taxpayer which had been rejected at first instance: no assistance could be obtained, on the court's reasoning, from the context of s. 222 when interpreting 'residential' as it appears in s. 223(4). In that section the word has no necessary implication of permanence and is used, on the Court of Appeal's view, merely in distinction from 'business', 'storage', or other alternative qualifying words.

In the light of the Court of Appeal's decision, s. 223(4) relief will be available to any hotelier who has his main residence on the hotel premises, and will extend at least to all the let bedroom areas, together (arguably) with the public rooms such as lounges, restaurants and bars, and service facilities such as kitchens, possibly subject to a restriction to the extent that the hotel is also used by customers not staying overnight.

By the same reasoning there should be relief for owners of furnished properties which are normally let to holiday-makers (see ¶711). Given that the licensees will be using the property 'residentially' in the broad sense adopted by the Court of Appeal in *Owen v Elliott (HMIT)*, it would be possible for an owner who established factual or elected MR status to use s. 223(4) relief to cover gains attributable neither to the MR period nor to the 'final 36 months'; the only arguments against such a position available to the Revenue would be (1) under s. 224(3) by reference to the motive behind the acquisition (see ¶307), or (2) that the owner's period of residence was a mere sham, perhaps because it was very brief. This could be attractive to those who are unwilling to reinvest their gains to obtain roll-over relief, or who are too young to claim retirement relief. See also the discussion about farmworkers' cottages at ¶714(1). Another use of s. 223(4), on

¶708

this view, might be available to, say, a householder in Wimbledon who let his entire home to tennis fans during Wimbledon fortnight.

(4) Computational considerations

The computation prescribed by s. 223(4) rests on the presumption that there will be an apportionment of consideration under s. 222(10) (see ¶703). Having first computed any restriction to PRR necessary for other reasons, such as non-permitted absences, it is then necessary, in effect, to compare three numbers:

(a) The amount of PRR due, after any such other restrictions, and before considering relief for lettings;
(b) The gain which is attributable to the letting period(s); and
(c) A fixed amount, which is £40,000 (s. 222(4)(b)).

The smallest of these three numbers is then deducted from the otherwise taxable gain to give the s. 222(4) relief. (Taper relief, for disposals after 5 April 1998, is then applied to the taxable gain *after* the lettings relief thus found – see ¶1104 below.)

Often, but not inevitably, this means that the lettings relief in effect exempts the first £40,000 of the otherwise taxable gains.

It is important to note that the lettings relief must be calculated as the final step (apart from taper relief) in the overall computation.

Example

Vernon bought his house on 6 April 1992 and sold it on 6 April 2002 for a total gain of £200,000 after indexation. He lived there as his only residence from 6 April 1992 to 5 April 1995. From 6 April 1995 to 5 April 1996 it was wholly let to a residential tenant. From 6 April 1996 to the date of sale he lived elsewhere and elected for that other residence to be his main residence under s. 222(5)(a). The relief for the final 36 months of ownership (s. 223(2)(a)) covers the period from 6 April 1999 to 6 April 2002, but the three years from 6 April 1996 to 5 April 1999 do not qualify for PRR.

The first step is to compute the taxable gains and PRR due over the whole of the ten years of ownership, before considering the lettings relief:

Period	Circumstances	Years of actual/ deemed residence	Years not eligible for PRR	Total
6/4/92–5/4/95	Actual residence	3		
6/4/95–5/4/96	Let		1	
6/4/96–5/4/99	Other property elected		3	
6/4/99–6/4/02	Final 36 months	3		
Totals		6	4	10

Total gain as above	£200,000
PRR before lettings relief:	
6/10 × 200,000 =	(120,000)
Taxable gain before lettings relief	80,000

The three relevant numbers to compare are therefore:

(a) PRR before lettings relief	120,000
(b) Gain attributable to let period: 1/10 × 200,000	20,000
(c) Fixed amount	40,000

In this case (b) is the smallest number and therefore the s. 223(4) relief is £20,000. The taxable gain (before taper relief) is therefore £80,000 less £20,000 making £60,000.

If Vernon's total gain was £500,000, the lettings relief would be £40,000 being the smallest of (a) £300,000, (b) £50,000 and (c) £40,000, and the taxable gain (before taper relief) would be £500,000 less PRR of £300,000 less lettings relief of £40,000, i.e. £160,000.

Unfortunately, the figure of £40,000 has been fixed since 19 March 1991 and is probably overdue for an increase.

There are further examples of the computation of s. 223(4) relief at CGT 64735–64739.

(5) Co-owners and s. 223(4) relief
Where more than one person owns a property which has been let residentially in his ownership period, the £40,000 deduction seems to be potentially available to each co-owner. This is because s. 223(4) refers to a gain 'accruing *to any individual*' if the property has 'at any time in *his* period of ownership been ... let by *him*' (emphasis added). Such co-owners could include a married couple (both before and after 6 April 1990). The Revenue accepts this view (see CGT 64716)

¶708

although the caveat in that paragraph about the need for joint ownership to be genuine should be noted.

However, a co-owner at the time of sale would not appear to be entitled to a separate £40,000 allowance if all lettings occurred before his own personal ownership period, since the property would not have been let 'by him'. This would also seem to be true of a spouse who was not a party to lettings: although s. 222(7)(a) extends the ownership period back before marriage in such cases (see ¶314(3)), there are no provisions, in that sub-section or elsewhere, to deem lettings by one spouse to be lettings 'by' the other for s. 223(4) purposes.

This must be a powerful argument for married couples to hold such let property jointly wherever possible, and for tenancies to be granted by both spouses jointly. More adventurous planning might take the form of transferring the property prior to its being let to several trusts with interests in possession for the joint owners of the freehold; assuming that full PRR is due up to the date when letting begins this transfer would not attract CGT, and once ownership has been passed into the trusts there does not seem to be anything to stop each trust being entitled to a £40,000 allowance, so long as each set of trustees is party to the lettings. (See CGT 64717).

(6) Lodgers, service tenants and separate accommodation

The Revenue regards the relief in s. 223(4) as unnecessary where a tenant is merely a lodger, living with the owner as part of the same household and sharing meals. In this case no restriction under s. 224(1) is made (see SP 14/80, para. 2) since the owner has not given up the use of any part of the property as his residence.

The relief is also unnecessary where part of the house has been let on a service tenancy to employees (see CGT 64704–64705), because in these cases the owner/employer has not given up legal occupation of the relevant parts.

The s. 223(4) relief is regarded as applicable only where the tenant (being more than a lodger) occupies part of the owner's dwelling-house which is let to him without significant structural alterations; whether there are separate washing and cooking facilities seems to be irrelevant. But if the property is subdivided so that the tenant's accommodation is self-contained, especially if it has its own entrance from the road, the Revenue view is that the owner is not letting part of his dwelling-house as required by s. 223(4), and no relief is due (see SP 14/80, para. 4, and also CGT 64724–64725). This view seems to rest on the premise that the tenanted portion will be a separate asset which can never fall within s. 222.

Whether this is in fact the case will depend on specific circumstances; the test would seem to be whether the owner could, at the time of the disposal, have made a separate disposal of the let portion. In that light the Revenue's attachment to the 'separate entrance' point may be misleading, since it would be quite possible to dispose of, say, a first floor flat on a long lease even if it was reached by a common front door and staircase. Separate cooking and lavatory facilities are more significant since their absence would make a separate disposal difficult in practice.

¶708

If a separate asset has been created it may be irrelevant that it was not created with a view to letting: if the owner created a separate 'granny flat' for an elderly parent who has since died, he may have to reintegrate it with the rest of the house in order to use s. 223(4) relief later.

SP 14/80 refers to 'a' lodger in the singular, and the Revenue believes that if there is more than one lodger at a time the statement may not apply, because it was not intended to apply to the running of a lodging house as a business (CGT 64703). In the writer's view this may not be soundly based. The statement is not a concession but an interpretation of the law; what matters is not the number of lodgers but whether the owner has given up legal occupation of part of the house, and whether the taking in of lodgers amounts to a trade. If the property is large enough, the owner may remain in legal occupation while taking in several lodgers at once. In particular there would seem no reason to deny the SP 14/80 treatment merely where there are two lodgers sharing a room. If there is any justified denial of SP 14/80 relief, the Revenue accepts that partial relief may be due under s. 223(4) as explained earlier.

¶709   The 'rent-a-room' scheme – interaction with PRR

Legislation was introduced in s. 59 and Sch. 10 of F(No. 2)A 1992 to allow relief from income tax on rental income from letting furnished accommodation in an individual's main residence. This is commonly known as 'rent-a-room' relief. Very broadly, it exempts from tax altogether gross furnished letting income (before expenses) not exceeding £4,250 in a tax year, and where gross income exceeds that figure, the taxpayer can elect to adopt the so-called 'alternative' basis, under which he is taxed on the gross receipts less £4,250. The relief covers cases where lettings are sufficiently organised, and include sufficiently extensive other services, to qualify as a trade in their own right under Case I of Sch. D, as well as the more familiar case where liability arises under Case VI.

The relief is only due where the furnished accommodation which is let is in a 'qualifying residence' (F(No. 2)A 1992, Sch. 10, para. 2(1) and 4). This is defined as a residence which is the individual's only or main residence in the basis period for the tax year in question. 'Residence' includes a part of a building (thus including flats), and also houseboats and caravans (F(No. 2)A 1992, Sch. 10, para. 7).

The rules contain no provision to deem a particular dwelling to be the claimant's only or main residence for this purpose if he has more than one. The test of what is a main residence will thus depend on the factual position, as it does for PRR in cases where no election has been made under TCGA 1992, s. 222(5)(a) – see the discussion at ¶503. Any election made under that section for a particular property will be irrelevant in determining whether 'rent-a-room' relief is due on that property.

The rules contain no specific provisions on CGT. Thus normal principles will apply, and where the letting is to a lodger who shares meals or a bathroom with the owner, it is unlikely that the Revenue would seek to tax any capital gain made on sale merely because accommodation had been let in this way (see ¶708(7)). If the tenant is more than a mere lodger, has his own cooking and bathroom facilities and takes his meals separately, there seems no reason why the lettings relief in s. 223(4) should not be due on the lines described above (see ¶708).

The 'rent-a-room' rules do not prevent the income tax relief from applying where the let residential accommodation is not occupied on a permanent basis; but even if the tenant has his 'main' home elsewhere – e.g. if he occupies furnished rooms during the working week but returns to his family at weekends – or spends only a few weeks in residence, there seems to be no reason why s. 223(4) relief should not be due following the Court of Appeal's decision in *Owen v Elliott (HMIT)* [1989] BTC 19 (see ¶708(3)).

However, if the letting is of self-contained accommodation within SP 14/80 para. 4 (see ¶708(7)), it appears that 'rent-a-room' relief will not be due, since the taxpayer will not be letting accommodation in his 'qualifying residence' (F(No. 2)A 1992, Sch. 10, para. 2(2) and 4), and in such a case there will be no s. 223(4) relief either.

¶710 Commercial lettings

A commercial letting of part of a dwelling-house (e.g. a ground floor let as office accommodation while the owner occupies the upper floors) is clearly outside TCGA 1992, s. 223(4). Section 222(10) would apply to restrict PRR and unless the let portion had at some time been occupied as a dwelling by the owner, no relief would be due for the 'final 36 months' on the fraction apportioned to the commercial letting.

¶711 Furnished holiday lettings

This expression is used here to denote lettings which qualify for the special income tax and CGT treatment afforded by ICTA 1988, s. 503, 504 and TCGA 1992, s. 241.

(1) Interaction with PRR

If a property which ranks as furnished holiday lettings is also at some point the factual or elected MR, the owner's PRR will be restricted under s. 223(2). This will apply whether the whole property is successively owner-occupied and let, or there is simultaneous partial use for both purposes. However, it may be possible to apply

s. 223(4) to such lettings, on the reasoning adopted by the Court of Appeal in *Owen v Elliott (HMIT)* [1989] BTC 19 (see ¶708(3)).

(2) Roll-over relief implications

Where a furnished holiday letting property is sold and roll-over relief claimed on a replacement property which is similarly used for a time, but then becomes the owner's residence, s. 241(6) imposes a rule to prevent the rolled-over gain from being 'washed' via PRR. The gain to which s. 222 applies on the second property is reduced by the rolled-over gain, leaving the balance taxable (subject to the possibility of further roll-over or, for disposals before 6 April 2003, retirement relief).

Example 1

Olwen, a farmer's wife in Wales, has let a cottage to holiday-makers, qualifying for furnished holiday letting treatment, for some years. She sold it – having never lived there herself – in 2000 for a gain of £30,000. In 2001 she bought a similar property for £180,000, claiming roll-over relief. From 2001 to 2002 it is let on a furnished holiday letting basis. Olwen and her husband, Emrys, then move in themselves and two years later she sells the property for £190,000.

Apart from s. 241(6), Olwen's gain of £40,000 on the second cottage would be wholly exempt under s. 222 and 223(4), including the additional part (£30,000) effectively representing the gain on the first cottage. But the application of s. 241(6) reduces the PRR by £30,000 (being the rolled-over gain), leaving only £10,000 eligible for PRR and recapturing the rolled-over gain from the earlier cottage.

(3) Avoiding s. 241(6)

Can this recapture charge be avoided? The key to this question is that, by s. 241(6)(b), it only applies where the base cost of the second property is reduced under s. 152 or 153 as applied by the furnished holiday letting rules. If it is reduced under the normal roll-over relief rules, the charge should be avoided.

Example 2

Olwen, in Example 1 above, instead ceased furnished holiday letting activities at the first cottage at the end of the 1999 season. She then made a gift of the cottage to Emrys, and from then until its sale in 2000 he used it to house a farm-worker. Thereafter the facts are as in Example 1, except of course that it is Emrys who lets, and eventually sells, the second cottage.

When the first cottage is sold the authority for roll-over is the normal rule in s. 152(1), since Emrys has occupied the cottage (through the worker) and used it for his business throughout his ownership: by virtue of s. 58(2) he inherits

Olwen's base cost and can roll-over the whole gain without recourse to the furnished holiday letting rules. Section 241(6) does not therefore apply and, provided that Emrys's business use of the first cottage, and his furnished holiday letting activity and factual residence at the second cottage, are all substantial, the recapture charge is avoided and all the gain on the second cottage, including the rolled-over gain from the first, should be covered by PRR. In practice the time scale would need to be sufficiently lengthy, and the transactions sufficiently lacking in 'pre-ordination', to avoid an attack on *Furniss (HMIT) v Dawson* [1984] BTC 71, lines.

It should, of course, be remembered that although furnished holiday letting is treated as a trade for certain purposes the property does not become trading stock.

PROBLEMS FOR FARMERS AND LANDOWNERS

¶712 The farmhouse
PRR restrictions should not normally arise on the sale of a farmhouse which has been owner-occupied, unless a dedicated area has been used exclusively for business purposes: see ¶703 above and the Revenue's views in CGT 64680.

¶713 Estate management – the manor house
If a landowner is not a working farmer but has used part of his own house exclusively for estate management, there will be a PRR restriction: the authority being either TCGA 1992, s. 222(10) or possibly s. 224(1), on the footing that the activity was a 'business' in general law.

¶714 Workers' cottages
The disposal of such cottages will not usually raise any PRR issue unless it can be said that they are part of the dwelling-house by reason of their situation (see ¶319). Even if this is the case PRR will not be due if the occupants have historically been employed on the farm or let estate, rather than in some role connected with the owner's enjoyment of the dwelling-house as a residence.

Two subsidiary points may, however, arise:

(1) Can s. 223(4) apply?
A cottage occupied solely by estate or farmworkers throughout the period of ownership will not qualify for s. 223(4) relief because it will never have been the

landowner's residence, and thus there will be no question of s. 222 applying: see the opening words of s. 223(4) and ¶708(1).

However, what would be the position if there had been some period of factual or elected MR by the owner? Would s. 223(4) then be in point on the grounds that the cottage had been 'let' by the owner at other times 'as residential occupation'? Since 'let' carries no implications of an exclusive tenancy, and there is no doubt that the occupant would be 'residing' in the cottage in the everyday sense of the word, the Court of Appeal's reasoning in *Owen v Elliott (HMIT)* [1989] BTC 19 (see ¶708(3)) could lead to the conclusion that s. 223(4) relief was available in such cases.

(2) Other methods of minimising the gain?

There may be other methods of achieving the same objective of minimising gains on such disposals. Consider, for example, a gift to a connected person, with hold-over relief under s. 165(2)(a) in the case of 'in hand' land or Sch. 7, para. 1 for tenanted land, followed by use as a factual MR by the donee for a significant period. This should enable the donee to dispose of the cottage with PRR on his own gain and the held-over gain – provided that the gift is not in any way conditional on the donee's sale, and is not made when a third party sale is virtually certain (see *Craven (HMIT) v White* [1988] BTC 268), or, bearing in mind Lord Jauncey's cautionary remarks about auction sales in that case at p. 312, when an auction of the cottage has already been arranged.

Example
Jack Broadacre has farmed Down Farm for many years. He and his wife live at Down Farmhouse, but a few years ago he bought an adjoining farm, Manor Farm, which also has a sizeable farmhouse. Jack has been using this to house his cowman, Fred. Seeking to reduce a substantial overdraft, Jack realises that Manor Farmhouse would be valuable on the open market. Fred is coming up to retirement and has already been allocated a council house in the village. Jack's son, John, aged 24, who lives with his parents, agrees to move into Manor Farmhouse when Fred retires. Jack gifts the house to John who moves in and lives there for 12 months. John then sells the farmhouse on the open market and becomes a partner in the farming business, reinvesting some of the proceeds in the business and using the rest as the deposit for a mortgage on a cottage in the village which he buys and into which he moves.

Jack's gift qualifies for hold-over relief under s. 165(2)(a), and as a potentially exempt transfer for IHT. John acquires the house at Jack's base cost for CGT and his own sale ranks for PRR on the whole gain, including the held-over gain from Jack. The year's factual residence should be enough to dispel any Revenue challenge, and John's buying a different home for himself should avoid any suggestion of circularity which might arise if he simply moved back into his parents' home. Jack would, of course, have to trust his son not to 'walk away' from the business with the benefit of Manor Farm house.

¶715 Exchanges of land

Where joint owners of land exchange their interests so that each thereafter becomes a sole owner for CGT purposes, each strictly makes a taxable disposal in consideration of the asset he acquires. However, Revenue practice is to allow a form of roll-over relief so that no immediate charge to tax arises (see ESC D26). This treatment is specifically denied where the property includes a house eligible for PRR. However, where there is more than one such house, and the transaction results in each party becoming the sole owner of the house which is his residence, PRR is allowed, on the basis that each treats his base cost and acquisition date as those applicable to his original acquisition of a joint interest.

Following *Jenkins (HMIT) v Brown* [1989] BTC 281 and *Warrington (HMIT) v Sterland & Ors and related appeals* [1989] BTC 281, however, there is some doubt as to whether the Revenue's practice is a 'concession' after all. In those cases joint owners of a 'pool' of land each removed particular holdings of land from the 'pool', equivalent in value to their initial contributions: it was held that none of them made taxable disposals. Knox J regarded the transactions as covered by the principle in *Booth v Ellard (HMIT)* (1980) 53 TC 393, since the measure of each party's interests was unchanged. The Revenue's view seems to be that the decisions in these cases were based on their own facts but they are not disapproved in the official manuals (see CGT 34411).

Since these decisions have not been overturned by a higher court, the principle seems equally applicable to an exchange involving a private residence; the judge was clear that the nature of the assets concerned (shares in *Booth v Ellard (HMIT)*, land in the cases before him) had no effect on the principle.

So on that basis, if (A) and (B) jointly owned a farm which included (A's) home, they could execute a deed of partition under which each took a 100 per cent interest, (A) in the house and (B) in the farm, without either making a taxable disposal.

8 Trustees and Personal Representatives

THE EXTENT OF THE s. 225 EXEMPTION

¶801 Disposal of settled property

Section 225 of TCGA 1992, affords an extension of PRR where trustees make a disposal of settled property consisting of or including a dwelling-house occupied by someone entitled to do so under the settlement terms. The mention of 'settled property' takes us to the definition in s. 68, so that the property must be held in trust, but other than as bare trustee or nominee property (see s. 60(1) and (2) and see CGT 65411). Thus, s. 225 would not appear to apply to co-ownership situations, where a house is beneficially owned by more than one person (see *Kidson (HMIT) v Macdonald & Anor* (1974) 49 TC 503) – in these cases relief will be due, if at all, under the main rules in s. 222. Also excluded from s. 225 will be properties held for a minor child or other incapacitated person absolutely (s. 60(2)). It seems that 'pools' of property of the *Jenkins (HMIT) v Brown* ([1989] BTC 281) type will also be excluded (see ¶715), but not cases where there are several beneficiaries, none of whom can force a sale without the consent of the others (see *Crowe (Bird Will Trustee) v Appleby (HMIT)* (1975) 51 TC 457).

¶802 An asset within s. 222(1)

The disposal in question must be one to which TCGA 1992, s. 222(1) applies, but this is not cut down further, e.g. to a disposal within s. 222(1)(a). It seems, therefore, that s. 225 can operate on a disposal of land within s. 222(1)(b), i.e. a separate sale of land within the permitted area: this will, however, only be the case if, at the time of that disposal, the dwelling-house is occupied as required by s. 225.

Example

A settlor gives an unoccupied house and one acre of garden to a settlement in April 2001. It remains vacant until April 2003. In December 2002, the trustees sell 0.75 acres of the garden to a builder. In April 2003 they resolve to allow a beneficiary to occupy the house. A subsequent sale of the house would, prima facie, be within s. 225, but the previous sale of the garden cannot so qualify, even though it fell within s. 222(1)(b), because in 2002 there has been no time 'in the period of ownership of the trustees' when the house was occupied as s. 225 requires.

If the beneficiary had been in residence at the time of that sale, however, s. 225 would have been available and, in this case, the gain would have been wholly exempt.

¶803 A person entitled to occupy under the terms of the settlement

For TCGA 1992, s. 225 to apply the house in question must be the only or main residence (as to which see ¶804) of a person entitled to occupy it under the terms of the settlement. The meaning of this 'entitlement' was considered in *Sansom & Anor (Ridge Settlement Trustees) v Peay, (HMIT)* (1976) 52 TC 1.

(1) Entitled to occupy

Before *Sansom v Peay (HMIT)*, the Revenue argued that s. 225 only covered a situation where the settlement terms specifically provided for the house in question to be occupied by a particular beneficiary. By what was then thought to be a concession, the relief was extended to permissive occupation by a beneficiary who was entitled under those terms to the whole income from the house or the whole proceeds of its sale (see para. (8) of the agreed statement of facts in *Sansom* at p. 2G.)

Sansom showed that this view was not concessional but a correct view of the law. The phrase 'entitled to occupy' was held to be equivalent to 'permitted to occupy for the time being' (as well as for a fixed term) under the exercise of a power. The beneficiary was 'thereupon' (per Brightman J *Sansom* at p. 7B) entitled to go into occupation and remain there until permission was withdrawn. It did not matter that the beneficiary could not obtain possession in law against the trustees, as a life tenant might.

Thus it is clear that while occupation of a specific property under a specific provision in the deed will qualify under s. 225, so also will occupation permitted under a discretionary power. Rent-free occupation would not seem to be necessary (see the Revenue's views at CGT 65448), since in *Sansom* the trustees had power to charge rent, although they did not do so (see *Sansom* at p. 4E).

So, following this case, a common sense approach seems the right one: is the occupier entitled to be where he is by virtue of the legitimate exercise of the trustees' powers? If so, then *prima facie* s. 225 can run.

Since s. 225 refers merely to 'a person' who is entitled to occupy, there seems to be no reason why s. 225 cannot apply where a succession of beneficiaries occupy the property, so long as each is 'entitled' to do so.

(2) Under the terms of the settlement

In *Sansom*, the trustees had power 'to permit any beneficiary to reside in any dwelling-house, or occupy any property or building which ... may for the time being be subject to the trusts ...' (per the quotation of Brightman J p. 4E). The Crown conceded in argument that the exercise of a power was part of the 'terms'. Brightman J said, obiter, (at p. 5H) that he thought a tenant for life under the *Settled Land Act* 1925 would also occupy as required by s. 225.

New trusts under the *Settled Land Act* have not been possible since 1 January 1997. Under the *Trusts of Land and Appointment of Trustees Act* 1996, which came into force on that date but can apply to many settlements created earlier, a beneficiary with an interest in possession has a right to occupy land if the purpose of the trust includes making land available for him, or for a class of beneficiaries of which he is a member, or if the trustees hold land which is available for that purpose (see s. 12(1) of that Act). A beneficiary whose rights fall within this provision would seem to meet the conditions of s. 225.

However, s. 225 will not apply where an entitlement to occupy stems from the use of the trustees' administrative or managerial powers. Thus, occupation under a lease granted for consideration would normally mean that the occupier's rights stemmed from that lease, and s. 225 relief would not be due (see CGT 65450–65451). But where, for example, there are several beneficiaries but not all occupy houses under the trust, and the trustees, to achieve equity between them, grant the occupier a lease under which rent accrues for the benefit of the others, the rights of the actual occupier, in the Revenue's view, still stem from the terms of the settlement and relief can be due (see CGT 65448).

¶804 Residential status of the property

(1) Occupation

Section 225 of TCGA 1992, requires the property to be the only or main residence of the beneficiary during the trustees' ownership. Subsection (a) then requires that in examining occupation, one looks at the individual who so occupies: subs. (b) adds that a s. 222(5)(a) election is to be a joint act by that individual and the trustees. It follows that s. 222–223 are to be read on the assumption that the occupier was the owner, asking whether the property was his factual or elected MR. The inclusion of s. 223 (by the plural 'sections' in the opening words of s. 225) may also involve applying the 'absence' rules in s. 223(2) and (3) to the beneficiary, by reference to his own circumstances as regards employment, etc. In a simple case this poses no problems:

Example 1
Edward owns Mon Repos, a house in the town where he works. He is also the life tenant under his father's Will trust, and entitled under its terms to reside at Keeper's Cottage, on the trust estate in Devon, where he spends weekends and some holidays, and which is not otherwise occupied.

Edward has two factual residences and can, if he wishes and they agree, join with the trustees in a s. 222(5)(a) election for Keeper's Cottage since his occupation of the latter is clearly within s. 225. He might, of course, refuse an invitation so to elect from the trustees, on the grounds that this would be disadvantageous to his position in respect of Mon Repos.

However, in more complex cases the construction of s. 225(a) may be less straightforward, since it is possible for the same trust property to be successively occupied by more than one beneficiary.

Example 2
The ABC Trust owns a dwelling-house. Its terms grant the house to Tom for life, then to Dick for life, with remainder to Harry. Tom occupies the house as his only residence for years 1–3, after which he is required by his employer to live elsewhere in the UK until year 5, when he dies. Dick then moves in and occupies the house as his only residence.

Are the two years of Tom's absence covered by s. 223(3)(c), since he never re-occupies the house as his residence and the 'before and after' rule (see ¶606) is not satisfied *by him*, although it could be said to be satisfied by Dick?

It is submitted that Tom's absence can be so covered. Section 223(3)(e) refers to the condition about re-occupation being satisfied where 'both before and after the period there was a time when the dwelling-house was *the individual's* only or main residence' (emphasis added). Section 225(a) says that in applying s. 222–224 to situations where settlement property is involved, 'references to the individual shall be taken as references to the trustee *except in relation to the occupation of the dwelling-house* ...' (emphasis added). In applying s. 223(3)(c) it seems clear, therefore, that for 'the individual' we should read 'a person entitled to occupy [the house] under the terms of the settlement', as in s. 225; on that interpretation, so long as the property is occupied by Dick as his residence under the terms of the settlement, Tom's absence will not cause any lack of PRR.

(2) Ownership
Section 225(a) requires attention to the *trustees'* period of ownership when considering whether the occupation test is met. So it seems that one disregards occupation under any previous ownership, even by someone who was connected

with the trustees. Where the previous owner was the settlor this is unlikely to be disastrous if he was entitled to PRR in his own right on the disposal by gift, or was able to claim hold-over relief on the gift into settlement, e.g. to a discretionary trust *via* s. 260: in the latter case, if the occupation test is passed during the trust period, s. 225 will apply, on a later disposal by the trustees, to the whole gain, including the held-over gain (see the example at ¶714(2)).

(3) Duration of occupation rights

There was argument in *Sansom* as to whether or not the required entitlement to occupy had to exist throughout the period of occupation (see p. 6C–E). Brightman J thought either view possible but said: '… looking at the matter *at the date of the disposal*, the beneficiaries were persons who, *in the events which happened*, were entitled to occupy the house … under the terms of the settlement.' (p. 7B, emphasis added). It seems therefore that it is necessary to ask the question 'What entitles the beneficiary to be here'? at the point of disposal.

¶805 User-related restrictions

Since the trade, etc. referred to in TCGA 1992, s. 224(1) need not be that of the owner, the use of part of the property exclusively for a business of the beneficiary would trigger a restriction under those rules.

¶806 Interaction with let property relief

No relief under TCGA 1992, s. 223(4) would be due where a property is let by trustees throughout their ownership to a non-beneficiary. There must be both occupation within s. 225 *and* residential letting within s. 223(4): if so, the explicit reference to s. 225 in s. 223(4)(a) supports the view that the latter relief is due. Although at first sight s. 223(4) seems to apply exclusively to individuals, the deeming mechanism runs from the references to an individual in s. 223(4), back to s. 222, and into s. 225(a), where in the context of ownership, references to an individual are to be taken as references to a trustee: and since, in the 1992 consolidation, s. 225 begins explicitly with the words 'Sections 222 to 224 shall apply …' there is now no doubt, if there ever was any, that it can apply where a trust property is both occupied by a beneficiary *and* let to a third party within s. 223(4).

The relief in s. 225 also seems, by similar reasoning, to include a case where a beneficiary has occupied, under the settlement terms, a property which is later appointed to him absolutely, so that when he sells the property PRR is capable of covering the whole period of his occupation.

¶807 Interaction with other CGT legislation about trusts

(1) UK resident trusts

Where a settlor or his spouse may themselves benefit under a trust, gains on disposals after 5 April 1988 are, broadly, taxed on the settlor as if they had accrued to him (s. 77). However, this rule does not appear to override TCGA 1992, s. 225 if the trustees dispose of a dwelling-house which was the main residence of a person entitled to occupy it under the settlement terms. Section 77 applies only where *chargeable* gains accrue to the trustees (see s. 77(1)(a)) and to the extent that s. 225 applies, then by s. 223, any trust gains are not chargeable gains.

Thus a settlor could create a UK resident settlement under which he was himself entitled to occupy a trust property as his main residence, without falling foul of the 'settlor interest' rules.

(2) Offshore trusts

The same result would follow if the trustees were resident outside the UK. If the settlor or his spouse, or certain other related or connected persons (as defined in Sch. 2, para. 2(3)), were interested in the settlement, the rules in s. 86 and Sch. 5 would apply to make gains in the trust potentially taxable in the hands of the settlor. However, as with the legislation considered in (1) above, this only applies where there are gains on which the trustees would be liable to CGT if they were resident in the UK throughout the tax year in question (s. 86(1)(e), (2) and (3)). To the extent that relief would be due under s. 225 to UK resident trustees, such gains would not be chargeable on them, and so to the same extent the settlor cannot be liable for CGT under s. 86.

If the s. 86 legislation does not apply to an offshore trust capital gains made in the trust may be visited on UK-resident and domiciled beneficiaries when they receive capital payments from the trust, under s. 87. However, this regime can, again, only apply where the trust gains would be taxable on UK-resident trustees. It follows that to the extent that s. 225 relief would be due, no gains can arise to offshore trustees for later attribution to UK-resident beneficiaries (s. 87(2)). See also the discussion below at ¶1012.

AVOIDING AN INTEREST IN POSSESSION

¶808 The problem

A practical difficulty with TCGA 1992, s. 225 is that for CGT purposes trustees wish to demonstrate the clearest possible 'entitlement to occupy', yet the existence of an interest in possession in the house, though undoubtedly bringing the case potentially within s. 225, will leave the value of the house in the life tenant's estate at death for IHT by IHTA 1984, s. 49(1).

¶809 Interest in possession

This is classically regarded, for IHT purposes, as the 'present right to present enjoyment' of property, even if subject to the possibility of a later appointment away (see *Pearson & Ors v IR Commrs* [1980] Ch 1). There is no such right if the enjoyment is subject to a power to accumulate which may put a stop to it (as in *Pearson*.) The Revenue may attempt to show that even where there is merely permissive occupation, as in *Sansom v Peay (HMIT)* (1976) 52 TC 1, there is nevertheless an interest in possession for IHT (see SP 10/79). This statement points to the following features as indicating in the Revenue's view, an interest in possession:

(a) a power drawn in wide enough terms to cover the creation of an exclusive or joint right of residence, albeit revocable for a definite or indefinite period; *together* with,

(b) the exercise of such a power with the intention of providing a particular beneficiary with a permanent home.

However, where there is no existing interest in possession, the Revenue does not regard the exercise of the power to permit a beneficiary to occupy the house as creating such an interest if the effect is merely to allow non-exclusive occupation or to create a contractual tenancy for full consideration.

¶810 Avoiding the difficulty?

Often the very conditions which will ensure PRR under TCGA 1992, s. 225 are those which also create IHT liability on the occupier's death. For IHT purposes, a permissive occupation from minute to minute seems, if it is exclusive, to run the risk of 'solidifying' for IHT into a right to occupy, and attempts to dress it up otherwise, especially when the beneficiary is elderly and has been in occupation for a lengthy period, may well fail.

Cases in which residential property occupied by a beneficiary has been held to be part of their estate for IHT purposes include *IR Commrs v Lloyd's Private Banking Ltd (as Trustee of Evans dec'd)* [1998] BTC 8,020 which went to the High Court, and two Special Commissioners' decisions, *Woodhall (as Personal Representatives of Woodhall dec'd) v IR Commrs* (2000) Sp C 261, and *Faulkner (as Trustee of Adams dec'd) v IR Commrs* (2001) Sp C 278. In each case an individual was permitted to reside in a particular property on condition that certain out-goings were paid. In each case the stipulations of the testator appear to have made it clear that the intention was to provide the occupier with a permanent home.

CGT was not involved in any of the cases, but in the writer's view there would have been little doubt that s. 225 relief would have been available for a disposal while the beneficiary was in occupation.

It may be possible to take the words of the final part of the SP as they stand and to create a non-exclusive lease for the occupier, or to charge them a full rent (which would reflect any out-goings paid by them such as repairs and insurance). Otherwise, more complex planning will be needed to take the value of the house (or perhaps its value at the date of the operation) outside IHT and this may not be compatible with PRR (see also ¶1105).

In any event, where the beneficiary is elderly and unlikely to leave the property, great care is needed to avoid IHT liabilities on his or her death.

DOES THE s. 225 EXEMPTION HAVE OTHER PLANNING USES?

¶811 Use of a gift

Section 225 of TCGA 1992, is still a useful planning tool in other ways, especially since the abolition of general hold-over relief in FA 1989 (see ¶1015). Since that change it is no longer possible to 'wash' a substantial gain on a dwelling-house which does not in itself rank for PRR, through a gift to a connected individual who occupies it for a while and then sells it, unless the gift could qualify for hold-over under the present restrictive rules (cf. ¶714(2)).

However, s. 225 can provide an alternative route to the same destination provided that the IHT cost is not too great, by the use of a gift which is an immediately chargeable IHT transfer and therefore qualifies for hold-over relief by s. 260.

> **Example**
> Mr and Mrs Wrinkly own a country property which is their factual MR, and a flat in London which they use when visiting their son, Paul, who is a medical student at Guy's Hospital. They foresee a time when the flat will no longer be needed and will be sold, but they do not want to deprive their country house of PRR by electing for the flat under s. 222(5)(a). The flat is currently worth £450,000 and they have made no IHT chargeable transfers in the last seven years.
>
> The Wrinklys, as joint settlors, set up a discretionary trust, for the benefit of their children and grandchildren, with a nominal cash sum. They then gift the flat to the trust. After an interval of several months the trustees resolve to allow

Paul to occupy it rent-free. He moves in (vacating his present accommodation) and lives there for 18 months until he graduates and takes a hospital job in Leeds. The flat is then sold.

The gift to the trust is covered by s. 260 since it is an immediately chargeable IHT occasion. Thus the gain is held-over but the Wrinklys' two NIL rate bands ensure that no IHT is payable. The gain on sale, including the held-over gain, is all exempt by, s. 225. The s. 222 exemption on the country house is unaffected. The only hazard is the potential erosion of the NIL rate bands should the Wrinklys wish to make further large gifts in the next seven years.

An obvious method by which the Revenue could try to counteract transactions such as these is to argue that the settlement is an interest in possession settlement from the outset, so that no hold-over relief is due. It is therefore important that the trustees exercise genuine, unfettered discretion.

Such a strategy would have been vulnerable to the proposals for the reform of the taxation of UK-resident trusts published in an Inland Revenue consultative document in March 1991, which would, inter alia, have prevented hold-over relief from applying where there was an occasion of charge to IHT, yet because of exemptions (as here), no IHT was actually due. Although this idea was dropped, it could well re-appear in any general reform of CGT. The Revenue is well aware of the possibilities (see CGT 65455–65458) and will be concerned to establish that those alleged to have occupied trust properties in fact did so. They are likely to be sceptical about attempts to use hold-over relief and s. 225 relief in tandem in this way where the alleged occupying beneficiaries are young children who would not in practice be likely to live alone without adult supervision (see CGT 65455) – a scepticism shared by the writer.

DEATH

¶812 Generally

Even if full PRR would not have been due on a sale by the owner of a dwelling-house in his lifetime, death washes out all gains by TCGA 1992, s. 62(1)(b). However, personal representatives risk a tax charge from any increase in value on a post-death sale.

¶813 Occupation by beneficiary of estate

Extra-Statutory Concession D5 allows TCGA 1992, s. 225 to operate concessionally where the personal representatives allow property to be occupied as a residence by a beneficiary who:

(1) used it as his only or main residence before the death,

(2) continues so to use it, and

(3) is entitled to the whole or substantially the whole of the proceeds of sale, absolutely or for life, even if no such authority exists in the Will or the terms of any testamentary trust.

If the beneficiary's only right is to a proportion of the whole estate this concession appears not to apply.

'Substantially the whole' is regarded as meaning at least 75 per cent (see CGT 65472).

¶814 Post-death variations

It often happens that a house is left in equal shares to several beneficiaries, one of whom has resided with the deceased but the remainder of whom have homes of their own (e.g. where an unmarried daughter has looked after an elderly parent but the other children are married with families). The 'carer' may wish to remain in the property at least for a while, and there may not be significant other assets. This can pose problems in relation to PRR on gains made on the property after the death of the parent.

Extra-Statutory Concession D5 will not apply where, for example, a dwelling-house is left equally to two beneficiaries of a Will, and one of them remains in occupation, since neither beneficiary will be entitled to 'substantially the whole' of the proceeds of sale. It may not be possible, without inequity to the other beneficiary, to execute a deed of variation so that the house is left wholly to one beneficiary who resides there until sale, so as to make the case comply with the requirements of the concession. In such a case it might, however, be possible to vary the Will so that the property was left in trust for the beneficiary who will in fact occupy the house, on terms that he or she is exclusively entitled to occupy it from the date of the death of the deceased. The personal representatives can then pass the property to the trustees and elections can be made under IHTA 1984, s. 62(7) and 142(2) to prevent any CGT or IHT liabilities arising from the variation.

The trust deed can provide that the trust capital is to be held for the two beneficiaries equally. Thus, when the property is sold, the proceeds will pass as the deceased intended. However, if the resident beneficiary remains in occupation of the house as his or her OMR until the date of sale, or until some point in the three years prior to sale, any gain on sale will be exempt under TCGA 1992, s. 225. It would probably be prudent to insure against IHT liability in the event of the resident beneficiary's death prior to the sale (see ¶808–¶810). This arrangement

¶814

achieves a similar effect to that of ESC D5 while having the advantage of using statutory provisions rather than the less certain provisions of a concession.

9 Marital Breakdown and the Private Residence Relief

¶901 Generally

Marital breakdown regularly gives rise to problems with PRR, unless the case is a simple one where there is only one factual residence where both parties remain until sale, so that TCGA 1992, s. 222 operates on all gains. More commonly, however, one or both will move out before any sale occurs.

The attitude of professional advisers to these problems will often vary according to which party is being advised. However, if the object of the exercise is to reach a settlement acceptable to both parties, it is necessary to avoid unforeseen tax burdens on either of them, since these can only deplete the available funds, to the detriment of everybody involved (including any children).

Generally in what follows, it is assumed that the husband leaves the matrimonial home and the wife stays, but naturally, the reverse may well occur.

SEPARATION PRIOR TO SALE

¶902 Sale after both parties have left

In this situation one needs to consider each party separately and ask whether any gains are chargeable on the basis of TCGA 1992, s. 223(1) and (2). So if a third party sale takes place within three years of the first departure, no special problems arise. The facts have to be examined separately for each spouse. Whether the third party sale occurs before or after decree absolute is irrelevant here. See ¶910 for problems where there is only one legal owner.

¶903 Inter-spouse transfers

(1) The spouse exemption

Section 58(1) of TCGA 1992, which deems inter-spouse transfers to give rise neither to a gain nor to a loss, only applies to transfers between spouses living together (as to which see ¶516(6)). It does, however, apply throughout the tax year of separation, so if a transfer is made in that tax year, there can be no taxable gains for the transferor, even if full PRR would not otherwise apply, e.g. by reason of non-privileged absences. The transferee then inherits the transferor's indexed base cost for the share acquired. However, such an outcome is often impossible to engineer.

(2) Connected persons and hold-over relief
Spouses are connected persons so long as they are legally married to each other (see s. 286(2)), so if any use is to be made of hold-over relief the vital date is that of the decree absolute. This may be important if a transfer is not at full market value. In any event following the abolition of general hold-over relief in FA 1989, any under-value element could no longer be held over on a dwelling-house since s. 165 would not be in point, nor would s. 260 apply, since for IHT such a transfer is either regarded as non-gratuitous (IHTA 1984, s. 10) or as exempt by s. 11(1) and (6), or failing both of these, as a PET. In the days of general hold-over relief the Revenue sometimes resisted claims under the former FA 1980, s. 79 on the grounds that such transfers were in consideration of the dropping of financial claims by the donee, an argument which they still use as a basis for their view that transfers after decree absolute take place at market value because the consideration cannot be valued (s. 17(1)(b) and see CGT 22506). Overall, then, hold-over relief is unlikely to be available.

(3) Timing of transfers
For that reason, those advising a 'quitting' spouse will wish to arrange any transfer of the property to the 'staying' spouse in such a way that no gain arises. This requires a transfer within three years of the date of permanent separation, so that the absentee's gain is fully covered by s. 223(1).

A transfer within this period would be covered even if made after decree absolute.

Those advising a 'staying' spouse may have different priorities; that spouse may need to compare (1) the potential CGT advantage of acquiring the other spouse's share at current market value rather than at original cost, with (2) the effect of any immediately payable CGT on the funds available to the other spouse for the financial settlement.

(4) Establishing the three-year time limit
If the transfer is to benefit fully from the 'final 36 months' relief in s. 223(1), there must be a disposal within that time. If disposal occurs under a contract, that means there must be an unconditional contract within that time (see s. 28(1)). But a consent order may not be in the nature of a contract: *Harvey (HMIT) v Sivyer* [1985] BTC 410, which suggests that s. 28(1) is inapplicable to consent orders, and

¶903

for the Revenue's views on this see CGT 22410–22426. In many cases – especially where it is handed down after the decree absolute – it is likely that the date of disposal will be the date of the order, so it will often be advisable to aim for this to be granted within the three-year period.

A more difficult problem may be to decide when that period began. Trial separations and failed reconciliations may confuse the issue, but it is suggested that while they are in progress, factual MR status should continue for both parties (unless a s. 222(5)(a) election was in force for another property – a most unwise course, see ¶904). It will be important to pinpoint the date of actual permanent separation and to diarise the expiry of the three-year limit.

¶904 Concession for inter-spouse transfers

(1) The terms

Extra-Statutory Concession D6 applies where one separated spouse (say, the husband) transfers his interest in the property to the other (in that case, the wife), *at any later time*, even after the TCGA 1992, s. 223(1) period, provided that the transferee has occupied it as her main residence throughout the intervening period. The effect is to deem the transferor to have continued in occupation during that period. However, it does not apply if he has elected to treat any other property as his MR in that period.

(2) Effects

This limitation will not matter in the simple case where one spouse (say, the husband) moves out of the property and into a new residence (owned or rented or possibly with relatives); he has only had one factual residence at a time, so there would be no need for a s. 222(5)(a) election, and even if he attempted to make one it would seem to be strictly incompetent (see ¶506). (Presumably if an election had been made in the mistaken belief that it was needed, and accepted in error, the concession could be claimed once the error had been demonstrated.)

Even if there has been no need for an election, because the quitting spouse has only one factual residence after the separation, under the Revenue's practice (see CGT 65358) he will not obtain PRR on that residence for periods during which PRR is running on the former matrimonial home by virtue of ESC D6. While not unreasonable in itself, this could usefully be made more explicit in the wording of the ESC. The Revenue could not insist on the ESC being applied if it was disadvantageous, as acknowledged in CGT 65375. That paragraph gives an example of how the gain on the matrimonial home is computed using the ESC. In practice, the husband in the example would have to consider whether he was likely to be selling his 'new' home in the near future, and whether the expected gain would be much larger than that on the matrimonial home. (Incidentally, this example treats the date of the court order as the date of disposal of the matrimonial home.)

(3) Practical value of the concession
If the inter-spouse transfer was made just prior to a sale by the 'remaining' spouse who would thereby cover all his or her gains by PRR, especially if there was some quid pro quo as to maintenance which enabled the transferor effectively to enjoy the gain, it is possible that the Revenue might deny ESC D6 on the grounds that it was being used for avoidance: see *R v HMIT, ex parte Fulford-Dobson* [1987] BTC 158. So if a sale is imminent the importance of a transfer within three years of separation is increased. If the concession is to be used the transfer should occur well in advance of any third party sale: the transferor will, of course, have to balance any loss of future equity appreciation against the immediate tax savings.

OTHER PLANNING POSSIBILITIES

¶905 Postponed sales and *Mesher* orders

(1) Nature of a *Mesher* order
Where there are minor children, the modern divorce law directs that their interests shall be the first consideration in any division of property (*Matrimonial Causes Act 1973*, s. 25(1)). In such cases the court may make a so-called *Mesher* order (see *Mesher v Mesher and Hall* [1980] 1 All ER 126), which has the effect of retaining the matrimonial home in the joint names of both spouses on a trust for sale for themselves in specified proportions, and postpones the sale of the house until the youngest child reaches a specified age.

It might be thought that for CGT purposes there was a significant disadvantage in agreeing to such an order for the departing spouse, because except for the 'final three years' relief, he would lose PRR for the period of non-occupation by him before sale; and although in theory he could use ESC D6, this might deprive any new home he had later bought of PRR (see ¶904(2)) for perhaps 15 to 20 years if the marriage ended when there were several young children.

(2) *Mesher* orders – the Revenue view
However, the Revenue views *Mesher* orders, or even binding agreements between the parties which have the same effect without a formal court order, as creating a settlement for CGT purposes (see CGT 65367). This opens up the way to relief under TCGA 1992, s. 225 for the 'gap' period between separation and eventual

sale, without prejudicing the PRR of the quitting spouse on a subsequently acquired home.

(3) Implications of the Revenue view
On this view, when the court order is made, both spouses make a disposal of their interests to the trustees of the settlement, who will presumably be themselves. This takes place at market value since, as settlors, they will both be connected with the trustees (s. 286(3)). Any gain made by the 'staying' spouse will rank for PRR in full assuming she has fulfilled the relevant conditions in s. 222. Any gain made by the 'quitting' spouse will also be exempt so long as the order is granted not more than three years after he moves out; but if this does not apply, it seems that ESC D6 (see ¶904) cannot strictly apply since he will not be disposing of his share to the other spouse, but to the trustees. However, the example of this situation in CGT 65376 extends the ESC to such a disposal – a view with which taxpayers are unlikely to argue.

When the youngest child reaches the specified age, the 'settlement' terminates and the spouses become absolutely entitled to the property as against themselves as trustees, so there is a deemed disposal and re-acquisition by them at current market value under s. 71(1). Presumably any taxable gain would be charged on the spouses as settlors, since they both have an interest in the settled property as defined in s. 77(3), if only by virtue of the fact that the proceeds of sale will revert to them; indeed, the wife (assuming that she remained in residence) would appear to have such an interest by virtue of her occupation rights in any event – see s. 77(3)(b). However, those rights are clearly enjoyed by her as a beneficiary under the terms of the settlement, so that to the extent to which the property has been her main residence since the settlement was created, any gain arising between that time and the termination of the order will be exempt under s. 225 (see ¶801). There may be a taxable gain if the property appreciates in value between the date of termination of the *Mesher* order and its sale, but this may be small enough to be covered by the parties' annual exemptions, and if the wife remains in occupation until sale, her share will be exempt in any event under s. 222 (1).

There is an example of the effect of this practice at CGT 65376. It should be noted that the husband in that example is said to have moved into rented accommodation after the separation, but in the writer's view if he was able to afford to buy a new home for his own occupation, PRR could run on this between 1988 and 1992, while the *Mesher* settlement was in operation.

¶906 Deferred charges
Alternative provisions ordered by the courts may include the transfer of the home to the 'staying' spouse but with the imposition of a charge on its sale proceeds at a specified future date, e.g. when the youngest child reaches 18, in favour of the

other spouse. The Revenue appears to regard this as a disposal by the latter of his interest in the property in return for a different asset in the form of the charge. On this view, the disposal of the interest in the home would appear to be treated in the same way as under a *Mesher* order (see ¶906(3)). When the charge is enforced and the absent spouse receives a capital sum, he appears to make a further disposal of the *chose-en-action* which it represents. If the charge is for a fixed amount, this would appear to be a simple debt for CGT purposes and no chargeable gain would arise (TCGA 1992, s. 251(1)). However, if it is for a variable sum (normally a percentage of the sale price), the position is much less clear; it may be that it can be argued that this is also the realisation of a simple debt and exempt under s. 251(1), but the Revenue (in correspondence with the writer) has argued that this is not the case and that a taxable gain would arise. Such a gain would not, of course, qualify for any PRR since it arises on an asset which is quite distinct from the dwelling-house (see *Marren (HMIT) v Ingles* (1980) 54 TC 76). The absent spouse would, on this view, lose the benefit of the final three years' 'ownership' which is available in arrangements of the type illustrated at ¶905.

¶907 Formal Trusts

A further alternative would be the creation of a formal trust under which the 'staying' spouse and any minor children were beneficiaries, with entitlement to occupy the home, as suggested at ¶903(3), with the object of ensuring that TCGA 1992, s. 225 relief is due on eventual sale. Thought will have to be given to the distribution of the proceeds of sale. However, in the light of the Revenue's view of the effect of a *Mesher* order (see ¶906(2) and (3)), this may be an unnecessary complication since that view seems to provide the benefit of s. 225 relief on sale without the attendant problems of deciding what is to happen to the trust fund after that event.

¶908 Overview

The Revenue's view of *Mesher* orders suggests that in many cases such an order is likely to prove the best solution to the problems of the absent spouse in CGT terms, though of course many other non-tax factors need to be considered. The uncertainties and possible tax costs inherent in deferred charges – especially variable charges – make them unattractive unless there are overriding non-tax advantages.

WHO OWNS THE MATRIMONIAL HOME?

¶909   How the difficulty may arise

If the home, when disposed of, is in the legal and beneficial ownership of only one of the parties, the other cannot strictly enjoy PRR since no part of the gain 'accrues' to him or her (see TCGA 1992, s. 222(1)). This problem may occur where (say) the husband had the home in his sole name, but moved out more than three years before a disposal to a third party (so that ESC D6 cannot apply), whereas the wife remained in occupation until sale. Are there any circumstances where it could be said that some of the gain 'accrued' to the wife so that she (as the occupier) could use PRR?

¶910   Possible arguments

By TCGA 1992, s. 2(1), it is the person to whom gains accrue who is chargeable to tax, and therefore apparently only that person can enjoy PRR. Further, only a disposal of a dwelling-house or an interest therein can attract the relief (s. 222(1)).

But suppose that the sale of the home is caused by an order of the court which directs that a capital sum from the sale be paid to the non-owning spouse (say the wife), under *Matrimonial Causes Act* 1973, s. 24, 25. The basis of such an order may be that the wife is considered to have a beneficial interest in the home. If the property was bought in the husband's sole name but with the help of funds from the wife, it may be that matrimonial law would regard the former as a trustee as to 50 per cent for the latter – see *Gissing v Gissing* [1971] AC 886. Arguably it follows that for CGT, the husband realises 50 per cent of the gains as a bare trustee within s. 60(1), and the wife should have a separate title to PRR as regards that portion by reference to her own circumstances and occupation, thus avoiding the loss of relief on part of the gain stemming from the husband's absence.

The apportionment of beneficial interests in such cases will be a matter for the court, which must make inferences as to the parties' intentions from their conduct and actual contributions (*Bernard v Josephs* [1982] Ch 391).

The position is less clear where the property was in the husband's sole name and he provided all or most of the purchase money (or mortgage deposit) but the wife helped to make mortgage payments or pay for repairs, or helped to keep the home going with her own labour. The House of Lords has held that it is 'at least extremely doubtful' whether anything less than direct contributions to the purchase price, whether initially or by sharing mortgage instalments, would suffice to support a claim to beneficial ownership (see *Lloyd's Bank plc v Rosset* [1991] 1 AC 107, per Lord Bridge).

It is also possible that substantial contributions in money or money's worth towards improvements to the home may confer or enlarge a beneficial interest, subject to any express or implied agreement to the contrary (see *Matrimonial Proceedings and Property Act* 1970, s. 37 and as to the meaning of 'substantial', *Re Nicholson* [1974] 2 All ER 386).

Finally, even if one spouse lacks any beneficial interest, he or she has certain occupation rights under the *Matrimonial Homes Act* 1983, s. 1(1): such rights could perhaps be seen as an 'interest' in a dwelling-house, a payment for extinguishing which could attract PRR. (The position for unmarried couples here may well be different, and legal advice will be needed.)

¶911 Important distinctions – interest in property or proceeds?

The Revenue is alive to such situations and its views are in CGT 65310–65319. Inspectors are advised to accept any agreement by the parties, or recognition by the court, of an equitable interest of up to 50 per cent without query unless there is obvious evidence to contradict it. There is an example of the resulting computation at CGT 65319 in which, on sale, the wife whose interest has been recognised is treated as if her payment is part of the sale proceeds and receives PRR accordingly.

However, the recognition of an equitable interest in the home needs to be distinguished from a court order which merely makes financial provision for a spouse out of the proceeds of sale (see CGT 65335). Here no equitable interest in the home has arisen and the computational effect is very different, as shown by the example at CGT 65377. It can be seen that the 'owning' spouse (Mr C in that example) suffers a severe disadvantage in that he can only retain two-thirds of the sale proceeds of the home, yet must pay CGT on 100 per cent of the gains after PRR. This, in the writer's view, is the correct arithmetical consequence if the legal analysis of the parties' position is correct; it can be compared with that of the taxpayer in *Burca v Parkinson (HMIT)* [2001] BTC 64, who was held to have owned 100 per cent of a holding of shares but subject to an obligation to pay away part of the proceeds of sale, and was unable to deduct the value of the shares whose proceeds he could not keep.

In divorce negotiations, therefore, in cases where the property is not in joint ownership, it should be borne in mind that a 'non-owning' spouse who received a capital sum derived directly from the sale of the matrimonial home might be able to argue the existence of an equitable interest in the property. This is likely to be much more advantageous to the 'owning' spouse where there is otherwise a large potential loss of PRR, but the interest will need to be agreed or established before the divorce is finalised to be effective for tax purposes. Those advising the 'owning' spouse, who will otherwise bear all the tax, may suggest that the possibility of a claim by the other spouse should be investigated.

10 Miscellaneous Problem Areas

PLANNING FOR LOSSES ON PRIVATE RESIDENCES

¶1001 The problem
Everyone hopes to make a gain on their home, but reality is sometimes otherwise. Where losses are likely to occur, it may be possible to turn some of the planning considerations discussed elsewhere in this text on their heads with the object of realising an allowable loss which can be set against the client's other gains (assuming these exist).

¶1002 Allowable losses
PRR operates by providing that a gain on a disposal which meets the relevant statutory conditions is not a chargeable gain (TCGA 1992, s. 223(1)). It follows, therefore, that since a loss will not be an allowable loss to the extent that a corresponding gain would not be chargeable (s. 16(2)), a loss on a property which qualifies for full PRR will not be allowable against gains on other assets. To realise an allowable loss it is therefore necessary to 'break the rules'.

¶1003 Some planning opportunities
Where significant taxable gains on other assets exist or are anticipated, it may be worthwhile to consider whether the rules which normally permit PRR can be broken to enable at least part of the loss on the dwelling-house to be allowed. Some of the possibilities in this area are set out below.

(1) 'Non-permitted' land as garden or grounds
Where there is a disposal of a large plot at a loss it will clearly be advantageous to restrict the 'permitted area' in TCGA 1992, s. 222(1)(b) to the basic 0.5 hectares. If the total plot exceeds this size it is clear that 0.5 hectares, including the site of the house, falls within the s. 222(1)(b) exemption and the relevant portion of the loss would not be allowable, unless there was non-domestic use or non-permitted absence (see (4) and (5) below). However, it appears that the taxpayer may then

quite properly decline to argue that a larger area is required for the reasonable enjoyment of the residence within s. 222(3), instead claiming an allowable loss on that area. Equally, though, there appears to be no reason why the inspector cannot ask the commissioners to rule that a larger area is 'required' under that subsection, applying objective criteria as suggested at ¶409; s. 222(3) is not activated solely on the taxpayer's motion. It would then be for the taxpayer to argue for a smaller area. The kind of arguments used by district valuers to restrict permitted areas (see ¶409(3), (8) and ¶411(2)) could then be deployed by the taxpayer.

(2) Reverse Varty v Lynes?
In periods when there is a decline in demand for residential building land, there may be cases where on the acquisition of a property (or at 31 March 1982 if acquired before that date) there was significant development or 'hope' value in part of the garden or grounds which has since declined or even disappeared. It might be possible to use the decision in *Varty (HMIT) v Lynes* (1976) 51 TC 419 in the taxpayer's favour in such cases (see ¶416).

Example
Victor acquired Grave Cottage, Slumpsville, in Year 1 for £400,000. It had a total plot of just less than 0.5 hectares. The vendor had obtained outline planning permission for four five bedroomed houses on the site and for the demolition of the cottage. However, the building company which had expressed interest in this development, Melldrew Estates Ltd, went into liquidation in Year 4 and no other developers have since shown any interest. The outline permission has now lapsed. Victor sells the whole plot to a residential purchaser in Year 6 for £350,000. The cottage has been his only residence throughout his ownership.

Victor has clearly realised a loss of £50,000 (before expenses of sale). A straightforward sale as described above would not permit any of this loss to be used against other gains. However, if he could arrange for the purchaser to acquire the house and necessary minimal access land before, and under a separate contract from, the balance of the garden, it would appear that he could insist on the application of the strict position regarding land sold after the sale of the house as established in *Varty (HMIT) v Lynes* – see Brightman J's illustration in that case (see ¶416(2) above). The present case, involving separate sales and development value (some of which may possibly remain in the form of 'hope' value) would seem to be 'caught' by the Revenue's interpretation of *Varty (HMIT) v Lynes* noted at ¶416(4). Thus, the value of the balance of the land at the date of acquisition would have to be established (reflecting its development value at that date) and that amount, plus indexation, would be set against the value on sale in Year 6. This should throw up an allowable loss. In practice, of course, the purchaser may be unwilling to run the risk of buying the house and access land only to find that he cannot acquire the remainder.

(3) Withdrawal of elections

An election to deem a property to be a main residence for PRR purposes can be varied by a further notice in respect of any period beginning not earlier than two years prior to the date of the further notice (s. 222(5)(a), and see ¶521). If it is likely that an elected MR will be sold at a loss, it might therefore be possible to withdraw the election in favour of another property, leaving the first property to produce an allowable loss. However, the scope for this is limited by the two-year time limit and the 'last 36 months' relief given by s. 223(1).

Example

Sangeeta has two homes, a country cottage which she inherited from her parents in Year 1, and a flat in London which she bought on 6 April in Year 5. At the time she was advised to make an election under s. 222(5)(a) in respect of the flat, because it was thought – wrongly as matters turned out – that this would grow substantially in value, and she did not envisage selling the cottage. The election was made with effect from the date of purchase of the flat. In Year 6, having recently been made redundant, she resolves to sell the flat, which stands at a loss (before indexation). Contracts are exchanged on 5 April in Year 7. Sangeeta gives the inspector a notice of variation of her election, effective from 6 April in Year 5, switching the election to her cottage. This has the effect of setting aside the election completely, as if it had never been made. Accordingly the flat, when sold, is not, and never was, her main residence and the loss is allowable against any other gains she has made in that or later tax years.

However, if Sangeeta had been unable to sell the flat within two years of the election being made, she would not have been able to invalidate its effect completely by the notice of variation, because of the two-year time limit. There would have been a period, however short, when it remained effective and in that period the flat would have been her deemed MR. If the disposal had produced a gain, it would have been at least partly exempt, because of the automatic relief for the final 36 months of ownership afforded by s. 223(1) and (2) where some PRR is due under s. 222. To the same extent that a gain would have been exempt under these rules, the loss actually made would not be allowable.

(4) Non-permitted absences

The rules about 'permitted absences' in s. 223(3) (see ¶603–¶605) are relatively easy to break in one respect. The strict position is that in order for any of these periods of absence from the residence to be ignored and effectively treated as a period of presence, there must be a time both before and after the absence when the property was the main residence (see ¶606). Thus, if it is known that a sale is imminent and a loss will result, the taxpayer may simply fail to re-occupy the property at all before sale. If a gain had occurred, this would have had the effect of denying PRR for the entire absence period; it follows that an equivalent part of the loss is allowable.

The concession which applies where re-occupation is impossible because of an employer's requirements (see ¶606(3)) cannot, in the writer's view, affect the matter in this case. A concession cannot be forced on the taxpayer by the Revenue if it is not to his advantage. In this case he would simply insist on being treated in accordance with the strict legal position.

(5) Business use

Exclusive business use of part of the property denies PRR to the extent and for the duration of that use. Thus, where losses arise such use may make them partly allowable (see ¶707(6)). In the most extreme case, turning the entire property into business premises prior to sale might enable the owner to claim that what he sold was not a dwelling-house at all, thus enabling the entire loss to be used. There are obvious practical problems about this, however, and in most cases business use is likely to help only with a fraction of any overall loss.

(6) Intention to realise a gain

Finally, an owner who in fact realises a loss might attempt to argue that his intention when acquiring the property, or more likely when making certain improvements, was to realise a gain on eventual disposal; so that when events turn out precisely opposite, his loss is allowed because, had he made a gain, it would have been taxable (wholly or partly) under s. 224(3).

This ingenious argument failed, on the facts, before the special commissioners in *Jones v Wilcock* (1996) Sp C 389, when it was held that the taxpayer's intentions had simply been to buy himself and his wife a home and nothing more. Anyone tempted to use this argument would be handicapped if, like the taxpayer in that case, he had no record of expenditure on improvements and could not show that he had a plan to minimise costs and maximise profits.

RE-BASING OF CGT-ELECTIONS UNDER s. 35(5) AND THE PRIVATE RESIDENCE

¶1004 Whether to elect

Section 35(5) of TCGA 1992 allows a taxpayer to elect that the CGT base cost, on a disposal after 5 April 1988, of all his assets held at 31 March 1982, shall be their value at that date, thus avoiding the usual comparison with gains using 1982 values and historical cost.

The decision to elect for wholesale re-basing of one's assets under this provision is unlikely to be much influenced by the private residence unless there is more than one such property. In almost all such cases, taking 31 March 1982 value, plus indexation allowance, as the base cost is almost always likely to yield a smaller gain than taking historical cost. There are dangers in so electing where a significant part of one's assets is such that 31 March 1982 was a 'trough' in value compared both to historical cost and subsequent value: but in the residential field such cases are likely to be very rare, unless there were wholly local factors in operation at 31 March 1982, such as a temporary 'planning blight', which would have made properties in the area almost unsaleable (see the effect on the market in parts of Kent of the Channel Tunnel project in 1989/90).

¶1005 Effect on other assets

Since the election covers all the taxpayer's assets the totality of them must be considered: but it is also irrevocable (TCGA 1992, s. 35(6)).

This could cause problems, since although a secondary MR may never, in fact, produce a gain, other assets will be 'tainted' with compulsory re-basing if an election is made.

Example
Harold owns Whiteacre, a property in the suburbs of London which is his main residence, and Blackacre which is a holiday home. (No s. 222(5)(a) election was made and is now out of time.) He inherited a silver tea service in 1980 worth £6,000; at 31 March 1982 it was worth £8,000. He also has a portfolio of engineering shares, for which 31 March 1982 happens to have been the bottom of a 'trough' in value: the shares cost £20,000 in 1980, but they were worth £5,000 in 1982. They are now worth £300,000. In 1988 Harold sold the silver tea service for £11,000. Since he thought that he would sell Blackacre eventually and it was then worth £150,000 as against a historic cost of only £25,000 while its 31 March 1982 value was £60,000 (Harold had improved it considerably before 1982) he decided to make a s. 35(5) election. He is now advised to retire to the countryside for health reasons.

The sale of Whiteacre will of course be covered by PRR but if Harold makes Blackacre his only residence and keeps it until death, he will never realise a gain from it, yet on a disposal of his shares the election will still apply: a sale now would yield a gain of £295,000 (before taper relief) whereas if he had never elected the gain would have been only £280,000 (being smaller than the 're-based' gain, see s. 35(3)(a)).

¶1005

The implication of the above is that care should be taken, in considering whether to elect under these rules, to calculate the likely effect on the sale of other assets if the secondary residence is never sold.

¶1006 Time limit

Under TCGA 1992, s. 35(6), the re-basing election has to be made within two years of the end of the tax year in which the first post-5 April 1988 disposal of an asset held at 31 March 1982 occurs.

On a strict interpretation, the time limit could be triggered by a disposal after 5 April 1988 of an asset held at 31 March 1982 which happened to be a private residence, even if it was wholly covered by PRR. SP 4/92, para. 6, largely removed that fear though its limitations should be noted.

PROPERTY OVERSEAS

¶1007 No territorial limitation to PRR

There is no territorial limitation to PRR and, in principle, an overseas property could attract the relief. In practice, it is only likely to do so where the owner has lived abroad for a significant period and comes to the UK permanently (so as to be ordinarily resident here) prior to the disposal. If the latter event occurs within three years of the owner's leaving the foreign property, having previously lived there continuously since purchase, the whole gain will, in principle, be exempt by TCGA 1992, s. 223(1) exactly as it would have been had the property been in the UK. (For those domiciled overseas the point cannot arise unless the proceeds of sale are remitted to the UK – see s. 12(1) – so returning UK expatriates are those most likely to be affected here.)

¶1008 Double taxation relief

If the owner in this kind of case remains taxable in the state where the property is situated, such tax will be lost for tax credit relief purposes to the extent that PRR is due in the UK (ICTA 1988, s. 796, applied to CGT by TCGA 1992, s. 277).

¶1009 Practical difficulties

(1) Valuation

If a valuation of an overseas property is needed (e.g. to obtain a 31 March 1982 or probate value where PRR is not fully due), the district valuer has no jurisdiction.

Miscellaneous Problem Areas

For the Revenue's practice, see CGT 75800–75820. In some cases the taxpayer's 31 March 1982 valuation may be accepted (apparently where the sale proceeds are less than £100,000) but in other cases it may instruct local valuers itself through the local British Embassy or High Commission. In the event of an appeal as to the valuation, it seems that the general or special commissioners would have to decide it; the lands tribunal has no jurisdiction (TMA 1970, s. 46D).

(2) 'Permitted area' or 'reasonable enjoyment' cases
Similar problems will arise in such cases, and the need for good plans and photographs (or even videos?) is even more pressing than where the land is in the UK (see ¶323(4) and ¶412(7)).

(3) *Force majeure* **and related issues**
If the owner is forced to leave a foreign property, e.g. because of political upheavals, there are no special provisions in TCGA 1992, s. 223(3) to assist in covering the resulting absence. If he cannot use the concession about re-occupation (see ¶606(3)) or has exceeded the time limits in that subsection by the date of sale, it seems that a specific Revenue concession is his only hope.

If the property is expropriated by a foreign power, he may not strictly make a disposal at all, but the Revenue seems to regard this as a disposal in some cases (see the old CGT 8 booklet, para. 108). It might be advisable to claim this treatment before the permitted period in s. 223(3)(b) expires if the concession in ¶606(3) can be used. However, the receipt of compensation later might be a separate disposal in itself, not covered by PRR (see *Davenport (HMIT) v Chilver* [1983] BTC 223), but here see ¶1017 regarding the *Zim* concession). If a sale has occurred but the foreign power blocks the proceeds there is a specific deferral relief in s. 279.

¶1010 Effect of foreign law

Sometimes problems may arise over foreign legal concepts which differ from those of the UK, for instance in TCGA 1992, s. 225 cases or over the question of an 'interest' in a residence (see ¶309). For example, if a non-UK resident trust governed by foreign law is the owner and s. 86 and 87 are in point, is the occupant 'entitled to occupy' in terms of the relevant foreign law? In such cases normal principles are likely to apply, as illustrated in cases such as *Dreyfus v IR Commrs* (1929) 14 TC 560; the right course will be to ask (1) what is the nature of the interest, etc., under the relevant law, (2) does that interest correspond to the required interest in the UK legislation? Thus, a non-resident trust in a common law jurisdiction, e.g. Canada or Australia, would probably be capable of affording the necessary 'entitlement' within s. 225, but questions might well arise if occupation was by permission of the founder of, say, a Liechtenstein *anstalt*.

¶1011 Let property

There is also no territorial limitation in TCGA 1992, s. 223(4), which is capable of applying to residential letting of foreign property so long as s. 222 applies to some part of the gain. Even holiday lettings would be included, following the Court of Appeal's reasoning in *Owen v Elliott (HMIT)* [1990] BTC 323 (see ¶708(3)).

UK RESIDENTIAL PROPERTY OCCUPIED BY FOREIGN EXPATRIATES

¶1012 Conflict between CGT and IHT planning

Individuals domiciled outside the UK have often held their UK residences through companies incorporated abroad, so as to hold excluded property (the shares in the company concerned, registered abroad) for IHT purposes (IHTA 1984, s. 6(1)). Sometimes the price of securing IHT exemption on death could be the risk of CGT liability if the residence is sold earlier, so this conflict always needs to be kept in mind.

¶1013 Ownership by a non-resident trust

As indicated above (see ¶1010) there is no reason why TCGA 1992, s. 225 relief should not operate within a non-resident trust structure; but for IHT this will not make the house excluded property, since within a trust this status only applies to property situated abroad (see IHTA 1984, s. 48(3)). The IHT charge on death will not be avoided if the trust grants an interest in possession. In a discretionary trust, although there will be no charge on death, there will be 'ten year' and exit charges under IHTA 1984, Ch. III, Pt. III. In practice, insurance can be taken against the death charge in a life interest trust (assuming the occupier to be insurable at reasonable rates), and in a discretionary trust the maximum charge at present under the 'ten year' regime is at six per cent of the opening value, which could itself be reduced by borrowings against the house.

¶1014 Ownership by a non-UK resident company

Such a structure will not, of course, attract PRR. It has also long tended to attract a Revenue attack on the occupier on the footing that he is a 'shadow director' of the company, thus incurring possibly substantial Sch. E benefit charges under ICTA 1988, s. 145, 146. Following the decision of the House of Lords in *R v Dimsey* [2001] BTC 408 and *R v Allen* [2001] BTC 421, this argument seems soundly based provided that the individual is indeed a person in accordance with whose directions the directors are accustomed to act (see ICTA 1988, s. 168(8)); and the income tax cost of such a structure is likely to be prohibitive. For IHT purposes, however, such a structure will produce excluded property in the occupier's estate in the shape of shares registered abroad. The need to avoid the Sch. E charge will now tend to make such structures unpopular and IHT may instead be mitigated by insurance, if possible (see ¶1013).

LIFETIME GIFTS OF THE PRIVATE RESIDENCE

¶1015   Business assets

Since the abolition of general hold-over relief by FA 1989, s. 124, it is not possible to use the 'business asset' holdover relief in TCGA 1992, s. 165 to 'wash' a gain on a dwelling-house which has not ranked for PRR through a donee who occupies it as his main residence.

However, where there is partial business use for a trade carried on by the transferor, some hold-over relief could be possible through s. 165(2)(a). Simply arranging for a short period of such use by the transferor of a property which then becomes the donee's MR will achieve little, because Sch. 7, para. 6(1) will restrict the held-over gain to the 'business use' fraction, and the balance will crystallise on the gift. However, there may be at least two other possible strategies.

(1)   Agricultural property hold-over

The restriction in Sch. 7, para. 6(1) does not apply if the transferor could obtain agricultural property relief (APR) on the presumption that the gift was an immediately chargeable IHT transfer – see Sch. 7, para. 6(2). For this purpose it is immaterial whether the APR would have been at 100 per cent or 50 per cent of the IHT value. Thus, this rule seems to offer an opportunity to disregard earlier non-business use.

To qualify for APR, the value transferred must be wholly or partly attributable to agricultural property – (see IHTA 1984, s. 116(1)), and the Revenue accepts that hold-over relief is due on the whole gain even if only part of it is so attributable (see ICAEW Technical Release TR 759 para. 155). 'Agricultural property' includes 'such cottages ... and farmhouses ... as are of a character appropriate to the property' – see ibid. s. 115(2). No APR, and therefore no hold-over relief is due unless the property was occupied by the transferor throughout the two years before the transfer (ibid. s. 117(a)). This may be turned to advantage:

Example 1
Phil Archer, a working farmer, owns a cottage which he inherited in 1988 at a probate value of £40,000 with a sitting non-agricultural tenant. In 1999 the tenant died. A sale would attract CGT. Phil arranged for Ned, one of his farmworkers, to occupy the cottage for two years until 2001 when the value was £160,000. Ned then moved out, and Phil gave the cottage to his daughter, Shula, who used it as her only residence for a further year. It is sold in 2002 for £180,000.

Without Sch. 7, para. 6(2) the whole of the gain on the gift to Shula would be taxable except for two-tenths representing the business use fraction under para. 6(1) of ibid. But the two years' occupancy by Phil (in law) through Ned disapplies para. 6(1) and creates a claim to APR, thus enabling hold-over relief to be claimed on the full £120,000 gain from 1988 to 2001, and on her sale Shula will be entitled to PRR on that and her own additional £20,000 gain. (If Shula were herself employed on Phil's farm it would seem that she could herself have been the occupier from 1999 onwards, as a service tenant until 2001 and as owner thereafter.)

(2) A transfer via s. 162?
Hold-over relief is also still available on a gift of shares in a family trading company, by s. 165(2)(b)(ii). If a business is incorporated wholly in exchange for shares, s. 162 enables the gain on the assets up to that time to be rolled into the value of the shares, and for the CGT base cost of the assets to be uprated to current market value. A combination of these reliefs may be a further method of obtaining PRR which would not otherwise be due.

Example 2
Asif, in addition to his factual MR, also owns a secondary residence on which no PRR appears to be due. He also runs a building business which he is thinking of incorporating, since a large contract is in the offing and the customer prefers to deal with a company. He brings the secondary house into his balance sheet and uses it as office accommodation for a reasonable period. He then sets up Newco Ltd, and transfers his entire business and assets, including the house, to Newco in exchange for shares. Section 162 applies so the latent gain on the house is rolled into the cost of Asif's shares. Newco continues to use the house in the same way. Some time later, Asif makes a suitable gift of Newco shares to his children, and at the same time the company sells the house on the open market.

The gain on the gift of shares – representing the value of the house – can be held-over by s. 165(2)(b)(ii). The 'non-business asset' restriction in those rules (Sch. 7, para. 7) does not apply, since the company used the house wholly for business throughout its ownership (Asif's use of it during *his* ownership is irrelevant) – see ibid. para. 7(3)(a). The base cost of the house in Newco is its market value at the time of incorporation and gains between its original cost and this figure effectively pass into the Newco shares. Any further gain on the property is taxed, eventually, in Newco at corporation tax rates.

The deferred gains will eventually emerge on a taxable disposal of the shares. It has been assumed here that Asif wanted to involve his children in the business and the gift would have been made in any event. But if Asif did not wish to do this (or had no children) he could simply retain his shares, and the gain would be washed out on his death. In practice, of course, care would be needed to ensure that the sale of the house was not pre-ordained when Newco was set up, and that the business use was real and substantial.

¶1016 Gifts to discretionary trusts

These still qualify for hold-over relief by TCGA 1992, s. 260, since they will be immediately chargeable for IHT. This opens up the possibility of a gift of a dwelling-house which has not qualified for PRR to such a trust, with hold-over relief, followed by 'entitled occupation' within s. 225 so that all gains rank for relief under that section on sale (see the example at ¶811). Depending on the figures and the donor's previous history of gifts this may have no immediate IHT cost.

THE ZIM PROBLEM AND PRIVATE RESIDENCES

¶1017 The problem

In *Zim Properties Ltd v Procter (HMIT)* [1985] BTC 42, it was held that a capital sum from an out-of-court settlement gave rise to a disposal by the recipient in its own right, and was not a part disposal of the asset which gave rise to the dispute (in that case an investment property). So the whole proceeds were consideration for a disposal within TCGA 1992, s. 22(1)(a). In such cases today, by virtue of s. 17(2)(a), there will now be no base cost or indexation relief to set against the consideration and it will be wholly taxable. In principle this could apply to disputes involving dwelling-houses.

¶1018 The concession

In ESC D33 the Revenue attempted to deal, inter alia, with some problems arising from *Zim* where the underlying asset would be exempt on disposal, including a

186 *Capital Gains Tax and the Private Residence*

private residence. The view taken was that in such cases the compensation would be treated as itself exempt, and the same would apply if there was no underlying asset.

¶1019 Implications for PRR

There is some doubt as to exactly how far this concession can be taken. A simple case might involve legal action by a private individual against an estate agent for damages arising out of the sale of his only residence, perhaps where it was alleged that the agent failed to obtain the best price. Since the disposal of the house attracted PRR, any compensation would also be exempt under the terms of the concession.

But what would be the position if the dispute arose out of an acquisition, e.g. a claim against a surveyor for negligent advice leading to a bad bargain for the purchaser of a private residence? There would be no problem if the purchaser occupied the house as his only residence throughout his ownership so that his eventual sale attracted PRR. But if it did not wholly qualify, e.g. because of absences outside TCGA 1992, s. 223(3) or exclusive business use of part, could part of the compensation later be taxed on sale? If the concession did not apply, there would have been a disposal at the time of the receipt of the payment (see s. 22(2)), but by the time the partially taxable nature of the asset emerged, the normal time limit for assessment might have expired.

The converse situation where the property so acquired is not the owner's residence on acquisition, but becomes such later, of course works against the taxpayer. If he was taxed on receipt of the compensation on the strict *Zim* basis, could he claim to re-open his liability later on the grounds that some of the tax should be repaid since the asset partially qualified for PRR (again he might be out of time)?

If the recipient of compensation never acquires the asset, e.g. where he is unsuccessful in his attempts to buy a house, and claims against his solicitor for delays which allegedly cost him the deal, is it exempt on the grounds that there was no underlying asset? In strictness there was such an asset, but the claimant never owned it!

The Revenue's practice here is unclear, but the writer would suggest that a robust view should be taken, applying the concession to the facts at the time of the receipt and not attaching the funds to an asset if the recipient never acquired that asset. Nevertheless, it seems unsatisfactory that such a complex matter is not clearly dealt with by statute.

It is always open to the taxpayer to claim the strict *Zim* basis if it is to his advantage: for instance where unrecovered costs were so heavy that he incurred a loss. The point of *Zim*, of course, in a private residence case would be that such a loss would be allowable against other gains, even though a loss on the residence itself would not be allowable (see ¶202).

¶1020 Shares of profits on sales by relocation agencies

Extra-Statutory Concession D37 applies where a relocated employee sells his house to a relocation agency on terms that he is entitled to a share in any profit when the agency resells the house. Any such profit share is regarded as attracting PRR to the same extent as the gain made by the employee on his own sale, provided that the 'right' is not held by the employee for more than three years.

The Revenue's view (CGT 14970 and 64611) is that for CGT purposes a right to share in profits in these circumstances is a separate asset from the house itself, and following *Zim*, the strict position would be that it is taxable in full (subject to taper relief) since it would have no base cost. The recognition in the concession that a *partly* exempt gain on the employee's own sale should result in a corresponding partial exemption on the profit share, might suggest that similar treatment should be applied to the receipt of compensation or damages in relation to a partly exempt sale (see ¶1019). Whether this treatment would in fact be applied is unclear. See also ¶309 regarding an 'interest in' a dwelling-house.

It should be noted that this concession is limited to employees and office-holders (such as directors) and to someone who owns property jointly with such a person (such as a spouse). It also appears to be confined to 'arm's length arrangements' involving sales to relocation agencies and does not seem to apply where it is the *employer* who actually buys the property and allows the employee to share the profit.

OCCUPATION BY A DEPENDENT RELATIVE

¶1021 Transitional reliefs still in force

Although the relief for the disposal of a property occupied by a dependent relative was withdrawn for the future by FA 1988, s. 111, significant transitional reliefs remain in force (TCGA 1992, s. 226), and it is likely to be some years before the last disposal occurs to which they may apply. It is therefore necessary to deal briefly with the conditions for such relief and the circumstances in which it may still be claimed.

¶1022 The conditions

Section 226(1) of TCGA 1992 allows a form of PRR on the disposal of a dwelling-house which was, or had at any time in his ownership been, the *sole residence* of a dependent relative of the individual making the disposal (emphasis added). It is essential, however, that the property was the OMR of the relative at 5 April 1988, or at some earlier time in the vendor's period of ownership. The dwelling-house has to be provided rent-free and without any other consideration (though see ¶1023(2) as to the latter point). It is necessary to claim the relief (s. 226(2)) within six years of the end of the tax year of disposal.

Section 226(2) involves the assumption that the property was the only or main residence of the claimant in the period of factual residence by the relative; thus if the relative was not in occupation throughout the period of ownership, an apportionment is necessary under s. 223(2), and the 'permitted absences' (see ¶603) may be used by reference to the relative's circumstances. It follows that relief for the final three years of ownership is still available (see CGT 65671), provided that the property was the relative's residence at the specified dates.

Relief under s. 226 can be claimed in addition to any PRR to which the claimant is entitled in his own right (s. 226(2)). However, no more than one dwelling-house can qualify as the residence of a dependent relative at any one time (s. 226(4)). This may mean that if the claimant simultaneously owns houses occupied by several relatives, and claims relief on the first such house to be sold, any subsequent sales will qualify for, at best, only partial relief since they will be deemed not to qualify during the period in which the first property to be sold was occupied by the relative in question. Such appears to be the Revenue view, although it could be argued that the statute means merely that if more than one house is provided at the same time *by the same claimant for the same relative*, relief is due on only one of them – though in that case it is not clear how one would decide which house so qualified. On that view, a taxpayer could provide houses for several *different* relatives simultaneously and obtain relief on each of them. (See the arguments of Counsel for the Revenue in *Honour(HMIT) v Norris* [1992] BTC 153 (see ¶320(6)) as described by the taxpayer himself in his article in *British Tax Review* (1993) pp. 36–37.) The point remains untested, although the writer inclines towards the Revenue's apparent view as being most in tune with the indefinite article in the phrase 'the residence of a dependent relative', rather than, for instance, 'any particular dependent relative'.

If the point were to be tested and the legislation held to be ambiguous or productive of absurdities, application of the so-called '*Hansard* doctrine' from *Pepper v Hart (HMIT) and related appeals* HL [1992] 591; CA [1990] 552; ChD [1989] 595 would seem to support the Revenue's view. What is now s. 226 originated in a government amendment at Report Stage in the *Finance (No. 2) Bill* 1965. A backbench MP, Mr John Hall, had put down an amendment to provide relief for dependent relatives' residences in Committee. The Financial Secretary, Mr MacDermot, had accepted the spirit of Mr Hall's proposal, but not the detailed drafting. Undertaking to table a government amendment to the same effect at Report Stage, he said:

'I think some limitation needs to be put upon the [dependent relative] exemption. At the moment [as drafted by Mr Hall] it could apply to any number of houses. We think that probably it is right that this concession should be extended to *only one other house beyond the taxpayer's own home*.'

At Report Stage, speaking to the government amendment, he said:

'... as I suggested in Committee, *only one dependent relative's house can qualify at any one period of time*. We have framed the provision so that it could apply to *more than one house in sequence*, but only to one at any particular time'. (*Hansard* Vol. 715, col. 1004 and 1753, emphasis added.)

If the courts accepted this as a clear statement of the government's intention, the Revenue's view would seem to be correct.

A married couple can only claim in respect of one such property between them (s. 226(4)), and for years before 1996/97 the inspector was empowered to check that the giving of relief in respect of one spouse's relative did not deprive the other spouse of similar relief (see the former s. 226(5)). For later years, under self assessment, the taxpayer is expected to check compliance with this condition himself, subject to the Revenue's right to enquire into his return.

'Dependent relative' for this purpose is defined in s. 226(6): it means any relative (see ¶1023(3)) of the individual or of his or her spouse who is incapacitated by old age or infirmity from maintaining himself (s. 226(6)(a)), or (regardless of age or infirmity) the claimant's mother or mother-in-law if she is widowed or separated, or if her marriage ended in divorce or annulment (s. 226(6)(b)).

If the occupier did not meet the conditions for being a 'dependent relative' throughout their period of occupation, the relief would be time-apportioned under s. 222(10) to the period when they were met.

For help in applying the various tests for this relief see the flow chart on page 190.

¶1023 Interpretational problems

Section 226 of TCGA 1992 contains some problems of interpretation which may be briefly noted.

(1) Sole residence

Relief is due only where the property was the sole residence of the relative. There is no provision for the use of elections by the relative as between several properties. Thus the relief could be denied if the relative spent significant periods elsewhere, unless these were merely temporary trips, e.g. for holidays or for health reasons (see ¶503).

DEPENDENT RELATIVES' RESIDENCES

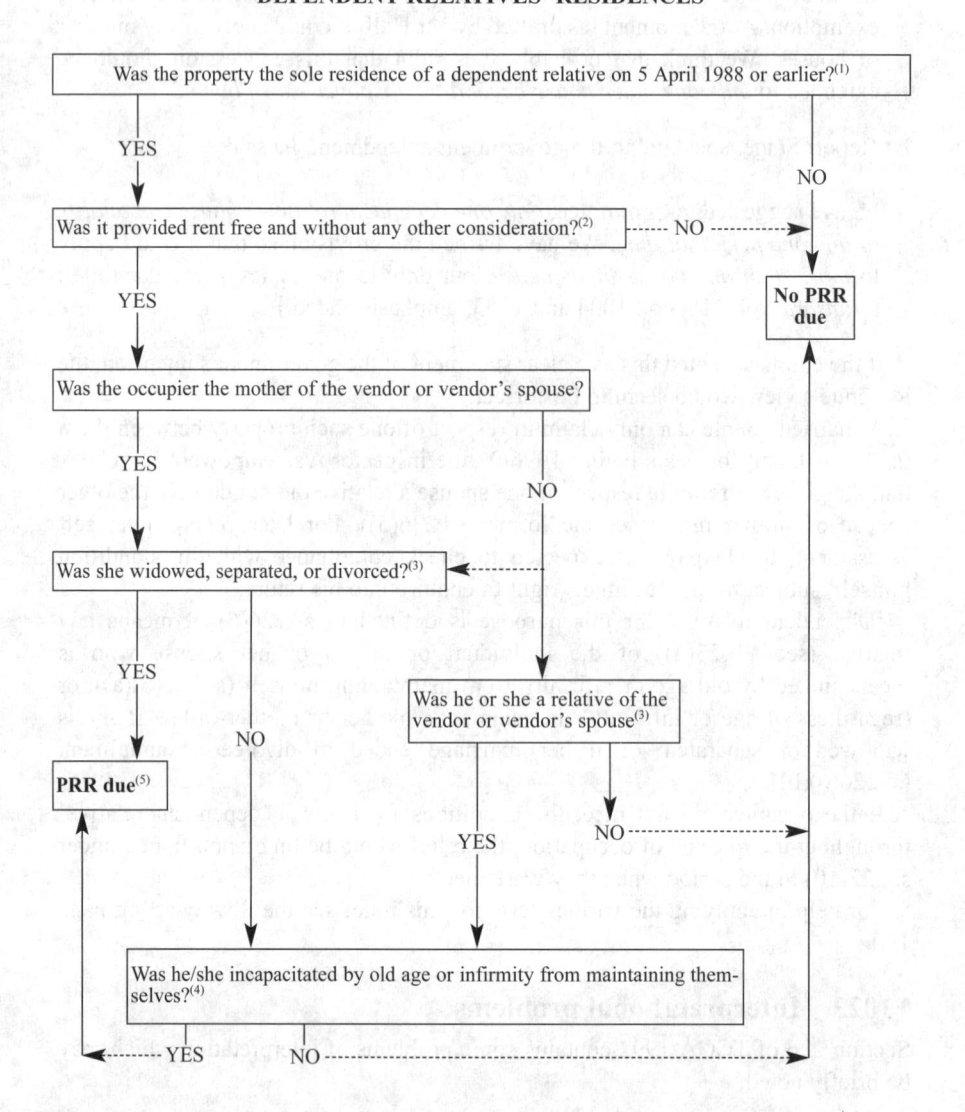

```
┌─────────────────────────────────────────────────────────────────────┐
│ Was the property the sole residence of a dependent relative on      │
│ 5 April 1988 or earlier?[1]                                         │
└─────────────────────────────────────────────────────────────────────┘
         │ YES                                          │ NO
         ▼                                              ▼
┌──────────────────────────────────────────┐      ┌──────────┐
│ Was it provided rent free and without    │─NO──▶│ No PRR   │
│ any other consideration?[2]              │      │ due      │
└──────────────────────────────────────────┘      └──────────┘
         │ YES                                          ▲
         ▼                                              │
┌──────────────────────────────────────────┐            │
│ Was the occupier the mother of the       │            │
│ vendor or vendor's spouse?               │            │
└──────────────────────────────────────────┘            │
         │ YES              │ NO                        │
         ▼                  ▼                           │
┌──────────────────────────┐                            │
│ Was she widowed,         │◀┄┄┄┄┄                      │
│ separated, or divorced?[3]│      ┆                    │
└──────────────────────────┘      ┆                    │
         │ YES         │ NO       ┆                    │
         ▼             │   ┌──────────────────────────┐ │
  ┌────────────┐       │   │ Was he or she a relative │ │
  │ PRR due[5] │       │   │ of the vendor or vendor's│ │
  └────────────┘       │   │ spouse[3]                │ │
         ▲             │   └──────────────────────────┘ │
         │             │       │ YES      │ NO ─────────┤
         │             ▼       ▼                        │
         │   ┌─────────────────────────────────────────┐│
         │   │ Was he/she incapacitated by old age or  ││
         │   │ infirmity from maintaining themselves?[4]││
         │   └─────────────────────────────────────────┘│
         └─────── YES ────────  NO ─────────────────────┘
```

Notes

(1) A different relative (as defined) may have occupied the house later without breaking this condition.
(2) For discussion of the meaning of this phrase see ¶1023(2) of this text.
(3) For interpretation see ¶1023(4) of this text.
(4) In practice over 65s qualify, regardless of health.
(5) PRR may have to be apportioned if the occupier did not fulfil the conditions throughout the period of occupation.

¶1023

Miscellaneous Problem Areas

(2) Rent-free and without any other consideration

In one respect, the Revenue in practice interprets this condition much less strictly than might be expected. By ESC D20, the relative can bear all or part of the occupier's council tax (see ¶1108) and repairs attributable to normal wear and tear, without infringing the condition (before 1990 the relative could bear the domestic rating charges, but the community charge ('Poll Tax') which was payable from 1990 to 1992 is ignored (see CGT 65615)). In fact, the maximum *financial* contribution which the relative can make is the amount which will ensure that the owner is not out of pocket taking one year with another; for this purpose a notional income calculation has to be performed by the owner under the rules of Sch. A, but also crediting any mortgage payments, whether capital or interest, which the relative makes either direct to the lender or via the owner. So long as this calculation does not produce a surplus in any year the relief is not endangered. A surplus in one particular year could, it seems, also be disregarded if 'taking one year with another' the owner was doing no more than breaking even; thus the relative might, for example, meet an exceptional repair bill in one year without necessarily infringing the condition. (Of course, if rent is charged and there is a surplus under the strict Sch. A rules, the owner may be liable to income tax in the normal way as well as losing the CGT relief on sale.) There are examples of this calculation at CGT 65616–65617.

However, any *non-financial* consideration might prejudice the owner's CGT relief, since the concessionary treatment described above applies only to 'payments in respect of the property'. An example of this situation might be where an elderly person made a gift of his house to a child on condition that he was allowed to live there rent-free for life. As well as being ineffective for IHT if made after 17 March 1986 (because it would be a gift with reservation, see IHTA 1984, s. 102) this appears to prevent the donee from claiming s. 226 relief on sale, since the donor's occupation is in consideration of the gift. Strictly, it appears that even the provision of services by the relative, such as agreeing to maintain the garden with his own labour, would deny the CGT relief if it was made in consideration for the right to occupy. It would thus seem to be advisable for such obligations to be covered by cash payments to third parties. These would then be taken into the notional calculation mentioned above and so long as they do not give rise to any net surplus to the owner, the CGT relief should not be lost.

(3) Some complications over 'consideration'

The requirement that the property must be 'provided rent free and without any other consideration' can, however, pose some further problems.

Example
Albert died in 1985, owning 100 per cent of his home. His Will left a 50 per cent share to his widow, Victoria, and 50 per cent to his son, Edward, who lives

¶1023

elsewhere. Victoria lives on in the home rent free until she dies in 2003. Her own Will leaves her share to Edward, who then sells the house. Can he claim s. 226 PRR on the half share he inherited from his father?

At first sight it seems that he could. Victoria occupied the whole house by virtue of her absolute ownership of a half share, but her son has not charged her rent for his half share.

However, inspectors may disagree. CGT 65628 suggests that if the true position is that the son would be unable to force a sale – because the court would be unlikely to grant an order for sale if his mother had nowhere else to live – he has not 'provided' anything. It argues that the word 'provided' implies some financial sacrifice beyond merely not charging rent – this would be sacrificing the chance to realise the value of the house until after the mother's death. If there is no such realistic chance, runs the Revenue's argument, there is no 'sacrifice' and no 'provision'.

This point is untested, but the writer believes that the Revenue's view should be resisted. The right reading of the Act is surely to read the phrase 'provided rent free and without other consideration' as a whole. On this reading 'provided' means something like 'made available as a residence', rather than implying some definable 'sacrifice' of the chance to sell. The 'other consideration' which the draftsman had in mind would surely be something passing from the mother in lieu of rent, such as an agreement that mother would pay all the running expenses. As noted above (¶1023(2)), even if she does, ESC D20 allows her to make a financial contribution to the running costs provided that the son does not make a profit taking one year with another. That concession would not be necessary if 'provided' meant 'foregoes the chance of forcing a sale'.

In any event, if Victoria does have enough resources to buy a home of her own, and especially if she actually has such a home (e.g. if she also inherited 100 per cent of a second home from Albert), it is arguable that even on the Revenue's view, the son has indeed 'sacrificed' something, since in those circumstances he might be able to obtain an order for sale of the former marital home, but has not attempted to do so.

Perhaps it is rather surprising, in view of this line of Revenue thinking, that in CGT 65645 there is an example where the relative and the child bought a home for the relative jointly before 6 April 1988 which the latter thereafter occupies rent free. Here it would seem to the writer that the child has literally 'provided' – in the 'sacrificial' sense favoured by the Revenue – some of the price, and the fact that the relative also did so does not, in the Revenue's view, prevent the relief being due on the child's share, even if the relative could have afforded to buy the house without assistance.

¶1023

Another surprising feature, though it is not a view which taxpayers would want to dispute, is the Revenue's view that a loss on a dependant's home is an allowable loss, since the s. 226 relief (unlike the main s. 222 relief for one's own home) requires a claim (s. 226(2)); the official view is that if there is no gain there will be no claim, and thus no reason for the loss to be disallowed because a gain in such a case, in the absence of a claim, would not be exempt (see CGT 65084). The writer finds this somewhat lacking in logic.

(4) Meaning of 'dependent relative'

'Relative' in s. 226(6)(a) is not defined. For the Revenue's quite generous interpretation, see CGT65574, which brings in blood relations and their spouses, the blood relations of the owner's spouse, and certain others. This would appear to include, for example, uncles, aunts, nephews and nieces, who are excluded from the narrower specific definitions for other purposes such as ICTA, s. 417(4).

In practice, the Revenue accept that a relative who is over 65 is 'incapacitated by old age' whatever his or her state of physical or financial health, as may be certain people over 55 who lack the capacity to work again in their industry. The latter rather oddly worded practice would seem to include, for example, redundant miners or steel workers in areas where the relevant industries have closed down, but not someone made redundant due to a general recession, or who has simply chosen to retire early (see CGT 65575–65576). 'Infirmity' is interpreted in its physical or mental sense, and not as equivalent to 'incapacity' in the legal sense; thus a relative under 65 (not qualifying for the 'redundancy' practice for over 55s) must be unable to support themselves because of illness or physical disability (CGT 65577). But minor children are not regarded as dependent relatives even if they happen to be infirm (CGT 65578). In the writer's view, this is probably right, since s. 226(6)(a) refers to someone who is prevented by infirmity from maintaining himself, and this would seem inapplicable to a child of school age, at least, who would be so prevented even if not infirm. Clearly, the Revenue is aware that interesting avoidance possibilities might have otherwise opened up, at least until 6 April 2004; after that, nobody still under 16 could have been in occupation at 5 April 1988 (see ¶1024 below).

The second leg of qualification, in s. 226(6)(b), is overtly sexist – there is no relief for a property occupied by the claimant's lone *father* if he is not 'incapacitated' within s. 226(6)(a) – and apparently fails to cater for a mother who never married, although in practice the surviving female partner of a relationship seems to be treated as a 'widowed mother' in relation to provision by a child of that relationship (see CGT 65582). A stepmother of the owner or owner's spouse, however, is not regarded as qualifying under this leg, but is a 'relative', and may thus come within the 'incapacity' test on the facts (CGT 65581). It is possible that some of these distinctions, both statutory and administrative, could be vulnerable to challenge under the *Human Rights Act* 1998.

¶1023

¶1024 Withdrawal of relief and the transitional rules

(1) General abolition

By FA 1988, s. 111(1), the relief in what is now TCGA 1992, s. 226 does not, in general, apply to disposals after 5 April 1988. At the same time, the former personal allowance for dependent relatives (ICTA 1988, s. 263) and the former mortgage interest relief for properties occupied by them (ICTA 1988, s. 355(3)) were also abolished.

(2) Where s. 226 relief may still apply

Section 226 relief will, however, still be available for a disposal after 5 April 1988 – subject to all the conditions in that section (see ¶1022) – if the relative in question was occupying the property as his sole residence (see ¶1023(1)) on that date, or at any earlier time in the owner's period of ownership (FA 1988, s. 111(2)). In a simple case, therefore, where the relative was living in the property at 5 April 1988 and remains there until it is sold or until a date not more than three years prior to sale there should be no loss of s. 226 relief, regardless of how long the relative remains in occupation.

The reference to 'any earlier time' in the period of ownership should mean that even if the relative ceased to occupy the property before 5 April 1988, some relief will still be available on sale, whenever this occurs.

Example

Frances bought a house for her father, aged 75 and crippled with arthritis, on 6 April 1983. He lived there as his sole residence, rent-free and without other consideration, until he died on 4 April 1988. Frances let the house until it was sold on 1 June 2002.

Since Frances's father was in occupation at a time earlier than 5 April 1988 it appears that the sale will still attract some s. 226 relief (which must be claimed by 31 January 2009 (see TMA 1970, s. 43(1)). Relief will be available for the actual period of occupation (6 April 1983 to 4 April 1988) plus the last three years of ownership (2 June 1999 to 1 June 2002), but in the Revenue's view, there can be no relief for the let period under the special rules in s. 223(4) (see ¶708), because this is only available to a gain which attracts some relief under s. 222 (see CGT 65562). A bold taxpayer might challenge this view by arguing that s. 226(2) grants 'such relief *as would be given under s. 222 to 224*' (emphasis added) if the property had been the owner's residence. It could be argued that this formulation also imports the relief under s. 223(4).

Frances could, however, consider moving into the house herself (making any necessary s. 222(5) election) for a period (cf the Example at ¶1025 below), in which case she would seem to have an indisputable claim for s. 223(4) relief as well as for her own period of residence.

However, note that where there was no occupation by a qualifying relative after 31 March 1982, it appears that no relief would be due on a post-5 April 1988 sale, because of the re-basing rule in s. 223(7) (see ¶618). This seems to follow because s. 226(2) explicitly imports s. 222–224 into the calculation of the relief. In such a case, it would appear that if, after 31 March 1982 but before 6 April 1988, occupation was resumed by the same or a different qualifying relative, some relief would be available. This interpretation seems to be supported by the Revenue's views at CGT 65671–65674.

(3) Events terminating the transitional relief

Transitional s. 226 relief stops when the property ceases to be the sole residence of the relative (or last such relative if there was more than one) who was in occupation before 6 April 1988 – subject to any relief for the final three years, as in the example at ¶1024(2)). It would also appear to terminate if any of the other conditions of s. 226 is breached, e.g. if the relative starts to pay rent beyond the terms of ESC D20 (see ¶1023(2)).

When sole residence status ceases will be a question of fact; cessation will not apparently occur until it is clear that there is no possibility of the relative returning to the property as a resident. The Revenue has said (see ICAEW Technical Release No. 739, para. 65) that residential status would not be lost simply because the relative goes into hospital for a temporary stay; in any event the relief for the final three years of ownership would normally obviate any problems here. If it is clear that the relative will not return, e.g. if he goes into an old people's home and sells most of his furniture, it seems that the relief will stop when he moves out. In such cases, therefore, the owner should ensure that he sells the property within three years to avoid any loss of relief.

The legislation makes it clear that once residential status is lost, any subsequent period of residence beginning after 5 April 1988, by the same or a different relative, will not confer additional s. 226 relief (s. 226(3), and see the example at CGT 65681). If a relative who was in occupation before 6 April 1988 spends substantial periods away from the property after that date, care should be taken, if practicable, to demonstrate that he has not given it up as his residence (see here the discussion at ¶504).

It is also clear that if the residence of a relative who was in occupation at 5 April 1988 is sold, with s. 226 relief applying to the gain, and the relative is then re-housed in another house owned by the claimant, no additional relief can be claimed under s. 226 on the sale of the second house; it is only the house in which the relative resided on 5 April 1988 or earlier which can so qualify (see CGT65674). However, this need cause little practical difficulty if the second house can be held

¶1024

in a suitable form of trust under which the relative has occupation rights, so that relief under s. 225 can operate in due course (see ¶801ff.).

¶1025 Combination of s. 226 relief and conventional PRR

It may be possible under both the old and transitional rules for TCGA 1992, s. 226 relief, to combine this relief with conventional PRR under s. 222.

Example

Norman bought a cottage for his elderly parents in 1983. His father lived there until he died in 1986 and his mother continued to live there until, in 2002, she became too infirm to look after herself and went into a nursing home as a permanent resident. In 2003 Norman sells his own residence and moves into the cottage.

Assuming that the Revenue accepts that Norman's parents were incapacitated within s. 226(6)(a), under the old and transitional s. 226 rules, the period from 1983 to 2002 qualifies for s. 226 relief. The period from 2003 to any eventual sale will qualify for PRR under the normal rules since the cottage is now Norman's only residence. There would be a loss of relief (possibly small) for the gap between 2002 and 2003, though Norman could eliminate even that problem if he started to use the cottage as an occasional residence as soon as his mother moved out and made an election in its favour under s. 222(5)(a) within two years (see ¶506). This would not, of course, have any adverse effect on his former home as long as that property was sold within three years of the effective date of the election.

If a property which has ceased to qualify for s. 226 relief cannot be used as a home by the owner, it may be possible to gift it to a discretionary trust under which it will be occupied by a younger relative, such as an adult child, as the latter's main residence, so that hold-over relief can be claimed on the gift and s. 225 relief will apply to any subsequent sale by the trustees – for the details see the example at ¶811.

COMPULSORY PURCHASE AND PRIVATE RESIDENCES

¶1026 The general deferral relief

There is a form of deferral relief from CGT where, after 5 April 1982, a taxpayer sells land to an authority possessing compulsory purchase powers (such as a local authority and certain government departments). Broadly, any gain realised on the disposal to the authority is deducted from the CGT base cost of new land which the taxpayer acquires with the full proceeds of the sale, and the disposal to the authority is treated as a 'no gain/no loss' event. In contrast to roll-over relief for business assets there is no time limit for reinvestment. It is, however, essential that the taxpayer (called 'the landowner' in the legislation) did not take any steps of any kind to dispose of the old land or make known to anyone, including the authority, his willingness to do so (TCGA 1992, s. 247).

¶1027 Restriction where new asset is a dwelling-house

However, this deferral relief may be denied where the replacement asset is a dwelling-house or part of a dwelling-house, or an interest therein (TCGA 1992, s. 248(1)(a)). In certain circumstances such a house will not qualify as an asset into which the gain on compulsory purchase can be 'rolled' under s. 247.

The circumstances which will operate to deny relief under s. 247 involve examining the history of the dwelling-house in the six calendar years beginning with the date of its acquisition. If, in that time, a disposal of the house by the landowner would give rise to *any* relief under s. 222–226, the deferral relief under s. 247 is not due and the gain on the land acquired by the authority becomes taxable in the normal way in the year of disposal (s. 248(1)(b)). If the circumstances of the house on its acquisition by the landowner are such that no PRR would be due, but at some time in the six-year period they change so that PRR becomes potentially due, the previously deferred gain can be assessed to CGT even though normal assessing time limits may have expired (s. 248(2)). In some cases a provisional claim can be made pending re-investment of the consideration (see s. 247A).

Example
Edgar is a farmer who is required by the Department of Transport to sell several fields which are needed for a new by-pass. He has not advertised the land previously or indicated his willingness to sell. The disposal takes place on 5 April 2003 for £100,000 giving him a gain (after indexation but before taper relief) of £75,000.

Edgar decides to spend this money (in addition to other funds which he has available) in buying a bungalow on a small plot of land adjoining the farm. The total expenditure on this is £200,000 and he exchanges contracts on 1 September 2003.

If Edgar immediately moves into the bungalow and uses it as his main or only residence, he will not be able to claim deferral relief at all under s. 247, because clearly he has used his compensation moneys to acquire a dwelling-house which, if he sold it at any time in the period from 1 September 2003 to 31 August 2009, would attract at least some PRR. His gain of £75,000, but with any applicable taper relief down to the date of disposal, on the farmland will therefore be taxable in 2003/04 in the normal way.

However, if on completion of the purchase of the bungalow, he uses it to house, say, one of his farmworkers, this does not infringe s. 248(1) because no PRR would be due if he sold it when so occupied. If that state of affairs continues until 31 August 2009 (or until an earlier sale) there will be no CGT liability on the sale of the farmland in 2003/04. Instead, when he sells the bungalow, its CGT base cost will be reduced by the untapered gain of £75,000 which was deferred in that year.

What is the position if Edgar uses the bungalow to house a farmworker initially, but the worker moves out in, say, April 2005? This is within the six-year period mentioned above and Edgar must be careful about the use of the bungalow if he is to avoid the re-opening of his liability for 2003/04 on the sale of the farmland. If, in the period from April 2005 to 31 August 2009, he has his only residence there, or his main residence (in fact or by election under s. 222(5)(a)), the inspector can issue a CGT assessment for 2003/04 on the gain of £75,000 less taper relief down to the actual disposal date of the farmland. This will apply even if the residential use starts on, say, 1 May 2009, by which time the six-year time limit for an assessment for 2003/04 (TMA 1970, s. 34) will have expired.

¶1028 Traps and problems

Several points arise on the detailed wording of TCGA 1992, s. 248 which could cause problems and unexpected liabilities.

(1) The deferral relief could be denied if the replacement asset is a dwelling-house (as to the meaning of which see ¶301) or part of such a house. Thus it seems that the expenditure of sums received as consideration for a compulsory purchase on some types of staff accommodation which are part of the same domestic entity as an existing house (see ¶315) could entail denial of s. 247 relief.

(2) The same effect could apply if the consideration was applied in purchasing an *interest* in a dwelling-house; so the acquisition of a leasehold interest at a premium would also need to be tested to see whether the landowner's interest qualified for any form of PRR within the six years from acquisition.

(3) However, s. 248(1)(a) refers only to the acquisition of a dwelling-house or part thereof. If the consideration was applied in acquiring, say, additional *land* to form part of the garden or grounds of an existing house occupied as a private residence, this would not seem to prejudice the deferral relief. Such land cannot be said to be a dwelling-house or part thereof (see the contrasting wording of s. 222(1)(a) and (b)), yet for s. 247 purposes it would

Miscellaneous Problem Areas

seem to be 'other land' into which the gain on the earlier sale could be 'rolled' (see s. 247(1)(c)). This raises interesting possibilities; a gain on compulsory purchase could be 'rolled' into the acquisition of such garden land, but the eventual sale of that land – especially if the total plot thus formed was less than 0.5 hectares and was sold with the house – could qualify for PRR under s. 222(1)(b) if the whole area sold was within the 'permitted area' on sale (see ¶408). Thus the 'deferred' gain would actually be 'washed' out of the CGT net.

(4) The deferral relief is denied if *any part* of the gain on the dwelling-house could attract PRR; thus even a fairly brief period of residential occupation, sufficient to attract PRR for up to the final 36 months of ownership, would involve forfeiture of s. 247 relief (as in the example in ¶1027 if Edgar occupied the bungalow from 1 May 2009.)

(5) *Any form* of PRR which would be available on a sale by the landowner in the six years following acquisition of the dwelling-house entails loss of s. 247 relief. Thus, the relief could be lost not only where an individual occupied the house as his only residence (as in the example at ¶1027) but also:

(a) where the replacement asset is, at any time in the six-year period, an *elected* main residence under s. 222(5)(a);

(b) where the replacement asset is a house which qualifies for PRR under s. 222(8) because the owner resides elsewhere in 'job-related' accommodation (see ¶610);

(c) where the 'landowners' are trustees and they allow a beneficiary to occupy the replacement asset so that relief under s. 225 would be due (see ¶801); or

(d) where the relief for occupation by a dependent relative would still be due (see ¶1021).

(6) If the land compulsorily purchased was *itself* the landowner's former private residence, there may have been full PRR on that disposal; if so, of course, s. 247 relief will not be necessary and s. 248 will not be relevant. However, if part of the gain on the compulsory sale of the former residence was taxable (e.g. because of non-exempt absences) s. 247 could apply, and s. 248 will then have to be considered.

¶1028

IMPLICATIONS OF PRR FOR COMPLETION OF TAX RETURNS

¶1029 Practical problems

As mentioned briefly at ¶20l, the PRR legislation does not strictly require a claim or impose a time limit. There are, however, some practical problems concerning tax compliance which accountants and others completing tax returns need to bear in mind.

¶1030 Suggested entries on returns

The relief in strict law applies automatically if the various statutory conditions are met. Under self assessment from 1996/97, the taxpayer is responsible for applying these conditions to the facts of his case and deciding whether PRR is due, and if so, how much, subject to the Revenue's powers of enquiry. (Thus the former power of an inspector to determine which of two or more factual residences was the MR in the absence of an election under TCGA 1992, s. 222(5)(a), contained in old s. 222(5)(b), was repealed when self assessment was introduced). In practice, however, the inspector will often have no means of knowing that this is the case unless the taxpayer takes the initiative and, in effect, makes a 'claim'. In the simplest cases, where only one private residence, with a site of less than 0.5 hectares, is owned at a time, it seems that no specific entry need strictly be made on the tax return for the year of disposal if full PRR is due, and the wording of Question 8 of the basic tax return form, and its accompanying guidance notes, for 2000/01, support this. If the facts are more complex, it would be advisable to include a 'white space' note explaining the reason why full PRR is thought to be due especially where there is more than 0.5 hectares involved. To do otherwise would, in effect, amount to saying that there are no taxable gains, without explaining why, and if the return is held to be wrong there is a risk of penalties under TMA 1970, s. 95.

A 'white space' note needs to make clear the grounds on which relief is 'claimed', for example 'Residence at [Address] and [x] hectares of land being its garden or grounds, private residence relief claimed'. This should protect the taxpayer against penalties, even if the Revenue take up an enquiry and he is later persuaded to concede that full PRR was not due.

In cases where a s. 222(5)(a) election was made, it is advisable to put the inspector on notice by entering the address of the property, followed by 'main residence election under TCGA 1992, s. 222(5)(a)'.

Similar disclosure should be made of other factors, such as business use, which may affect the computation, and where relevant a full computation should be included on a separate schedule. Reference should also be made, where appropriate, to any applicable ethical guidelines regarding disclosure published by the adviser's professional body.

¶1031 Records

Those who prepare tax returns will need to keep permanent records of elections made under TCGA 1992, s. 222(5)(a) (see ¶508) and to update these when necessary. Advisers should not rely on the Revenue retaining the original election; although this ought theoretically to be the case, frequent changes in the tax office network can result in Revenue files being less complete than they should be. It is also advisable to keep permanent records of other relevant matters, such as the extent of the plot if this exceeds 0.5 hectares (see ¶408), and the use of any ancillary dwelling-houses (see ¶323), the occupation of job-related accommodation (see ¶610) and the extent of any business use (see ¶707). A running record of any 'permitted absences' (see ¶603) may also save time and trouble later, and highlight the need for any necessary planning.

11 Interaction with Other Reliefs and Taxes

MORTGAGE INTEREST RELIEF

¶1101 The contrasting tests

The test for mortgage interest relief for income tax purposes, until its abolition from 6 April 2000, was whether the loan in question was to defray money applied in purchasing land (and certain caravans and houseboats) in the UK or Ireland, which was, at the time the interest was paid, used as the only or main residence of the taxpayer (see ICTA 1988, old s. 353(1), 354(1)(a) and 355(1)(a)). Thus the test was purely factual, and there was no deeming procedure equivalent to TCGA 1992, s. 222(5)(a). An elected MR (which was not the MR in fact) would therefore never have qualified for mortgage interest relief. The test of MR status depends on the factors discussed at ¶503 and glossed in *Frost (HMIT) v Feltham* (1980) 55 TC 10, *Hughes (HMIT) v Viner* [1985] BTC 156, and *Goodwin v Curtis (HMIT)* CA [1998] 176; ChD [1996] 501. If the factual MR is outside the UK or Ireland, it may qualify for PRR (see ¶1007) but could never have qualified for mortgage interest relief. It is thus quite possible for PRR to be due, by a s. 222(5)(a) election, on a property which did not qualify for mortgage interest relief, but in the absence of an election the fact that mortgage interest relief was given up to 5 April 2000 may assist in establishing factual MR status for PRR in the event of a dispute.

RETIREMENT RELIEF

¶1102 Property used partly for a trade

The conditions for CGT retirement relief are generally incompatible with those for PRR. However, the two reliefs may co-exist for a property which is used partly for a trade so that there is a TCGA 1992, s. 224(1) restriction for PRR (see ¶703). The taxable part of the gain on such a property could qualify for retirement relief. If the business is that of a partnership or 'family' company, the owner should take no rent from the business so as to avoid a restriction on the latter relief under Sch. 6, para. 10(1)(c). Retirement relief is being progressively reduced in amount and will disappear altogether for disposals after 5 April 2003 (FA 1998, Pt III, Sch. 27).

ROLL-OVER RELIEF

¶1103 Business use of a dwelling-house

Similar considerations may apply to roll-over relief where there has been business use of a dwelling-house. If this is non-exclusive there will be no PRR restriction under TCGA 1992, s. 224(1) and apparently no roll-over relief either since the terms of s. 152(5) will not apply. But if there has been exclusive business use of part of the property, or use of the entire property for part of the period of ownership, there will be some potential for roll-over relief under s. 152(5) or (6). A further opportunity to combine the two reliefs might lie in the fact that it is not necessary to use the replacement asset for the business throughout its ownership.

> **Example**
> Maurice is a dentist who has used part of his home exclusively as a surgery for the entire period of his ownership. He is advised that on a sale, PRR would only be due on 70 per cent of the gain. He now intends to move house and also to transfer his surgery to a health centre owned by the local health authority, for which he will pay rent. He will therefore have no new asset into which he can roll the other 30 per cent of his gain. He buys a new home and instead of moving immediately to the health centre he uses part of it as a surgery for six months, and only then moves his practice to the health centre.
>
> Depending on the exact figures, there seems little reason why Maurice cannot claim roll-over relief, and the cessation of business occupation of the new property does not trigger any clawback. The inspector may try to argue that the occupation of the new house for business was a mere sham, but this would be difficult to sustain if Maurice carries on the full range of his practice there for a significant period, and even harder if there was a good business reason (e.g. delays in building work) for not moving into the health centre immediately. If Maurice never sells his new home, the rolled-over gains will never be taxed; and even if he does sell it eventually, those gains will, at most, be taxed only to the extent required by the small restriction on PRR under s. 224(2) required by the business use of part of the new home for the first six months of ownership.

¶1104 Taper relief

Taper relief was introduced from 6 April 1998 for individuals and trusts, and although it has not been illustrated in detail in the examples in this text, in practice it is extremely important where PRR is not available or due only in part. The detailed rules, which have changed several times since their introduction, are not repeated here.

Taper relief, which reduces the otherwise taxable gains progressively with the length of ownership of the relevant asset, is given as the final step in the computation of a taxpayer's overall chargeable gains for a tax year, before applying the annual exemption (TCGA 1992, s. 2A(1)). If there are losses as well as gains the relief is applied to the net gains after losses (if any). However, to ascertain how much relief is due it is necessary to examine each separate disposal. Naturally, if a gain on a private residence is wholly eligible for PRR, taper relief is irrelevant because there is no otherwise chargeable gain to be reduced. It will become material, therefore, where PRR is not fully due for any reason; e.g. because of non-qualifying absences, exclusive business use of all or part of the property, or the presence of land outside the permitted area.

Indexation relief was abolished for the future from 6 April 1998, but relief accrued up to that date is not lost in respect of a later disposal and is effectively 'frozen' into the base cost of the property where relevant. Taper relief thus applies to the post-indexation gain for a property acquired before 5 April 1998.

Where full PRR is not available, taper relief is applied to the otherwise taxable gain after whatever PRR is due, after any letting relief under s. 223(4) (see ¶708(4)) and also after any other relief such as retirement relief. The amount of taper relief will depend on the 'qualifying holding period' for the property as defined in s. 2A(8) and the table in s. 2A(5). Broadly, this is the period from the date of acquisition, or if later, from 6 April 1998, to the date of disposal.

Normally, any taxable gain on a private residence will qualify only for the less generous 'non-business asset' taper scale, which means that no relief at all will be due where the 'qualifying holding period' is less than three complete years (s. 2A(3)(b)); but where acquisition occurred before 17 March 1998, an additional 'bonus' year is added to that period (s. 2A(8)(b)(i)).

However, sometimes the reason for PRR not being fully due will be a period of exclusive business use of all or part of the property (see s. 224(1) and the discussion above at ¶707). This will mean that some 'business asset' taper relief will be due, on the more generous scale for such assets; see the definition of a business asset in Sch. A1, para. 5(1),(2). This may be the case if the use was for the purpose of a trade carried on by the owner, or a partnership of which he was a member, or possibly for the purposes of his employment (see para. 5(1),(2)(d) and CGT 64690), so long as the employment was in a trading business. However, use for letting will not attract business taper relief because the taper definitions are tied to the existence of a trade.

When this situation arises there will be an apportionment for PRR purposes (see ¶701), and also for taper relief purposes (Sch. A1, para. 9). The part of the gain which does not attract PRR will have to be apportioned between periods which represented business use and those which did not; the respective taper scales are then applied to each portion.

Example
Henry bought his house in 1990 and sold it on 6 April 2002 for a total gain of £200,000 (after indexation to April 1998). It was his only residence throughout, but also throughout his ownership he used a workroom exclusively for his business of repairing computers. The business use fraction for PRR purposes is agreed with the Revenue to be ten per cent. In the writer's view the computation of taper relief is as follows:

Total gain not attracting PRR = 10% of £200,000 = £20,000

Apportioned for taper purposes:
Non-business portion = 90% of £20,000 = £18,000, which attracts non-business taper for five years (four years since 6 April 1998 plus the 'bonus' year for pre-17 March 1998 ownership); this gives a taxable gain on this portion of 85% of £18,000=£15,300.

Business portion = 10% of £20,000 = £2,000, which attracts business taper for four years, giving a taxable gain on this portion of 25% of £2,000 = £500.

The total taxable gain is therefore £15,800.

Some might argue that this produces the wrong result. Why should the gain not eligible for PRR be taken to arise on a wholly business asset which has been so used throughout Henry's ownership period? In that case should the taxable gain not simply be 25 per cent of £20,000 i.e. £5,000? In the writer's view this attractive, and arguably more equitable, solution for the taxpayer is prevented by Sch. A1, para. 9. This is a case of an asset (the whole house) which has been simultaneously used for private and business purposes; it is the whole house, not just the workroom, on which the otherwise chargeable gain accrues. Paragraphs 9(2) and (3) thus require 90 per cent of the ownership period to have represented non-business use of that asset. Ninety per cent of the otherwise chargeable gain must thus be taken to arise on a non-business asset.

(This interpretation appears to be consistent with the example at CGT 17958, although this does not concern PRR).

Finally, it is worth noting that taper relief is much more beneficial than indexation to the taxpayer where there has been enhancement expenditure after acquisition. Taper relief applies to the whole gain otherwise chargeable, after

¶1104

deduction of such expenditure, even if the latter was incurred only shortly before disposal; whereas indexation applies separately to each item of expenditure and only from the date when it was incurred. Thus, where a gain fails to attract full PRR because it was attributable to 'tainted' expenditure and the rule in s. 224(3) applies (see ¶307 above), the actual taxable gain will often be much less after taper relief than would have been the case before April 1998.

¶1105 Reverse premiums

Legislation was included in FA 1999, s. 54 and Sch. 6, to treat certain financial inducements given to tenants or prospective tenants by their landlords to enter into leases (commonly known as reverse premiums) as income for Sch. A purposes. Previously, these were normally capital receipts on first principles, but not subject to CGT because no disposal was involved. However, FA 1999, Sch. 6, para. 6 excludes from this legislation an inducement offered to an individual, where the premises to which it relates are occupied, or are to be occupied, by him as his only or main residence.

This ensures that a private individual tenant will not be taxed on a deemed rental receipt if these conditions are met. However, the limitations should be noted. The 1999 legislation can apply if the property is not a factual main residence, and the fact that it may be the subject of a valid TCGA 1992, s. 222(5)(a) election will not help. Also, the exemption does not apply to trustees, who would be caught by the 1999 rules which apply to 'persons', even if the property attracted relief under s. 225.

INHERITANCE TAX (IHT)

¶1106 'Carve out' schemes involving the private residence

Schemes to save IHT by a lifetime gift of most of the value of a private residence while retaining occupation are usually aimed at avoiding the 'reservation of benefit' rules (see FA 1986, s. 102–102C), by granting a lease to a nominee for the owner to run for his life expectancy plus a few years; the freehold reversion is then gifted subject to the lease. They are now much less likely to succeed since the decision in *Ingram v IR Commrs* [1998] BTC 8,047 was counteracted by the rules now included in FA 1986, s. 102A–C. Although there is no case law on the impact of such schemes on PRR, there seems no reason why a gift of the freehold reversion should not rank for PRR since it represents a gift of an 'interest' in the property within TCGA 1992, s. 222(1) (see ¶311).

In practice, the problem with most such schemes is that they store up a CGT problem for the next generation, even if they succeed in saving IHT for the present owner. For example, it may still, even after the post-*Ingram* legislation, be possible for the present owner to grant a lease of his home to a nominee or life interest settlement for himself, then wait for at least seven years, and then give away the freehold reversion; this should succeed in avoiding the reservation of benefit rules (see FA 1986, s. 102A(5)), and the reversionary gift will be capable of attracting PRR subject to the usual conditions. However, for CGT purposes the donees of the reversion are likely to acquire their interests at a value heavily depressed by the rights of the donor, and unless they are able to occupy the house themselves in due course, their own sale of the freehold after the donor's death will almost certainly create a large gain on which no PRR will be due. More sophisticated planning will be needed to avoid this problem.

¶1107 Shared occupation schemes

This method of avoiding the reservation of benefit rules previously relied on the parliamentary statement by Mr Peter Brooke QC, MP on 10 June 1986 in Standing Committee on the Finance Bill (see *Hansard* col. 425). Taking advantage of this, an elderly parent could make an unconditional gift of his home to one or more of his children, and all concerned could then make the house their family home, each co-owner bearing his share of the running costs. Statutory recognition of this method was given as part of the post-*Ingram* legislation by FA 1986, s. 102B(4). The donor's occupation is treated as for full consideration, so that there is no reservation of benefit (see FA 1986, Sch. 20, para. 6(1)(a)) and the gift takes effect as a PET.

For CGT, it seems clear that such a gift would be legally valid and PRR would, in principle, be due to the donor. Equally, the donees would occupy the whole property by virtue of their co-ownership rights and on a disposal by them, no restriction of PRR could arise under TCGA 1992, s. 224(2). A somewhat analogous situation arose in *Green v IR Commrs* [1982] BTC 378 (see ¶318(2)), where a co-owner and the taxpayer's father lived in parts of the house during the first two years of ownership, but any argument that the owner was not using the whole as his residence on that account was rejected. The specific mention of the 'family home' in Mr Brooke's statement also suggests that where the protection of that statement applied for IHT, all the owners would be able to show factual MR status.

¶1108 Stamp duty

Despite several substantial increases in the rates of stamp duty since 1997, there are no special reliefs from this duty in connection with the conveyance or letting of a private residence.

VALUE ADDED TAX (VAT)

¶1109 Impact on dwelling-houses

There is no direct correlation between the PRR rules and the impact of VAT on dwelling-houses. The sale of a new house by a builder will normally be a zero-rated supply and this will also cover materials (VATA 1994, Sch. 8, Group 5, items 1 and 2).

Such treatment covers *any* building 'designed as a dwelling', or a number of dwellings, regardless of whether it becomes anyone's main residence, though certain holiday homes may incur standard-rated VAT. Sales of existing houses will be exempt supplies (VATA 1994, Sch. 9, Group 1, item 1), again without the need to examine whether the house is anyone's main residence. It is interesting to note that in *Whiteley* (LON/92/2979) No. 11,292, the VAT tribunal rejected as irrelevant arguments based on *Batey v Wakefield* (1981) 55 TC 550 (see ¶320(1)) as to the extent of a 'dwelling-house' for VAT purposes, and ruled that an annexe and a swimming pool could not be regarded as a 'dwelling' for zero-rating. There are, however, numerous VAT tribunal cases on the extent of zero-rating relief on the construction or extension of residential properties.

Even if the 'taxation option' (which does not generally apply to residential property) has been exercised on a property or on bare land which is then sold to an individual, the supply is still exempt if the land is to be used for the conversion or construction, otherwise than in the course of a business carried on by him, of a building intended to be used by him as a dwelling (see VATA 1994, Sch. 10, para. 2(3)(b)). This test would cover the subsequent erection of a secondary residence as well as a sole or main residence, so that the fact that the option was disapplied by the vendor does not of itself assist in a later PRR claim by the purchaser. It could, however, be evidence, of no more than persuasive value, of the purchaser's intention to use the property as a residence, which could assist in making it the subject of a TCGA 1992, s. 222(5)(a) election. However, since the VAT rule is based on intention at the time of purchase of the site, the nature of the supply for VAT cannot assist if in fact there is no residential occupation of the completed house.

Similar considerations apply to the special VAT rules for 'DIY' builders. Here, again, the test for VAT repayment claims is the intention at outset that the property will not be built or converted in the course or furtherance of a business, and this includes no requirement about its intended use as a 'main' residence (see *Value Added Tax Regulations* SI 1995/2518 and VAT Notice No. 719 *VAT Refunds for 'Do-It-Yourself' Builders and Converters*).

THE COUNCIL TAX AND BUSINESS RATES

¶1110 Council tax and the factual main residence

The council tax was introduced on 1 April 1993 in England, Scotland and Wales to replace the community charge. Unlike its predecessor, it is fundamentally a property tax and in some ways resembles the pre-1990 domestic rating system. Very broadly, domestic properties are placed in bands according to their valuation at 1 April 1991. The charging authority then fixes a tax level for a property in the central band (D), and from this the tax payable on properties in other bands is derived by a simple formula.

Liability to council tax falls, initially, on a resident in the property, whether he or she is the freeholder or has a lesser interest. If there is no resident, liability falls on the owner (*Local Government Finance Act* 1992, s. 6(1)). 'Resident' for that purpose, in relation to any dwelling, means an individual aged 18 or over who has his sole or main residence there (*Local Government Finance Act* 1992, s. 6(5)).

'Sole or main residence' is an expression which also appeared in the community charge legislation (LGFA 1988, s. 2(1)(b)) and, as there, it is undefined for council tax purposes. Thus, the normal everyday meaning of the phrase applies (see ¶503), although since the tax is a daily tax it may be that the courts would require a lesser degree of permanence to be shown than would be the case for income tax or CGT. In most cases, however, it is likely that where a person has two or more homes the council tax liability will fall on the property where he spends the majority of his time, although alternative arguments might be possible, as they are for PRR in the absence of a TCGA 1992, s. 222(5)(a) election (see ¶503(3)). A more wide-ranging approach was taken by the Scottish Sheriff's Court in a community charge case, *Stevenson v Rogers* 1990 SLT (Sh. Ct.) 30, where it was held that it was relevant to look at the whole of the history and circumstances of each residence, their relative values, the quality of the respective accommodation and – as one only out of these factors – the time for which each is used. In the English community charge case of *Bradford City Council v Anderton The Times*, 15 February (1991), importance was attached to the place where the taxpayer's family normally resided in determining his main residence.

Thus, in many cases a property on which the taxpayer is paying the council tax will also prove to be his factual MR for PRR purposes, and the place of liability for the council tax may be of some assistance in resolving the main residence issue in the absence of a s. 222(5)(a) election. There is, of course, no facility in the council tax code for deeming a secondary residence to be the main residence.

¶1111 Property used in part for business

A property used in part for a business may be subject to partial business rating (see *Local Government Finance Act* 1988, s. 64(8)), which may lead the Revenue to argue that there should be a restriction on PRR under TCGA 1992, s. 224(1) (see ¶703). However, local authorities will not generally seek to levy business rates on domestic properties which have no exclusive business use, e.g. where the owner merely does some occasional work related to his business at home, or which have no parts which have been so altered or furnished that they can no longer be used domestically (see *'Non-Domestic Rates – the boundary between the Community Charge and Non-Domestic (Business) Rates: definition of non-domestic property'*, issued by the Department of the Environment, May 1990). This should often correspond to the CGT position in such cases, whereby such use does not give rise to a PRR restriction, and the fact that no business rates were charged may support an argument that PRR should be available in full.

Appendix A: Taxation of Chargeable Gains Act 1992, s. 222-226

PART VII – OTHER PROPERTIES, BUSINESSES, INVESTMENTS ETC.

PRIVATE RESIDENCES

Section 222 Relief on disposal of private residence

222(1) This section applies to a gain accruing to an individual so far as attributable to the disposal of, or of an interest in–

(a) a dwelling-house or part of a dwelling-house which is, or has at any time in his period of ownership been, his only or main residence, or

(b) land which he has for his own occupation and enjoyment with that residence as its garden or grounds up to the permitted area.

222(2) In this section "**the permitted area**" means, subject to subsections (3) and (4) below, an area (inclusive of the site of the dwelling-house) of 0.5 of a hectare.

222(3) Where the area required for the reasonable enjoyment of the dwelling-house (or of the part in question) as a residence, having regard to the size and character of the dwelling-house, is larger than 0.5 of a hectare, that larger area shall be the permitted area.

222(4) Where part of the land occupied with a residence is and part is not within subsection (1) above, then (up to the permitted area) that part shall be taken to be within subsection (1) above which, if the remainder were separately occupied, would be the most suitable for occupation and enjoyment with the residence.

222(5) So far as it is necessary for the purposes of this section to determine which of 2 or more residences is an individual's **main residence** for any period–

(a) the individual may conclude that question by notice to the inspector given within 2 years from the beginning of that period but subject to a right to vary that notice by a further notice to the inspector as respects any period beginning not earlier than 2 years before the giving of the further notice.

(b) [Repealed by FA 1996, s. 134 and Sch. 20, para. 59(3) and s. 205 and Sch. 41, Pt. V(10).]

222(6) In the case of a man and his wife living with him–

(a) there can only be one residence or main residence for both, so long as living together and, where a notice under subsection (5)(a) above affects both the husband and the wife, it must be given by both.

(b) [Repealed by FA 1996, s. 134 and Sch. 20, para. 59(4) and s. 205 and Sch. 41, Pt. V(10).]

222(7) In this section and sections 223 to 226, **"the period of ownership"** where the individual has had different interests at different times shall be taken to begin from the first acquisition taken into account in arriving at the expenditure which under Chapter III of Part II is allowable as a deduction in the computation of the gain to which this section applies, and in the case of a man and his wife living with him–

(a) if the one disposes of, or of his or her interest in, the dwelling-house or part of a dwelling-house which is their only or main residence to the other, and in particular if it passes on death to the other as legatee, the other's period of ownership shall begin with the beginning of the period of ownership of the one making the disposal, and

(b) if paragraph (a) above applies, but the dwelling-house or part of a dwelling-house was not the only or main residence of both throughout the period of ownership of the one making the disposal, account shall be taken of any part of that period during which it was his only or main residence as if it was also that of the other.

222(8) If at any time during an individual's period of ownership of a dwelling-house or part of a dwelling-house he–

(a) resides in living accommodation which is for him job-related, and

(b) intends in due course to occupy the dwelling-house or part of a dwelling-house as his only or main residence,

this section and sections 223 to 226 shall apply as if the dwelling-house or part of a dwelling-house were at that time occupied by him as a residence.

222(8A) Subject to subsections (8B), (8C) and (9) below, for the purposes of subsection (8) above living accommodation is job-related for a person if–

(a) it is provided for him by reason of his employment, or for his spouse by reason of her employment, in any of the following cases–

(i) where it is necessary for the proper performance of the duties of the employment that the employee should reside in that accommodation;

(ii) where the accommodation is provided for the better performance of the duties of the employment, and it is one of the kinds of employment in the case of which it is customary for employers to provide living accommodation for employees;

(iii) where, there being a special threat to the employee's security, special security arrangements are in force and the employee resides in the accommodation as part of those arrangements;

or

(b) under a contract entered into at arm's length and requiring him or his spouse to carry on a particular trade, profession or vocation, he or his spouse is bound–

  (i) to carry on that trade, profession or vocation on premises or other land provided by another person (whether under a tenancy or otherwise); and
  (ii) to live either on those premises or on other premises provided by that other person.

222(8B) If the living accommodation is provided by a company and the employee is a director of that or an associated company, subsection (8A)(a)(i) or (ii) above shall not apply unless–

(a) the company of which the employee is a director is one in which he or she has no material interest; and

(b) either–

  (i) the employment is as a full-time working director, or
  (ii) the company is non-profit making, that is to say, it does not carry on a trade nor do its functions consist wholly or mainly in the holding of investments or other property, or
  (iii) the company is established for charitable purposes only.

222(8C) Subsection (8A)(b) above does not apply if the living accommodation concerned is in whole or in part provided by–

(a) a company in which the borrower or his spouse has a material interest; or

(b) any person or persons together with whom the borrower or his spouse carries on a trade or business in partnership.

222(8D) For the purposes of this section–

(a) a company is an associated company of another if one of them has control of the other or both are under the control of the same person; and

(b) "**employment**", "**director**", "**full-time working director**", "**material interest**" and "**control**", in relation to a body corporate, have the same meanings as they have for the purposes of Chapter II of Part V of the Taxes Act.

222(9) Subsections (8A)(b) and (8C) above shall apply for the purposes of subsection (8) above only in relation to residence on or after 6th April 1983 in living accommodation which is job-related for the purposes of that subsection.

222(10) Apportionments of consideration shall be made wherever required by this section or sections 223 to 226 and, in particular, where a person disposes of a dwelling-house only part of which is his only or main residence.

Section 223 Amount of relief

223(1) No part of a gain to which section 222 applies shall be a chargeable gain if the dwelling-house or part of a dwelling-house has been the individual's only or main residence throughout the period of ownership, or throughout the period of ownership except for all or any part of the last 36 months of that period.

223(2) Where subsection (1) above does not apply, a fraction of the gain shall not be a chargeable gain, and that fraction shall be–

(a) the length of the part or parts of the period of ownership during which the dwelling-house or the part of the dwelling-house was the individual's only or main residence, but inclusive of the last 36 months of the period of ownership in any event, divided by

(b) the length of the period of ownership.

223(3) For the purposes of subsections (1) and (2) above–

(a) a period of absence not exceeding 3 years (or periods of absence which together did not exceed 3 years), and in addition

(b) any period of absence throughout which the individual worked in an employment or office all the duties of which were performed outside the United Kingdom, and in addition

(c) any period of absence not exceeding 4 years (or periods of absence which together did not exceed 4 years) throughout which the individual was prevented from residing in the dwelling-house or part of the dwelling-house in consequence of the situation of his place of work or in consequence of any condition imposed by his employer requiring him to reside elsewhere, being a condition reasonably imposed to secure the effective performance by the employee of his duties,

shall be treated as if in that period of absence the dwelling-house or the part of the dwelling-house was the individual's only or main residence if both before and after the period there was a time when the dwelling-house was the individual's only or main residence.

223(4) Where a gain to which section 222 applies accrues to any individual and the dwelling-house in question or any part of it is or has at any time in his period of ownership been wholly or partly let by him as residential accommodation, the part of the gain, if any, which (apart from this subsection) would be a chargeable gain by reason of the letting, shall be such a gain only to the extent, if any, to which it exceeds whichever is the lesser of–

(a) the part of the gain which is not a chargeable gain by virtue of the provisions of subsection (1) to (3) above or those provisions as applied by section 225; and

(b) £40,000.

223(5) Where at any time the number of months specified in subsections (1) and (2)(a) above is 36, the Treasury may by order amend those subsections by substituting references to 24 for the references to 36 in relation to disposals on or after such date as is specified in the order.

s. 223(1)

223(6) Subsection (5) above shall also have effect as if 36 (in both places) read 24 and as if 24 read 36.

223(7) In this section–
   "**period of absence**" means a period during which the dwelling-house or the part of the dwelling-house was not the individual's only or main residence and throughout which he had no residence or main residence eligible for relief under this section; and
   "**period of ownership**" does not include any period before 31 March 1982.

Section 224 Amount of relief: further provisions

224(1) If the gain accrues from the disposal of a dwelling-house or part of a dwelling-house part of which is used exclusively for the purpose of a trade or business, or of a profession or vocation, the gain shall be apportioned and section 223 shall apply in relation to the part of the gain apportioned to the part which is not exclusively used for those purposes.

224(2) If at any time in the period of ownership there is a change in what is occupied as the individual's residence, whether on account of a reconstruction or conversion of a building or for any other reason, or there have been changes as regards the use of part of the dwelling-house for the purpose of a trade or business, or of a profession or vocation, or for any other purpose, the relief given by section 223 may be adjusted in a manner which is just and reasonable.

224(3) Section 223 shall not apply in relation to a gain if the acquisition of, or of the interest in, the dwelling-house or the part of a dwelling-house was made wholly or partly for the purpose of realising a gain from the disposal of it, and shall not apply in relation to a gain so far as attributable to any expenditure which was incurred after the beginning of the period of ownership and was incurred wholly or partly for the purpose of realising a gain from the disposal.

Section 225 Private residence occupied under terms of settlement

225 Sections 222 to 224 shall also apply in relation to a gain accruing to a trustee on a disposal of settled property being an asset within section 222(1) where, during the period of ownership of the trustee, the dwelling-house or part of the dwelling-house mentioned in that subsection has been the only or main residence of a person entitled to occupy it under the terms of the settlement, and in those sections as so applied–

(a) references to the individual shall be taken as references to the trustee except in relation to the occupation of the dwelling-house or part of the dwelling-house, and

(b) the notice which may be given to the inspector under section 222(5)(a) shall be a joint notice by the trustee and the person entitled to occupy the dwelling-house or part of the dwelling-house.

Section 226 Private residence occupied by dependent relative before 6th April 1988

226(1) Subject to subsection (3) below, this section applies to a gain accruing to an individual so far as attributable to the disposal of, or of an interest in, a dwelling-house or part of a dwelling-house which, on 5th April 1988 or at any earlier time in his period of ownership, was the sole residence of a dependent relative of the individual, provided rent-free and without any other consideration.

226(2) If the individual so claims, such relief shall be given in respect of it and its garden or grounds as would be given under sections 222 to 224 if the dwelling-house (or part of the dwelling-house) had been the individual's only or main residence in the period of residence by the dependent relative, and shall be so given in addition to any relief available under those sections apart from this section.

226(3) If in a case within subsection (1) above the dwelling-house or part ceases, whether before 6th April 1988 or later, to be the sole residence (provided as mentioned above) of the dependent relative, any subsequent period of residence beginning on or after that date by that or any other dependent relative shall be disregarded for the purposes of subsection (2) above.

226(4) Not more than one dwelling-house (or part of a dwelling-house) may qualify for relief as being the residence of a dependent relative of the claimant at any one time nor, in the case of a man and his wife living with him, as being the residence of a dependent relative of the claimant or of the claimant's husband or wife at any one time.

226(5) [Repealed by FA 1996, s. 134 and Sch. 20, para. 61 and s. 205 and Sch. 41, Pt. V(10).]

226(6) In this section "**dependent relative**" means, in relation to an individual–

(a) any relative of his or of his wife who is incapacitated by old age or infirmity from maintaining himself, or

(b) his or his wife's mother who, whether or not incapacitated, is either widowed, or living apart from her husband, or a single woman in consequence of dissolution or annulment of marriage.

226(7) If the individual mentioned in subsection (6) above is a woman the references in that subsection to the individual's wife shall be construed as references to the individual's husband.

Appendix B: Inland Revenue Extra-Statutory Concessions

ESC D3 PRIVATE RESIDENCE EXEMPTION: PERIODS OF ABSENCE (A)

In determining how far an individual's gain on the disposal of his residence is exempt from capital gains tax under sections 222 to 226, TCGA 1992, sub-section (3) of section 223 provides that within specified limits, periods of absence are to be treated as periods of residence if, inter alia, the absence was as a result of his employment. Where in the case of a husband and wife who are living together this condition is satisfied as regards one spouse, it is treated as satisfied as regards the other.

ESC D4 PRIVATE RESIDENCE EXEMPTION: PERIODS OF ABSENCE (B)

In determining how far an individual's gain on the disposal of his home is exempt from capital gains tax under sections 222 and 226, TCGA 1992, certain periods of absence are treated as periods of residence if he resumes residence there at some time after the absence. This condition will be treated as satisfied where after a period of absence falling within section 223(3)(b) (absence on duties overseas) or (c) (other absences due to conditions of employment) an individual is unable to resume residence in his previous home because the terms of his employment require him to work elsewhere.

ESC D5 PRIVATE RESIDENCE EXEMPTION: PROPERTY HELD BY PERSONAL REPRESENTATIVES

Section 225, TCGA extends the exemption from capital gains tax given for private residences to cases where a trustee disposes of a house which has been the only or main residence of an individual entitled to occupy it under the terms of a settlement. Relief is also given where personal representatives dispose of a house which before and after the deceased's death has been used as their only or main residence by individuals who under the will or intestacy are entitled to the whole or substantially the whole of the proceeds of the house either absolutely or for life.

ESC D6 PRIVATE RESIDENCE EXEMPTION: SEPARATED COUPLES

Where a married couple separate or are divorced and one partner ceases to occupy the matrimonial home and subsequently as part of a financial settlement disposes of the home, or an interest in it, to the other partner the home may be regarded for the purposes of sections 222–224, TCGA 1992 as continuing to be a residence of the transferring partner from the date his or her occupation ceases until the date of transfer, provided that it has throughout this period been the other partner's only or main residence. Thus, where a husband leaves the matrimonial home while still owning it, the usual capital gains tax exemption or relief for a taxpayer's only or main residence would be given on the subsequent transfer to the wife, provided she has continued to live in the house and the husband has not elected that some other house should be treated for capital gains tax purposes as his main residence for this period.

ESC D20 PRIVATE RESIDENCE EXEMPTION: RESIDENCE OCCUPIED BY DEPENDENT RELATIVE

D20 [Classified as obsolescent by IR 1 (1994). Reproduced below for information.]

Where relief is claimed under section 105, CGTA 1979 in respect of the disposal by an individual of a dwelling house which has at any time been the sole residence of a dependent relative, the condition that the dwelling house must have been provided rent free and without any other consideration will be regarded as satisfied where the dependent relative pays all or part of the occupier's council tax and the cost of repairs to the dwelling house attributable to normal wear and tear.

Additionally, the benefit of the relief will not be lost where the dependent relative makes other payments in respect of the property either to the individual or to a third party, provided that no net income is receivable by the individual, taking one year with another. For this purpose the net income will be computed in accordance with the normal rules of Schedule A, except that any mortgage payments (including both income and capital elements) and any other payments made by the dependent relative as consideration for the provision of the property, whether made directly to the mortgagee or other recipient or indirectly by the individual, will be credited as receipts. The deductions to be debited will be computed in accordance with the normal rules of Schedule A.

ESC D21 PRIVATE RESIDENCE EXEMPTION: LATE CLAIMS IN DUAL RESIDENCE CASES

Where for any period an individual has, or is treated by the Taxes Acts as having more than one residence, but his interest in each of them, or in each of them except one, is such as to have no more than a negligible capital value on the open market (e.g. a weekly rented flat, or accommodation provided by an employer) the two year time limit laid down by section 222(5)(a), TCGA 1992 for nominating one of those residences as the individual's main residence for capital gains tax purposes will be extended where the individual was unaware that such a nomination could be made. In such cases the nomination may be made within a reasonable time of the individual first becoming aware of the possibility of making a nomination, and it will be regarded as effective from the date on which the individual first had more than one residence.

ESC D26 RELIEF FOR EXCHANGE OF JOINT INTERESTS IN LAND

Where interests in land which is in the joint beneficial ownership of two or more persons are exchanged after 19 December 1984, and

either

- a holding of land is held jointly, and, as a result of the exchange, each joint owner becomes sole owner or part of the land formerly owned jointly,

or

- a number of separate holdings of land are held jointly, and, as a result of the exchange, each joint owner becomes sole owner of one or more holding,

a relief along the lines of Sections 247 and 248 TCGA 1992 (relief on compulsory acquisition of land) may be claimed to alleviate the charges to capital gains tax which would otherwise arise.

If the consideration received or deemed to be received for the interest relinquished is less than or equal to the consideration given or deemed to be given for the interest acquired, relief will be allowed on the lines of that provided by Section 247(2) and (5), TCGA 1992; where the consideration is greater, greater relief will be allowed on the lines of Section 247(3) and (5). For this purpose the interest relinquished will be treated as the "old land" and the interest acquired as the "new land". "Land" includes any interest in or right over land and "holding of land" includes an estate or interest in a holding of land, and is to be construed in accordance with Section 243(3) TCGA 1992.

Relief will not be allowed to the extent that the "new land" is, or becomes, a dwelling house or part of a dwelling house within the meaning of Sections 222 to 226, TCGA 1992. However where individuals who are joint beneficial owners of dwelling houses which are their respective residences become sole owners of those houses in consequence of an exchange of interests, concessionary relief may be claimed if, by virtue of Sections 222 and 223, TCGA 1992, each gain accruing on a disposal of each dwelling house immediately after that exchange would be exempt. Each individual must undertake to accept for capital gains tax purposes that he or she is deemed to have acquired the other's interest in the dwelling house at the original base cost and on the original date on which that joint interest was acquired.

Where

- interests in land are exchanged after 29 October 1987; and
- this concession applies to that exchange; and
- there is a parallel exchange of interests in milk or potato quota associated with the land; and
- after the exchange each joint owner becomes sole owner of the part of the quota relating to the land he now owns;

ESC D26

then this concession will apply to the exchange of interests in quota as it applies to the exchange of interests in the land.

For the purposes of this concession a married couple is treated as an individual, so that an exchange of interests which results in a married couple alone becoming joint owners of land or of a dwelling house will meet the terms of the concession.

ESC D33 CAPITAL GAINS TAX ON COMPENSATION AND DAMAGES ZIM PROPERTIES LTD – COMPENSATION AND DAMAGES

Introduction

1 A person who receives a capital sum derived from an asset is treated for the purposes of capital gains tax as disposing of that asset. The case of Zim Properties Ltd v Proctor [[1985] BTC 42] has established that the right to take court action for compensation or damages is an asset for capital gains tax purposes. It follows that a person who receives compensation or damages, whether by court order or arbitration or by negotiated settlement as a result of a cause of action may be regarded as disposing of the right of action. A capital gain may accrue as a result.

The strict position

Cost of acquisition

2 A capital gain will accrue if the capital sum received as compensation exceeds the amount which may be deducted as the cost of acquiring the right of action. A right of action will almost invariably be acquired otherwise than by way of bargain made at arm's length. Special rules for determining the cost of acquisition apply in these circumstances. Where the right of action was acquired on or before 9 March 1981, it is deemed to have been acquired for a sum equal to its market value on the date of acquisition. Where it was acquired on or after 10 March 1981 and there was no disposal of the right of action corresponding to the claimant's acquisition of it, then where – as is usually the case – the taxpayer gave no consideration to acquire it, it is treated as having been acquired without cost.

If the cause of action was held on 31 March 1982 and disposed of on or after 6 April 1988, it will, in accordance with the rebasing rules, be deemed to have been disposed of and immediately reacquired at its open market value on 31 March 1982.

If a right of action passes on the death of the claimant, it is treated as acquired at its open market value on the date of death.

In computing the gain or loss, a deduction may be made for any legal and professional fees incurred in pursuing the claim. If the action in respect of a claim of substance fails, or if the expenses exceed the compensation, a capital loss may accrue.

Date of acquisition

3 A right of action accrues and so is acquired by a person for capital gains tax purposes when, for example as a result of a breach of contract or the negligent actions of another person (tort), he or she suffers actual loss or damage.

ESC D33

Appendix B: Inland Revenue Extra-Statutory Concessions

Market value on acquisition
4 In practice, where relevant, the Board of Inland Revenue will be prepared to accept a valuation which gives rise to neither chargeable gain nor allowable loss.

Date of disposal
5 The right of action is treated as disposed of when a capital sum derived from it is received, and if a series of capital sums is received, each receipt is the occasion of a separate disposal.

Rebasing to 31 March 1982
6 If an asset which was held on 31 March 1982 is disposed of on or after 6 April 1988, the gain or loss is normally computed as if it had been disposed of and immediately reacquired at its open market value on 31 March 1982. If an underlying asset were held on 31 March 1982, but a right of action related to that asset were acquired after 31 March 1982, the rebasing provisions would apply on the disposal of the underlying asset but not on the disposal of the right of action.

Reliefs and exemptions
7 Some forms of compensation are specifically exempted from liability to capital gains tax (see paragraph (12) below) and these remain exempt despite the decision in Zim Properties. But other statutory reliefs and exemptions are not available where the receipt of the compensation is regarded as giving rise to a disposal of the right of action, not of any underlying asset to which the relief or exemption might apply. These include deferment relief for compensation applied in restoring or replacing an asset, roll-over relief for the replacement of business assets, retirement relief and private residence relief.

Relief by concession
8 Where a gain arises on the disposal of a right of action, the case may alternatively, by concession, be treated in accordance with the following paragraphs of this statement.

Underlying assets
9 Where the right of action arises by reason of the total or partial loss or destruction of or damage to a form of property which is an asset for capital gains tax purposes, or because the claimant suffered some loss or disadvantage in connection with such a form of property, any gain or loss on the disposal of the right of action may by concession be computed as if the compensation derived from that asset, and not from the right of action. As a result a proportion of the cost of the asset, determined in accordance with normal part-disposal rules, and indexation allowance, may be deducted in computing the gain. For example if compensation is paid by an estate agent because his negligence led to the sale of a building falling through, an appropriate part of the cost of the building may be deducted in computing any gain on the disposal of the right of action.

The gain may be computed by reference to the original cost of the underlying asset, with time-apportionment if appropriate if the asset was acquired before 6 April 1965, or by reference to its market value at 6 April 1965. For disposals on or after 6 April 1988, the gain

ESC D33

may be computed in appropriate cases by reference to the value of the asset on 31 March 1982.

Other reliefs and exemptions
10   If the relief was or would have been available on the disposal of the relevant underlying asset, it will be available on the disposal of the right of action. For example, if compensation is derived from a cause of action in respect of damage to a building suffered by reason of professional negligence, and the compensation is applied in restoring the building, deferment relief under section 23, TCGA 1992 will be available as if the compensation derives from the building itself and not from the right of action.

Other reliefs which may become available in this way include private residence relief, retirement relief and roll-over relief. The Board of Inland Revenue will be prepared to consider extending time limits in cases where because of a delay in obtaining a capital sum in compensation, the normal time limit allowed for a relief has elapsed. If the right of action relates to an asset which is specifically exempt from capital gains tax, such as a motor car, any gain on the disposal of the right of action may be treated as exempt.

No underlying asset
11   A right of action may be acquired by a claimant in connection with some matter which does not involve a form of property which is an asset for capital gains tax purposes. This may be the case where professional advisers are said to have given misleading advice in a tax or other financial matter, or to have failed to claim a tax relief within proper time. Actions may be brought in relation to private or domestic matters. Where the action does not concern loss of or damage to or loss in connection with a form of property which is an asset for capital gains tax purposes, the approach in paragraph (9) above of treating the compensation as deriving from the asset itself is not appropriate. In these circumstances any gain accruing on the disposal of the right of action will be exempt from capital gains tax.

Other points
Personal compensation or damages
12   Section 51(2), TCGA 1992 provides that "sums obtained by way of compensation or damages for any wrong or injury suffered by an individual in his person or his profession or vocation" are not chargeable to capital gains tax. The words "wrong or injury" include breaches of contractual duties and torts (in Scotland, delicts). If the exemption would have applied to damages received for any wrong or injury, it also applies to any compensation for professional negligence in relation to an action in respect of that wrong or injury.

The words "in his person" are to be read in distinction to "in his finances" but they embrace more than physical injury so that distress, embarrassment, loss of reputation or dignity may all be suffered "in the person". Compensation or damages for unfair or unlawful discrimination suffered "in the person" and for libel or slander (in Scotland, defamation) would thus be included. Similarly the words "in his profession or vocation" refer to compensation or damages suffered by an individual in his professional capacity such as unfair discrimination, libel or slander (in Scotland, defamation) as distinct from "in his finances". If the compensation is received by the members of a partnership, each member, in Scotland as elsewhere, is treated as receiving a share of the compensation. The exemption is extended by concession to such compensation received by an individual in his trade or employment.

The exemption also extends to compensation received by a person other than the individual who suffered the wrong or injury, such as relatives or personal representatives of a deceased person. It also extends to compensation for emotional distress caused by the death of another person, and compensation for loss of financial support.

It does not apply to compensation for any other wrong or injury suffered by any person other than an individual.

Indemnity payments

13   The principle in Zim Properties Ltd is not regarded as applicable to payments made by the vendor to the purchaser of an asset under a warranty or indemnity included as one of the terms of a contract of purchase and sale.

Where such a contractual payment is made, then the cost of the asset to the person acquiring it will, on the occasion of a further disposal be reduced by the sum received. The sale proceeds of the person who makes (or is treated by section 171A TCGA as making) the disposal of the asset are adjusted under section 49, TCGA 1992 in respect of the sum received. Where a warranty or indemnity payment is not made in accordance with the terms of the contract, the principle in Zim Properties may apply and the sums received by the vendor or purchaser as appropriate may be identified as capital sums derived from the asset, or from the right of action, depending on the facts of the case.

Date of commencement

14   The concessions and practices set out in this statement will apply to all open cases on the date of issue, 19 December 1988

ESC D37 PRIVATE RESIDENCE EXEMPTION: RELOCATION ARRANGEMENTS

Where work is being relocated, the employer may set up arm's length arrangements under which an employee, who moves home because of the relocation, can sell his or her home to a relocation company or to the employer and have a right to a share in any later profit made when the relocation company or the employer later sells the home. Such arrangements may also exist where employees are required by their employer to transfer within an organisation and as a result have to move home.

In such circumstances, if the home is fully exempt from capital gains tax, the employee's right to the share in any later profit will be exempt too. Some employees' homes may be only partially exempt (for example they may have been used partly for business purposes, or may not have been the main home throughout an employee's period of ownership). In such cases, a corresponding proportion of any gain relating to the right to later profits will also be exempt.

The concession does not apply when the right is held by the employee for more than three years.

Where an employee owns his or her home jointly with others and moves home in the circumstances described above, the concession will apply to the other joint holders in the same way as to the employee.

ESC D37

The concession applies to office holders in the same way as to employees, and to arrangements involving unincorporated relocation businesses in the same way as to those involving relocation companies.

ESC D49 PRIVATE RESIDENCE RELIEF: SHORT DELAY BY OWNER-OCCUPIER IN TAKING UP RESIDENCE

This concession applies:

- where an individual acquires land on which he has a house built, which he then uses as his only or main residence.
- where an individual purchases an existing house and, before using it as his only or main residence, arranges for alterations or redecorations or completes the necessary steps for disposing of his previous residence.

In these circumstances, the period before the individual uses the house as his only or main residence will be treated as a period in which he so used it for the purposes of Sections 223(1) and 223(2)(a), TCGA 1992, provided that this period is not more than one year. If there are good reasons for this period exceeding one year, which are outside the individual's control, it will be extended up to a maximum of two years.

Where the individual does not use the house as his only or main residence within the period allowed, no relief will be given for the period before it is so used. Where relief is given under this Concession it will not affect any relief due on another qualifying property in respect of the same period.

Appendix C: Inland Revenue Statements of Practice

SP 10/79 POWER FOR TRUSTEES TO ALLOW A BENEFICIARY TO OCCUPY DWELLING-HOUSE

[15 August 1979]

Many wills and settlements contain a clause empowering the trustees to permit a beneficiary to occupy a dwelling-house which forms part of trust property as they think fit. The Board do not regard the existence of such a power as excluding any interest in possession in the property.

Where there is no interest in possession in the property in question, the Board do not regard the exercise of the power as creating one if the effect is merely to allow non-exclusive occupation or to create a contractual tenancy for full consideration. The Board also take the view that no interest in possession arises on the creation of a lease for a term or a periodic tenancy for less than full consideration, though this will normally give rise to a charge for tax under IHTA 1984, s. 65(1)(b). On the other hand, if the power is drawn in terms wide enough to cover the creation of an exclusive or joint residence, albeit revocable, for a definite or indefinite period, and is exercised with the intention of providing a particular beneficiary with a permanent home, the Revenue will normally regard the exercise of the power as creating an interest in possession. And if the trustees in exercise of their powers grant a lease for life for less than full consideration, this will be regarded as creating an interest in possession in view of IHTA 1984, s. 43(3) and 50(6).

A similar view will be taken where the power is exercised over property in which another beneficiary had an interest in possession up to the time.

SP 14/80 RELIEF FOR OWNER OCCUPIERS

[14 November 1980]

The Finance Act 1980 introduced a new relief from capital gains tax for owner occupiers who let living accommodation in their homes. The legislation has been consolidated as Section 223(4) TCGA 1992. The purpose of this statement is to give to people who are (or are thinking of) letting the whole or a part of their homes an indication whether they are likely to be liable to any capital gains tax when they dispose of them. Anyone who would like further information about the application to his own circumstances of the rules and practice described in this statement is advised to get in touch with his tax office which will be pleased to give further help.

Full exemption
Where the owner of a dwelling house has occupied the whole of it as his only or main residence throughout his period of ownership

- Since 6 April 1965 if he acquired it before then and disposed of it before 6 April 1988, or
- Since 31 March 1982 if he acquired it before then and disposed of it on or after 6 April 1988

any gain on disposal is entirely exempt from capital gains tax.

Lodger living with the family
Where a lodger lives as a member of the owner's family, sharing their living accommodation and taking meals with them, no part of the accommodation is treated as having ceased to be occupied as the owner's main residence, and the exemption will not be restricted at all.

Relief for lettings
The new relief will apply where the owner disposes after 5 April 1980 of a dwelling house which has been his only or main residence during his period of ownership but which he has wholly or partly let as residential accommodation. That part of the gain which would previously have been taxable will now be exempt from capital gains tax up to the lower of

- £10,000 for disposals before 6 April 1983
- £20,000 for disposals before 19 March 1991
- £40,000 for disposals on or after 19 March 1991

and the amount of the exemption attributable to his own occupation. The amount of the gain on the let part depends on two things–

i   how much has been let; and
ii the length of time during which it was let.

For example, someone occupies the whole of his home (acquired after 6 April 1982) for six years out of his 10 year period of ownership. He lets one-third of it throughout the other 4 years. The gain on the house as a whole is £30,000. Previously, he would have been exempt from capital gains tax on £26,000 and chargeable on £4,000 (1/3×4/10×£30,000).

The new relief applies to the £4,000 (which is less than the two limits referred to above) so that the whole of the gain of £30,000 is now exempt.

When relief will be available
Whether the let accommodation is part of the owner's dwelling-house or is itself a separate dwelling-house will depend on the facts of particular cases. The Board of Inland Revenue wish to make known, however, their view of the application of the new relief to the common case where the owner of a house, which was previously occupied as his (or the family) home, lets part as a flat or set of rooms without structural alteration (or with only minor adaptations). For the purposes of the new relief the Board will regard this as a letting of part

of the owner's dwelling house, whether or not the tenants have separate washing and cooking facilities. But the relief does not extend to property which, although it may be part of the same building, forms a dwelling house separate from that which is, or has been, the owner's (for example, a fully self-contained flat with its own access from the road).

Other capital gains tax changes in the Finance Act 1980 which affect owner-occupiers
Where a house has not been the owner's only or main residence for his whole period of ownership, relief is (subject to certain exceptions) restricted to the period of occupation. Previously, the last 12 months were disregarded in making this restriction but this period has now been extended to:

- 24 months where the disposal takes place between 6 April 1980 and 18 March 1991; or
- 36 months where the disposal takes place on or after 19 March 1991.

The FA 1980 [TCGA 1992 s. 3] also provides for 1980–81 onwards an exemption for the first £3,000 of an individual's total gains in a year. This exemption has been amended in later Finance Acts and stood at £5,800 for disposals in 1992/93. This replaces the previous system which gave exemption for an individual whose gains did not exceed £1,000 in a year with a restricted measure of relief where the total exceeded £1,000 but did not exceed £9,500.

SP 4/92 CAPITAL GAINS TAX: RE-BASING ELECTIONS

[14 May 1992]

1. Section 35(6) TCGA 1992 (Section 96(6) FA 1988) provides that an election under Section 35(5) (Section 96(5)) of that Act should be made within two years of the end of the year of assessment or accounting period in which "the first relevant disposal" is made, or such longer period as the Board of Inland Revenue may allow.

2. The Board will always exercise their discretion to extend the time limit to at least the date on which the statutory time limit would expire if disposals of a certain kind did not count as a first relevant disposal of either

  (i) an asset held at 31 March 1982; or

  (ii) an asset treated by paragraph 1 Schedule 3, TCGA 1992 (paragraph 1 Schedule 8 Finance Act 1988) as having been held at that date.

3. There are three kinds of disposals in relation to which the Board will exercise their discretion in this way.

4. *First*, those on which the gain would not be a chargeable gain by virtue of a particular statutory provision. Such disposals can be left out of account in deciding when to make an election.

5. The main examples of these provisions are in the annex attached to this Statement of Practice.

6. *Second*, those disposals which in practice do not give rise to a chargeable gain or allowable loss. The main examples of such disposals are:

Building society accounts
Withdrawals from building society accounts on which no chargeable gain or allowable loss arises.

Private residences
The disposal by an individual of his or her dwelling house where the whole of any gain would qualify for relief under Section 223(1) TCGA 1992 (Section 102(1) CGTA 1979).

No gain/no loss transfers
Transfers which give rise to neither a chargeable gain nor an allowable loss by virtue of the operation of statutory "no gain/no loss" provisions listed at Section 35(3)(d) TCGA 1992 (paragraph 1(3), Schedule 8, Finance Act 1988). These include gifts to charities and transfers between spouses.

7. *Third*, those disposals in respect of which a Section 35(5) (Section 96(5)) election cannot be made. These are specified in paragraph 7, Schedule 3 TCGA 1992 (formerly paragraph 12 Schedule 8 FA 88 and are, in general terms, disposals of:

(i) Plant and machinery

or

(ii) Assets used in connection with a trade of working mineral deposits but in either case only if capital allowances were or could have been given.

or

(iii) Oil licences

or

(iv) Shares deriving their value from oil exploration or exploitation

In each case, a rebasing election cannot apply to such disposals, but they will nevertheless count strictly as first relevant disposals. Consequently, in all cases the Board will exercise their discretion to extend the time limit to at least the date on which the statutory time limit would expire if such disposals did not count as a first relevant disposal.

Persons becoming resident in the UK after 6 April 1988
8. A person who is non UK resident on 6 April 1988 may make a disposal which will count as a first relevant disposal between then and the date on which they first become UK resident. The Board will generally give sympathetic consideration to extending the time limit to the end of the second year of assessment or, in the case of companies, accounting period after the year in which the first disposal is made after taking up UK residence. The extension will not normally be available where the taxpayer has disposed of an asset, held on 31 March 1982, within Section 10 TCGA 1992 (Section 12 CGTA 1979 and Section 11 ICTA 1988), in the period between 6 April 1988 and the date of becoming UK resident.

Other situations in which the statutory time limit may be extended
9. There are a variety of other circumstances in which the Board of Inland Revenue may exercise their discretion to extend the statutory time limit. In all cases an extension will depend on the particular facts and circumstances of each individual case.

SP 4/92

What may be regarded as a first relevant disposal?
10. There are also some circumstances where it may help to clarify what is regarded as a first relevant disposal:

Capacity in which person makes an election under Section 35(5)
Where a person makes an election under Section 35(5) in relation to assets held in one capacity the election does not apply to assets held in another capacity. This is because of the provisions of Section 35(7). For this purpose a person may hold assets in several capacities as, for example, an individual, trustee, partner or member of a European Economic Interest Grouping. It follows that there will be a first relevant disposal and a separate time limit for making an election for each holding of assets which a person holds in different capacities.

Individuals who hold assets in different capacities should indicate at the time they make an election in what capacity it should be regarded as applying.

Disposals of non-UK assets by an individual resident but not domiciled in the UK
In the case of individuals who are resident but not domiciled in the UK a disposal of an asset situated outside the UK may be a first relevant disposal. For Section 35(5) purposes the date on which the proceeds are remitted to the UK is taken to be the date on which the disposal occurs and not the date when the asset was disposed of. This means that the date of the first relevant disposal will therefore be the date on which remittances are received from an overseas gain after 5 April 1988 or the date of the first disposal of a UK asset, whichever occurs first.

Disposals by a UK resident during a period of non-residence
An individual who is UK resident on 6 April 1988 may then have a period of non-residence before resuming UK residence. In these circumstances the first relevant disposal will be treated as the first disposal after 5 April 1988 on which the individual is chargeable to UK capital gains tax. So if, for example, a disposal was made between 6 April 1988 and the date the individual became non-resident that will be treated as the first relevant disposal. If there was no disposal in this period the first relevant disposal will be the first disposal after residence is resumed. Where an individual is not entitled to be treated as resuming residence part-way through a tax year by virtue of Extra-Statutory Concession ESC D2, the first disposal will be the first made in the year in which residence is resumed.

11. This Statement of Practice provides an indication of the main circumstances where, and the extent to which, the Board of Inland Revenue will or may exercise their discretion under Section 35(6)(b) TCGA 1992. It is not intended to be an exhaustive list of disposals where, having regard to the individual facts and circumstances, such discretion may be exercised.

Annex to SP 4/92

Disposals on which any gain would not be a chargeable gain by virtue of specific statutory provisions are:

(i) Private cars (Section 263 TCGA 1992) [formerly Section 130 CGTA 1979]
(ii) Chattels, including household goods, and personal belongings, but excepting commodity futures and foreign currency, worth less than the chattel exemption at

the date of disposal (Section 262(1) TCGA 1992) [formerly Section 128(1) CGTA 1979]

(iii) All chattels that are wasting assets, except plant and machinery used in business (but see also (ii) above and paragraph 7(i) of the Statement of Practice) and commodity futures (Section 45(1) TCGA 1992) [formerly Section 127(1) CGTA 1979]

(iv) Government non-marketable securities, including savings certificates, premium and British Savings bonds (Section 121 TCGA 1992) [formerly Section 71 CGTA 1979]

(v) Gilt-edged securities and qualifying corporate bonds, except those received in exchange for shares or other securities (Section 115 TCGA 1992) [formerly Section 67 CGTA 1979]

(vi) Life assurance policies and deferred annuity contracts unless purchased from a third party (Section 210(2) TCGA 1992) [formerly Section 143(2) CGTA 1979]

(vii) Foreign currency acquired to meet personal or family expenditure abroad (Section 269 TCGA 1992) [formerly Section 133 CGTA 1979]

(viii) Rights to compensation or damages for any wrong or injury suffered by an individual in his person, profession or vocation (Section 51(2) TCGA 1992) [formerly Section 19(5) CGTA 1979]

(ix) Debts, other than debts on a security, held by the original creditor, his personal representative or legatee (Section 251(1) TCGA 1992) [formerly Section 134(1) CGTA 1979]

(x) Business expansion scheme shares in respect of which relief has been given and not withdrawn (Section 150(2) TCGA 1992) [formerly Section 149C(2) CGTA 1979]

(xi) Shares held as part of a personal equity plan investment (Regulation 1 SI 1989 No 469, as amended]

(xii) Gifts of eligible property, including works of art, for the benefit of the public (Section 258(1) and (2) TCGA 1992) [formerly Section 147(1) and (2) CGTA 1979]

(xiii) Decorations for valour or gallantry (Section 268 TCGA 1992) [formerly Section 131 CGTA 1979]

(xiv) Rights to or any part of an allowance, annuity or capital sum from a superannuation fund or any other annuity (except under a deferred annual policy) or annual payments receivable under a covenant which is not secured on property (Section 237 TCGA 1992) [formerly Section 144 CGTA 1979]

The disposal of sterling, which is not an asset for capital gains tax purposes (Section 21(1) TCGA 1992) [formerly Section 19(1) CGTA 1979] does not count as a first relevant disposal.

SP 4/92

Appendix D: ICAEW Technical Releases

Set our below are the relevant extracts from Technical Resleases 211, 500 and 730 which are referred to in the text of this book. They are reproduced with the kind permission of the ICAEW.

TAXATION OF AMONALIES AND PRACTICAL DIFFICULTIES – 1976 [ICAEW Technical Release TR211, December 1976]

Gardens: loss of exemptions
The Revenue stated that they would not take the point established by *Varty v Lynes* ... that the private residence exemption might be lost in respect of the garden if the taxpayer ceased to occupy the house before he sold it, unless the garden had development value.

TAXATION: POINTS OF PRACTICAL INTEREST [ICAEW Technical Release TR500, 10 March 1983]

Private residences
13. The Inland Revenue take the view that where absences from the dwelling-house exceed the three years or four years mentioned in section 102(3), Capital Gains Tax Act 1979, then it is only the excess which does not qualify for the exemption. Where the other conditions are satisfied the three or four years out of the longer period of absence would qualify as the "period of absence" for which exemption under section 102(3) would be available.

THE FINANCE (NO. 2) BILL 1988 – NOTE OF MEETING WITH THE INLAND REVENUE IN JUNE 1988 [ICAEW Technical Release TR 739, 1 February 1989]

Schedule 7: Capital gains: assets held on 31 March 1982
Paragraph 7: Private residence relief (paragraph 80)
58. The Revenue said that paragraph 7 of Schedule 7 did *not* operate to deny private residence exemption under section 102(3)(b), CGTA 1979 where a taxpayer occupied a property as his residence before 31 March 1982 and also moved abroad before that date. Periods prior to 31 March 1982 would be disregarded *only* for the purposes of apportioning any gain/loss and not for the purpose of considering whether the property was occupied as

a residence before and after the absence (nor for securing relief in respect of the final two years of ownership).

Clause 103: Dependent relative's residence (paragraph 93)
65. The Revenue said that where a dependent relative was obliged temporarily to live elsewhere – nursing home, hospital etc. – that absence would not normally be treated as a cessation of occupation. But all cases necessarily turned on their particular facts.

Appendix E: Extracts from Inland Revenue Tax Bulletins

February 1992

CAPITAL GAINS TAX: PRIVATE RESIDENCE RELIEF – PERMITTED AREA PROCEDURES

When a disposal occurs of land associated with a dwelling house, and the total holding of land exceeds half a hectare (for disposals prior to 19 March 1991, 1 acre), it may be necessary to determine the size and location of the "permitted area". This can involve both the Inspector and the District Valuer. In this article we describe the process and suggest how you – the practitioner – may be able to help.

The questions to be answered in such cases are

- is the land at the date of sale "garden or grounds"?
- what is the size and character of the dwelling house at the date of sale?
- what is the corresponding size of the permitted area?
- where should the permitted area be located?
- how should disposal proceeds and acquisition costs be apportioned between the exempt and non exempt areas?

The first question is relevant because if the land is not "garden or grounds" at the date of sale it cannot qualify for relief. In general, land is treated as "garden or grounds" if it is enclosed land serving chiefly for ornament or recreation, surrounding or attached to a dwelling house or other building. Land used for agriculture, for commercial woodlands, or letting, for example, will not qualify. If the land does qualify as "garden or grounds" the second question becomes material. Section 101(3) CGTA 1979 allows a permitted area in excess of half a hectare if **required** by the **size and character** of the dwelling house. The permitted area must include the site of the dwelling house (Section 101(2)) and must be located on the land most suitable for occupation with the residence (Section 101(4)).

A major factor in dealing with this question is how to treat structures other than the main building. Following Batey v. Wakerfield 55 TC 550 it is clear that the dwelling house may include more than one building. Whilst the cases to date have been concerned mainly with servants' cottages, the principle can apply to any other outbuildings. The Inspector will therefore try to distinguish between those outbuildings which form part of the entity comprising the dwelling house, those which are ancillary to the garden or grounds, or in some circumstances those which fall within neither of those categories.

Clearly, in the first category will be buildings close to the main house which serve in its function as a residence, such as garages used for private cars and fuel stores. In the second category will be non-commercial greenhouses, gazebos, garden sheds etc. The third category will include, for example, buildings in use for the purposes of a trade or letting.

The distinction between the three categories above is relevant because as well as affecting the size and character of the dwelling house, any building forming **part** of the entity comprising the dwelling house is considered for relief by reference to the Section 101(1)(a) test, that is, relief is available if it is or has been all or part of the main residence any building merely **ancillary** to the garden or grounds is considered only by reference to the Section 101(1)(b) test, that is, relief will only be available if it stands within the permitted area.

Buildings which fall into neither of these categories will not qualify for any private residence relief.

When considering whether land is within Section 101(1)(b) the Inspector and the District Valuer will only need to consider the relevant questions as at the date of sale. This is because that subsection uses only the present tense. The relevance of this distinction was shown by the case of Varty v. Lynes 51 TC 419. However, if the Inspector has to deal with a disposal that also includes part of the dwelling house he may need details at other dates because the test in Section 101(1)(a) is a historic test – "is, or has at any time been".

Thus, a building that is not part of the dwelling house at the date of sale but had previously been a part, will not be taken into account in determining the permitted area. But it may still qualify for partial private residence relief by reason of Section 101(1)(a).

ROLE OF THE DISTRICT VALUER

The first two questions above are questions of fact. As such they are the responsibility of the Inspector. The Inspector may seek information from the District Valuer before coming to a decision. On the other hand the District Valuer may bring to the Inspector's attention material which is relevant but about which the Inspector was not aware.

When the first two questions have been answered the Inspector will pass the information to the District Valuer. The District Valuer will advise the Inspector on the size and location of the permitted area (the third and fourth questions) and on any consequential apportionments required by the fifth question.

In considering these questions the District Valuer has to decide what is **required** by the size and character of the dwelling house. This is considered to be an objective test. To be **required** the land must be needed by each and every occupant of the dwelling house, not just by a particular occupant who has special needs. Although there is not direct judicial guidance, the view taken is that the corresponding legislative context makes the compulsory purchase case of In Re Newhill Compulsory Purchase Order 1937, Payne's Application [1938] 2 All E R 163 useful guidance on the meaning of this word. Du Parcq J said at page 167C:

> "'Required', I think, in this Section does not mean merely that the occupiers of the house would like to have it, or that they would miss it if they lost it, or that anyone proposing to buy the house would think less of the house without it than he would

if it was preserved to it. 'Required' means, I suppose, that without it there will be such a substantial deprivation of amenities or convenience that a real injury would be done to the property owner."

The District Valuer's opinion will be based on a comparison of the size of garden and grounds held with other houses in the locality which are of a comparable size and character to the subject house. An initial review will be made which may not include an inspection of the property. If this supports the taxpayer's claim the District Valuer will inform the Inspector. Otherwise the District Valuer will undertake further work. This will include a sufficient inspection of the property to enable the District Valuer to take into account the attributes of the land. If the Inspector has not yet made an assessment the opinion formed by the District Valuer at that stage will be used as a basis for making an estimated assessment. The District Valuer will then enter into negotiations with the taxpayer's representatives and it will be necessary to inspect the property fully.

The Inspector retains responsibility for settling any appeal against a capital gains assessment. If the District Valuer cannot reach agreement with the Taxpayer, it is for the Inspector to take the matter forward to the Commissioners for a decision. If the disputed point, before the Commissioners, is a question of interpretation, for example, of the word 'required' in Section 101(3), this may be wholly a matter for the Inspector. However, if the dispute is over the District Valuer's opinion the Inspector will wish to call the District Valuer as an expert witness at any appeal hearing.

In order to introduce expert evidence a proof of that evidence must be prepared and exchanged with the other side before the appeal hearing. Our advice is that this should be done 2-3 weeks before the hearing date. Ensuring that an appropriate proof is available at that date is, however, a complex and time consuming procedure.

Sometimes there is also a dispute about the apportionment of sale proceeds. If the dispute is about the manner of apportionment, for example, that sale proceeds should be apportioned by regard to area rather than by reference to valuations, the dispute will be within the jurisdiction of the Commissioners (Section 43(4)). The Commissioners will normally consider the point when dealing with the permitted area point. Again the District Valuer may appear as the Inspector's expert witness. If the Commissioners find that apportionment should be by reference to valuations then they cannot determine the apportionment dispute. Jurisdiction over such matters lies with the Lands Tribunal (Section 47 TMA 1970).

WHAT PRACTITIONERS CAN DO TO ASSIST

It will greatly assist the Inspector if you submit as much information as possible when a claim is made. The following information will be particularly useful a full description of the dwelling house and any associated outbuildings and structures, preferably including some historical background if available

a full description of the holding of the land including whenever possible a plan of the property. Photographs will be helpful details of the use made of any outbuildings and structures. If only the permitted area point is relevant you may restrict this to the period immediately preceding the date of sale. But otherwise details for the full period of ownership would be appropriate details of the use made of the associated land and, in any borderline case, the reasons for considering the land to be garden or grounds at the date of sale a clear statement of what you claim is the permitted area with a plan setting out the location of the area claimed, if this is less than the whole proposals for apportionments of sale proceeds and costs where relevant.

Where a dispute proceeds to a contentious appeal hearing, an early indication of whether you or you client will call expert evidence would be appreciated. In such a case we would expect all parties to aim to comply with the appropriate advance time limits for exchange of proof of evidence.

May 1992

CAPITAL GAINS TAX: PRIVATE RESIDENCE RELIEF – JOINT BUT UNRELATED OWNER OCCUPIERS

There is some uncertainty as to whether joint owner occupiers of a property who are not husband and wife are entitled to full private residence relief. We take the view that in general they will be entitled to relief.

Where people jointly own a home we consider each to have an undivided share in all of the property – see Tod v Mudd 60 TC 237 for a case involving tenants in common. If they have unrestricted access to the whole property, even though some areas may in practice not be used by all of the joint owners, private residence relief may be available under Section 222 TCGA 1992 (formerly Section 101 CGTA 1979). Provided it is their only or main residence, relief will be available on each owner's share of any gain on disposal in the normal way.

Occasionally property in joint ownership may be divided into separate and identifiable homes, each exclusively occupied. In these cases the statute does not provide relief in respect of any gain on the part not occupied by each owner. Extra Statutory Concession D26 (third paragraph) may however enable joint owners to exchange their interests so as to acquire sole ownership of the part each occupies without a charge to capital gains tax.

[Section 222 TCGA 1992 (Section 101(1)(a) CGTA 1979)]

August 1994

PRINCIPAL PRIVATE RESIDENCE RELIEF

We have been asked to clarify our interpretation of a number of points that arise on principal private residence relief (Sections 222-226 Taxation of Chargeable Gains Act (TCGA) 1992).

SCOPE OF THE DWELLING-HOUSE – MEANING OF CURTILAGE

Lewis v Rook (TL 3308) gave guidance on determining whether a building, with one or more ancillary buildings, could together form a single dwelling-house for the purposes of Section 222. In cases where there is an identifiable main house it was held that no building can form part of a dwelling-house with the main house unless that building is appurtenant to, and within the curtilage of, the main house. Curtilage is defined by the Shorter Oxford

Dictionary as "a small court, yard, or piece of ground, attached to a dwelling-house and forming one enclosure with it". This definition has been adopted by the Courts in non-tax cases and emphasis is placed on the smallness of the area comprised in the curtilage. Buildings standing around a court yard together with the main house will be within the curtilage of the main house.

Where more dispersed groups of buildings have a clear relationship with each other they will fall within a single curtilage if they constitute an integral whole. In the Leasehold Reform Act case of Methuen-Campbell v Walters, quoted with approval in Lewis v Rook, the Court held that "For one corporeal hereditament to fall within the curtilage of another, the former must be so intimately associated with the latter as to lead to the conclusion that the former in truth forms part and parcel of the latter". Whether one building is part and parcel of another will depend primarily on whether there is a close geographical relationship between them. Furthermore, because the test is to identify an integral whole, a wall or fence separating two buildings will normally be sufficient to establish that they are not within the same curtilage. Similarly, a public road or stretch of tidal water will set a limit to the curtilage of the building.

Buildings which are within the curtilage of a main house will normally pass automatically on a conveyance of that house without having to be specifically mentioned. There is a distinction between the curtilage of a main house and the curtilage of an estate as a whole and the fact that a whole estate may be contained within a single boundary does not mean that the buildings on the estate should be regarded as within the curtilage of the main house.

SALE OF A HOUSE AND GARDEN AFTER IT HAS CEASED TO BE USED AS A RESIDENCE

Varty v Lynes (51 TC 419) established that no principal private residence relief was due on the sale of a garden where it was sold separately and after the dwelling-house. Certain dicta in that case also suggested that where a dwelling-house and garden were sold together, but after the taxpayer had ceased to occupy the property, the sale of the garden would not qualify for relief. This particular point was not directly in issue in that case, and so was not decided by it, but the case provided grounds for taking that view. Since then we have not taken this line in cases where house and garden were sold together and not for development. Recently we have received advice that arguments based on those dicta are misconceived and we no longer seek to apply them at all.

We do however apply the decision itself, so that no relief is due on the sale of a garden which takes place after a prior sale of the dwelling-house.

STATEMENT OF PRACTICE D4

Statement of Practice D4 explains that certain delays in occupying a dwelling-house as a residence at the start of a period of ownership will be regarded as a period of residence in that dwelling-house for the purposes of Private Residence Relief. For SP D4 to apply the delay must not exceed a period of one year, or somewhat longer if there are good reasons for exceptional delay. Where a period of delay falls within SP D4 the dwelling-house must be occupied as a residence immediately thereafter. Otherwise no extension to the actual period of residence is allowed.

What constitutes a good reason for exceptional delay is a matter left to the discretion of local District Inspectors, subject to an overall time limit of two years. Where the period of delay is greater than two years no extension is allowed. We expect good reasons for exceptional delay to be factors outside the taxpayer's control.

Where SP D4 does apply, and as a result two houses are treated as residences for the same period, no Section 222(5) election is required. Relief can be given on both houses for the period covered by SP D4.

PERIODS OF ABSENCE

Relief is only due for periods of absence from the home falling within Section 223(3) if both before and after the period of absence there was a time when the home was the taxpayers residence. We take the same view of residence for this purpose as we take for determining whether Section 222 applies generally, so that the question is whether during the period concerned the property has as a matter of fact been a residence.

A minimum period is not specified and we do not attempt to impose one. We take the view that it is quality of occupation rather than length of occupation which determines whether a dwelling-house is its owner's residence. As Millet J in Moore v Thompson, 61 TC at page 24 comments:

> ". . . the Commissioners were alive to the fact that even occasional and short residence in a place can make that a residence; but the question was one of fact and degree . . ."

APPORTIONMENTS

- In broad terms the apportionment rules work as follows:
- Section 222(10) apportions consideration where required;
- Section 223 apportions the gain over time;
- Section 224(l) restricts relief to parts of the property not used exclusively for a business etc;
- Section 224(2) provides for a just and reasonable apportionment to apply where there is a change in use.

Section 224(1) only applies where the part of the property concerned has been exclusively so used throughout the period of ownership. It does not refer to use only at the date of disposal. Where Section 224(1) applies no relief is due on the part of the dwelling-house used for business etc, even for the last 3 years of ownership. This is because Section 224(1) only applies Section 223 to the part of the dwelling-house not exclusively used for business etc. Section 223 specifies how much relief is due, and since it does not apply to the business part no relief can be given for that part for any period.

Section 224(2) provides for a just and reasonable apportionment to apply where there is a change in use, and for this purpose commencement or cessation of use of a dwelling-house as a residence is not a change of use. Section 223 already gives the rules required for such cases and there is therefore no need to apply Section 224(2). Our approach in cases falling within Section 224(2) is to deal with each case on its merits, and to produce an adjustment which so far as possible reflects:

- the extent to which, and
- the length of time over which,
- each part of the dwelling-house has been used as part of the residence.

This approach broadly follows the statutory method of apportionment for more straightforward cases set out in Section 223 and Section 224(1). We do not normally consider it is appropriate to take into account intervening market values when apportioning gains to different periods in Section 224(2) cases since Section 223 clearly provides for time apportionment as the appropriate method.

ELECTIONS BY MARRIED COUPLES

When a couple marry and both spouses own a residence a new two year period for making an election under Section 222(5) begins.

Where one spouse owns more than one property, and the other owns no property, and there is no change on marriage, then we take the view that a fresh period does not begin since there has been no change in the combination of residences owned by either spouse, and neither spouse needs to become a party to any existing election to which they had not previously been a party. Section 222(6)(a) only requires a notice to be given by both spouses where it affects them both. Where only one spouse owns property only that spouse is affected and he or she will already have had a two year period in which to make the election.

Where the spouses jointly own more than one property at marriage but neither separately owns any other property, a new two year period for making an election would still begin. Although both parties own the same properties as before, and have previously had a two year period in which to elect, they now have to make a joint election and a new period is required accordingly.

The right to receive a notice under Section 222(6)(b) only applies to a spouse who owns a residence. Otherwise a spouse, who had no financial interest in a property, would be given a right of appeal against a determination relating to that property owned by the other spouse, and with possibly adverse consequences for that other spouse.

SUCCESSIVE INTERESTS

Section 222(7)(a) stipulates that where a spouse inherits a dwelling-house from the other spouse he or she also inherits the other spouse's period of ownership for principal private residence relief purposes. This is not overridden by Section 62 TCGA 1992 which provides that a legatee acquires an inherited asset for CGT purposes on the date of death. Section 62 sets out the rules for computing the gain arising to a legatee, but says nothing about how any private residence relief which might be due is to be calculated, the rules for which are in Section 222 etc. Thus Section 222(7) continues to apply with the result that periods of ownership prior to the death of the first spouse to die fall to be taken into account in determining qualifying periods of residence.

One effect of this is to produce results different to those which would be obtained by only looking at the period after the death of the first spouse to die. This can work to the advantage or to the disadvantage of the taxpayer.

SECTION 224(3)

To prevent abuse of principal private residence relief there is anti-avoidance legislation at Section 224(3) which is widely drawn. Section 224(3) applies

- where a dwelling-house is acquired wholly or partly for the purpose of realising a gain from its disposal, or
- where there is subsequent expenditure on the dwelling-house wholly or partly for the purpose of realising a gain from its disposal.

Where the first part of Section 224(3) applies no relief is due on any gain arising from the disposal of that dwelling-house. Where the second part applies no relief is due on any part of the gain attributable to the expenditure.

Anyone who buys a dwelling-house is likely to hope that, in the fullness of time, they will make a gain on its disposal. One house may be chosen over another because its value is more likely to appreciate over time. These cases could be said to fall within the first part of the Section but, if the house was genuinely acquired and used as a residence and the conditions for relief are met, relief will not be restricted. The legislation will only be applied when the primary purpose of the acquisition was an early disposal at a profit. The same approach will be taken when considering whether a restriction of relief is appropriate under the second part of the Section.

In many cases in which the first part of Section 224(3) would be applied the transaction of purchase and sale will amount to an adventure in the nature of trade. In these cases the charge to income tax will take priority over the charge to capital gains tax. In some cases subsequent expenditure on the dwelling-house may also be part of an adventure in the nature of trade, giving rise to an income tax charge. The income tax charge will again take priority.

The second part of Section 224(3) is more often applied than the first. It denies relief on the part of a gain which is attributable to particular expenditure. Common circumstances in which it may be applied are acquisition by a leaseholder of a superior interest in the property conversion of an undivided dwelling-house into flats barn conversions and other developments of outbuildings or of the land attached to the dwelling-house.

The legislation does not dictate how this part of the gain should be computed but in practice it implies a comparison between the gain which accrues and the gain which would have accrued if the relevant expenditure had not been incurred.

In deciding whether a restriction to relief is appropriate under the second part of Section 224(3) we ignore cases in which the only relevant expenditure is incurred on obtaining planning permission, or removing restrictive covenants.

Where there is a delay between the expenditure and the disposal the effect of inflation may need to be considered. The part of the gain which is excluded from relief is the part attributable to the expenditure incurred. This part may have been increased by the effect of inflation. If so, the effect of inflation will be mitigated by indexation allowance.

DECEASED PERSON'S ESTATES – ESC D5

Extra-Statutory Concession D5 provides relief to Personal Representatives where they dispose of a house which before and after the deceased's death has been used as their only or main residence by individuals who under the will or intestacy are entitled to the whole or substantially the whole of the proceeds of the house. This is aimed at beneficiaries who have been living in the dwelling-house prior to and at the time of death, where there has therefore been continuity of occupation, and 'before' is interpreted accordingly. The intention is that beneficiaries who have lived in the house throughout should not be deprived of relief because their home happened to be sold by the Personal Representatives rather than by themselves as legatees. It is not intended that relief should as a result be extended to beneficiaries for whom the house has not been their only or main residence. To avoid this would mean insisting that resident beneficiaries should have a 100% interest in the dwelling-house which in turn could operate harshly against resident beneficiaries with very nearly a 100% interest. Hence the reference to 'substantially the whole' which we interpret as 75% or more.

DISPOSALS BY BENEFICIARIES

Where there is a disposal by a beneficiary of an inherited property the combined effect of Section 62(4) and Section 222(7) is that the beneficiary's period of ownership begins on the date of death. Where the beneficiary does not become resident until a later date the period prior to taking up occupation will not qualify for relief (unless it falls within the final 36 month period prior to disposal (Section 223(2)).
[Sections 222–226 TCGA 1992]

October 1994

PRINCIPAL PRIVATE RESIDENCE RELIEF: RESIDENCES OCCUPIED UNDER LICENCE

We have been advised that our view of the application of Section 222(5) TCGA to residences occupied under licence is incorrect. The circumstances in which an election is now no longer appropriate are discussed below. These are likely to be very rare and the vast majority of elections under Section 222(5) will not be affected.

Section 222(5) concerns the need for, and method of, determining which of 2 or more residences is an individual's main residence. We have previously taken the view that Section 222(5) applies to all residences, including residences occupied under licence such as a hotel or club room where that was in fact a person's place of residence, and a house in which someone lived with relatives (where there is no tenancy). An individual had to make an election under Section 222(5)(a) where he or she occupied a residence under licence, as well as an owned residence. If an election was not made and the owned residence was sold, the inspector had to make a determination under Section 222(5)(b).

Our new advice is that Section 222(5) is to be interpreted purposively, considering the aim of Section 222 as a whole. The section gives relief from capital gains tax on disposals of residences in which an individual has a legal or equitable interest. A "legal or equitable interest" in a property includes all forms of ownership, from that of the sole owner of a fee simple absolute in possession to that of the co-owner of a minimal tenancy. It does not include a residence occupied under licence. Elections or determinations are not appropriate where an individual has a legal or equitable interest in only one property but occupies another property under licence.

Where an individual's main residence is a residence occupied under licence, in which no legal or equitable interest is held, relief will still be available on one other residence which is owned even though an election cannot be made. This is because the owned residence will be the only residence in which that individual has a legal or equitable interest. An election will still be appropriate whenever an individual owns more than one residence each of which consists of a dwelling-house or an interest in a dwelling-house.

Job-related accommodation may be occupied under either a service occupancy or a tenancy. Under a service occupancy any rights derive from the service contract and there is no legal or equitable interest in the property which is occupied under licence.

Any notice of election given under Section 222(5) which relies on a residence occupied under licence for its effect and which is made after 16 October 1994 will not be regarded as valid. This change of view does not affect the need for an election under Section 222(5) in the majority of cases where an individual owns one property and rents another property, since the rented property will normally be occupied under a tenancy rather than under a licence.

Existing elections in favour of residences which fall within Section 222(1) will continue to be regarded as valid even if they relied on a residence occupied under licence for their effect. An example would be where the occupation under licence was at the time treated as a change in the combination of residences beginning a new period for which it was necessary to determine the main residence; and hence as beginning a new two year period in which a notice of election could be and was made.

Existing elections made in respect of residences occupied under licence will be regarded as ceasing to have effect from 16 October 1994. Where there is only one other residence in which a legal or equitable interest is held that residence will become the only or main residence for the purposes of Section 222 from that date, and the normal rules of time apportionment etc. (Section 223) will apply accordingly.

Where an existing election is in favour of a residence occupied under licence and there are two other residences in which a legal or equitable interest is held, a new two year period for making an election between them will be regarded as beginning when the existing election ceases to take effect on 16 October 1994. For this purpose only the lapsing of the existing election will be regarded as giving rise to a change in the combination of residences held. Any new election made as a result in this new two year period can only be backdated to the beginning of the period. This does not mean that an election made now cannot be backdated further if there was an earlier change of residences giving rise to a two year period which has not expired.

In any case where an assessment is not yet final and conclusive an individual may ask for an election which relied for its effect on a residence occupied under licence, and which is therefore not valid, to be disregarded completely. In that case the strict statutory rules will be applied in accordance with our new view to the whole of the period affected. This might mean, for example, that an election could not be made between two residences in which a legal or equitable interest is held, because the time limit for doing so has expired.

[Section 222(5) TCGA 1992]

August 1995

CAPITAL GAINS TAX: PRIVATE RESIDENCE RELIEF GARDEN OR GROUNDS

Section 222(1)(b) Taxation of Chargeable Gains Act (TCGA) 1992 provides for relief on the disposal of, or of an interest in, land which an individual has for his own occupation and enjoyment with his residence as its garden or grounds up to the permitted area.

The purpose of this article is to set out the Revenue's interpretation of this Section following comment on a recent Special Commissioner's decision in the case of Wakeling v Maidment, now correctly named Wakeling v Pearce SPC 32/1995. Mrs Wakeling succeeded in her appeals but the Revenue has decided not to test the matter in the High Court due to her particular circumstances. The facts of the case and the decision do not affect the Revenue's interpretation of this Section.

To qualify for private residence relief, the land must meet certain conditions **at the date on which it is disposed of.** The words "land which he has for his own occupation and enjoyment with that residence as its garden or grounds" in Section 222(1)(b) make this clear. They contrast with Section 222(1)(a) which applies to a dwelling-house, "which is, or has at any time in his period of ownership been his only or main residence" and thus looks both to the present and the past. This difference in interpretation was confirmed in the case of Varty v Lynes (51 TC 419) – Brightman J. at page 425. The use of the land other than that at the date of disposal is therefore irrelevant.

The conditions to be met are:

- it must be land which the owner has for occupation and enjoyment with the residence;
- it must be the garden or grounds of the residence;
- the area of land must not exceed the permitted area.

However, this does not mean that land which meets these conditions necessarily qualifies fully for relief. Section 222(1)(b) TCGA 1992 determines land which may qualify, whilst the amount of relief is then determined by Section 223 TCGA 1992.

It is for the Inspector to agree whether land can be regarded as occupied and enjoyed with the residence as its garden or grounds. The determination of what constitutes the permitted area, if over 0.5 of a hectare, (for disposals prior to 19 March 1991, one acre), rests with the District Valuer. (The procedures relating to the determination of the permitted area were reported in detail in Tax Bulletin Issue 2 (February 1992).)

The phrase "occupation and enjoyment" is understood by reference to the legal meaning of the words used. Occupation means possession of the land while enjoyment means possession without contested claims from third parties.

The phrase "garden or grounds" is not defined in the statute, nor is there judicial authority. The words must carry their everyday meaning and whether a piece of land can be regarded as the garden or grounds of a residence is a question of fact.

The word "garden" is taken to mean an enclosed piece of ground devoted to the cultivation of flowers, fruit or vegetables. The word "grounds" extends this and makes it more difficult to define. A useful dictionary definition of grounds is

> "Enclosed land surrounding or attached to a dwelling-house or other building serving chiefly for ornament or recreation".

In general, the Revenue accepts that land surrounding the residence and in the same ownership is the grounds of the residence, unless it is used for some other purpose. The Revenue would not regard land used for agriculture, commercial woodlands, trade or business as part of the garden or grounds. Also, land which has been fenced off from the residence to be sold for development is excluded. Land which has traditionally been part of the grounds of the residence but which, at the date of sale, is unused or overgrown is not excluded, nor are paddocks or orchards if there is no significant business use. Included in the definition is land which has a building on it, provided the building is not let or in use for a business, and also land which is not used exclusively for recreational purposes. For example, the owner-occupier of a guest house may allow guests to use the garden. The land would still qualify for relief providing the other conditions are satisfied.

Disposal of land which is physically separated from the residence may cause problems. The Revenue does not accept that land is garden or grounds merely if it is in the same ownership as the residence and is used as a garden. However, land which can be shown objectively, on the facts, to be naturally and traditionally the garden of the residence, so that it would normally be offered to a prospective purchaser as part of the residence, will be accepted. An example of this is where, as in some villages, it is common for a garden to be across the street from the residence. The separation itself would not be regarded as a reason for denying relief.

It must be stressed that these cases will be rare and if land is separated from the residence by other land which is not in the same ownership as the residence, it will usually not be part of the garden or grounds. For example, land bought some distance from the residence due to an inadequate garden at the residence and which is cultivated and regarded as part of the garden will not qualify for relief.

[Section 222 TCGA 1992]

Case Table

All references are to paragraph numbers

A

	Paragraph
A and GB Murdoch v Lethem (1904) 5 TC 76	317
Acme Flooring and Paving Co (1904) Ltd v IR Commrs [1948] 1 All ER 546	409
Annicola Investments Ltd v Minister of Housing and Local Government [1965] 3 All ER 850	316

B

	Paragraph
Batey v Wakefild (1981) 55 TC 550	319; 320; 321; 322; 323; 1109
Belfast Corporation v Kelso [1953] NI 163	316
Bernard v Josephs [1982] Ch 391	910
Booth v Ellard (1980) 53 TC 393	715
Bradford City Council v Anderton (The Times, 15 February 1991)	1110
Burca v Parkinson [2001] BTC 64	911
Byrne v Rowbotham (1969) 210 EG 823	504

C

	Paragraph
Craven v White [1988] BTC 268	411; 518; 714
Cresstock Investments Ltd v Commons Commissioner [1992] 1 WLR 1088	407; 408
Crowe (Bird Will Trustee) v Appleby (1975) 51 TC 457	801

D

	Paragraph
Davenport v Chilver [1983] BTC 223	1009
Dreyfus v IR Commrs (1929) 14 TC 560	1010
Drummond v Brown [1984] BTC 142	313
Dyer v Dorset County Council [1989] QB 346	321

E

	Paragraph
Edwards v Bairstow & Harrison (1955) 36 TC 207	316; 323

F

	Paragraph
Faulkner (as Trustee of Adams dec'd) v IR Commrs (2001) Sp C 278	810
Field Place Caravan Park Ltd v Harding [1966] 3 All ER 247	304
Fox v Stirk and Bristol Electoral Registration Officer [1970] 2 QB 463	503
Frost v Feltham (1980) 55 TC 10	502; 503; 504; 610; 615; 1101
Fulford-Dobson, ex parte [1987] BTC 158	904
Furniss v Dawson [1984] AC 474	711

G

	Paragraph
Gissing v Gissing [1971] AC 886	910
Goodwin v Curtis [1996] BTC 501	307
Grant v Langston (1900) 4 TC 205	317
Green v IR Commrs [1982] BTC 378	317; 318; 320; 323; 1107
Griffin v Craig-Harvey [1994] BTC 3	509; 518

H

	Paragraph
Harvey v Sivyer [1985] BTC 410	903
Hecquard, Re (1889) 24 QBD 71	302; 304
Hochstrasser v Mayes (1959) 38 TC 673	604
Honour v Norris [1992] BTC 153	320; 321; 1022
Hughes v Viner [1985] BTC 156	502; 1101

I

	Paragraph
Ingram v IR Commrs [1998] BTC 8,047	1106
IR Commrs v Joiner (1973) 50 TC 449	605
— v Lloyd's Private Banking Ltd (as Trustee of Evans dec'd) [1998] BTC 8,020	810

	Paragraph		Paragraph
— v Ross and Coulter [1948] 1 All ER 616	303	Moore v Thompson [1986] BTC 172	304; 305

J

		N	
Jenkins v Brown [198] BTC 281	715; 801	Newhill Compulsory Purchase Order, Re [1983] 3 All ER 163	408; 409
Jones v Associated Tunnelling Co Ltd [1981] IRLR 477	605	Nicholson, Re [1974] 2 All ER 386	910
Jones v Wilcock [1996] Sp C 389	1003	Northern Ireland Commr of Valuation v Fermanagh Protestant Board of Education [1969] 3 All	

K

Kelly, ex parte [1991] BTC 50	703	ER 352	322
Kidson v MacDonald (1974) 49 TC 503	801	**O**	
Kirkby v Hughes [1993] BTC 52	307; 502	1–4 White Row Cottages, Bewerley, Re (1991) Ch 441	304; 305
		Owen v Elliott [1990] BTC 323	103; 708; 709; 714; 1011

L

Land at Freshfields, Re (The Times, 1 February 1993)	407		
Leicester City Council, ex parte [1978] JPL 787	409	**P**	
Lewin v End [1906] AC 299	302	Paul v The Governors of the Godolphin and Latymer Girl's School (1919) 7 TC 192	319
Lewis v Lady Rook [1992] BTC 102	319; 320; 321; 322	Pearson v IR Commrs [1980] Ch 1	809
		Pepper v Hart [1992] BTC 591	410; 509; 604; 1022
Lloyd's Bank plc v Rosset [1991] 1 AC 107	910		
London County Council v Cook (1905) 5 TC 173	303	**R**	
		R v Allen [2001] BTC 421	1014
London County Council v Rowton House Co (1897) 77 LT 693	302	— v Dimsey [2001] BTC 408	1014
Longson v Baker [2001] BTC 356	103; 408; 409	— v HMIT, ex parte Fulford-Dobson [1987] BTC 158	904
Lucas v Cattell (1972) 48 TC 353	703	— v HMIT, ex parte Kelly [1991] BTC 50	703

M

		— v Secretary of State for the Environment, ex parte Leicester City Council [1978] JPL 787	409
McClelland v Commr of Taxation for Australia [1971] 1 WLR 191	307		
McGregor v Adcock (1977) 51 TC 692	706	— v Secretary of State for the Environment, ex parte Sharkey [1990] 45 EG 113	409
Macmillan & Co Ltd v Rees [1946] 1 All ER 675	302	Richart v J Lyons & Co Ltd [1989] BTC 337	618
Makins v Elson (1976) 51 TC 437	304; 305	Ricketts v Cambridge City Electoral Registration Officer [1970] 2 QB 463	503
Mallalieu v Drummond [1983] BTC 380	703		
Markey v Sanders [1987] BTC 176	319; 320; 321; 323	Riley v Read (1879) 1 TC 219	303; 304
Marren v Ingles (1980) 54 TC 76	906	Ripon Housing Order, Re [1939] 3 All ER 548	408; 409
Marson v Morton [1986] BTC 377	307(5)	Russell v Couts (1881) 1 TC 469	317
Mesher v Mesher and Hall [1980] 1 All ER 126	905	**S**	
Methuen-Campell v Walters [1979] 1 All ER 606	321; 407	Sansom (Ridge Settlement Trustees) v Peay (1976) 52 TC 1	103; 803; 809

	Paragraph		Paragraph
Sharkey, ex parte [1990] 45 EG 113	409	Warrington v Sterland [1989] BTC 281	715
Shepherd v Lyntress Ltd [1989] BTC 346	518	Whiteley (LON/92/2979) No. 11,292	1109
Stevenson v Rogers 1990 SLT 30	1110	Williams v Merrylees [1987] BTC 393	319; 320; 323; 502
V		Wisdom v Chamberlain (1968) 45 TC 92	307
Varty v Lynes [1976] 1 WLR 1091; (1976) 51 TC 419	408; 416; 417; 1003	Woodhall (as Personal Representatives of Woodhall dec'd) v IR Commrs (2000) Sp C 261	810
Vertigan v Brady [1988] BTC 99	614		
W		**Z**	
Wakeling v Pearce (1995) Sp C 32 ...	408; 409	Zim Properties Ltd v Procter [1985] BTC 42	1017
Ward-Stemp v Griffin [1988] BTC 12	508		

Legislation Finding List

All references are to paragraph numbers

Provision	Paragraph
Capital Gains Act 1979	
19(1)	101
115(6)	618
Common Land (Rectification of Registers) Act 1967	
1(3)	407
Finance Act 1962	
11(3)	101; 410(5)
Finance Act 1965	
29	103
29(13)(b)	204(1)
Sch. 6, para. 25	204(1)
Finance Act 1978	
50	610
Finance Act 1980	
79	903(2)
80(2)	205(1)
Finance Act 1984	
25(2)(b)	615
Finance Act 1986	
102–102C	1106
102A(5)	1106
102B(4)	1107
Sch. 20, para. 6(1)(a)	1107
Finance Act 1988	
64(8)	1111
104(1)	515
111	201
111(1)	1024(1), (2)
Finance Act 1989	
124	1015
Finance Act 1991	
93	203(3); 408
94(1)	205(1)
94(3), (4)	708(4)
Finance (No. 2) Act 1992	
59	709

Provision	Paragraph
Sch. 10	709
Sch. 10, para. 2(1), (4), 7	709
Finance Act 1998	
Sch. 27, Pt. III	1102
Finance Act 1999	
54	1105
Sch. 6	1105
Sch. 6, para. 6	1105
Housing Act 1936	
75	409(3)
Housing Act 1980	
Sch. 1, para. 1(1), (2)	321(3)
Human Rights Act 1998	1023(4)
Income and Corporation Taxes Act 1988	
19(1)	604(1)
74(a)	307(3); 702
145	1014
145(4)	610; 614(1)
145(4)(a), (b)	323(4)
146	1014
168(8)	1014
198(1)	702
263	1024(1)
282, 282(b)	514(6)
353(1)	1101
354(1)(a)	1101
355(1)(a)	1101
355(3)	1024(1)
356	203(5)
356(3)	503(3)
417(4)	1023(4)
503, 504	711
703(2)	605(2)
776	307(5)
776(2)	308(2)
776(9)	307(5); 308(2)
796	1008
Sch. 11A	605(5)
Sch. 11A, para. 3(2), 4(2), 25	605(5)

Provision	Paragraph
Inheritance Tax Act 1984	
6(1)	1012
10, 11(1), (6)	903(2)
18(2)	411(5)
48(3)	1013
49(1)	417; 808
62(7)	814
102	1023(2)
115(2)	1015(1)
117(a)	1015(1)
142(2)	814
Leasehold Reform Act 1967	
1(2)	504
2(3)	321(3); 407
Leasehold Reform Housing and Urban Development Act 1993	308(2)
Local Government Finance Act 1988	
2(1)(b)	1110
Local Government Finance Act 1992	
6(1)	1110
Matrimonial Causes Act 1973	
24, 25	910
25(1)	905(1)
Matrimonial Homes Act 1983	
1(1)	910
Matrimonial Proceedings and Property Act 1970	
37	910
Settled Land Act 1925	803(2)
Taxation of Chargeable Gains Act 1992	
2(1)	910
2A	202
2A(1), (3)(b), (5), (8)	1104
2A(8)(b)(i)	1104
12(1)	1007
16(2)	1002
17(1)(b)	903(2)
17(2)(a)	1017
21(1)	310
22(1)(a)	1017
22(1)(b)	305(3)
22(1)(c)	313
22(2)	1019
23(1)	305(3)
24(1), (3)	305(3)
28(1)	618; 903(4)
28(2)	618
35(5)	1004
35(6)	1005; 1006
44(1)	305(6)
45(1)	305(6)

Provision	Paragraph
52(4)	410(7)
58(1)	314(2); 903(10
60(1)	801; 910
60(2)	801
62(1)	314(3)
62(1)(b)	812
68	801
71(1)	905(3)
76(1)	312
77	417; 807(1)
77(3)	905(3)
85	312
86	807(2); 1010
86(1)(e), (2), (3)	807(2)
87	1010
87(2)	807(2)
91	411(5)
152	711(3)
152(5), (6)	1103
153	711(3)
157	704
158(1)(c)	705
161(1), (3)	411(5)
162	1015(2)
163	706
164	704; 706
164(1), (4), (6)	706
165	903(2); 1015
165(2)(a)	714(2); 1015
165(2)(b)(ii)	1015(2)
222–226	103; 104; 201; 707(1); 1027; App. A
222–224	209; 1024(2)
222	202; 204; 206(2); 509, 509(5); 707(2); 708(1), (3), (4), (6); 711(2); 714(1); 801; 804(1); 806; 901; 905(3); 1011; 1025
222(1)	203(1), (3); 305(4); 410(1); 802; 905(3); 909; 910; 1106
222(1)(a)	301; 302; 305(3); 309; 313; 802 315; 316(2); 322(2), (4), (6); 402; 410(1); 413; 416(2); 701; 707(1); 1028
222(1)(b)	305(5); 316(2); 319(1); 322(6); 401; 402; 405; 408; 409(3); 410(1), (3), (4), (5); 413; 416(2), (5); 418; 802; 1003(1); 1028
222(2)	203(3); 408; 410(1), (3)
222(2)(a), (b)	203(2)

Taxation of Chargeable Gains Act
1992 – continued

Provision	Paragraph
222(3)	203(3); 409(1), (2); (3), (4), (6), (10); 410(1), (3), (4), (8); 411(3); 1003(1)
222(4)	203(3); 410(1), (5), (6), (7); 412(1), (3)
222(5)	203(4); 209; 503(1); 504; 509
222(5)(a)	203(4), (5); 304; 307(1); 505; 509(4); 510; 513; 516; 518; 519; 520; 521; 601; 605(5); 606(1), (2); 611(2); 612; 617; 709; 804(1); 903(4); 904(2); 1003(3); 1027; 1031; 1033; 1101; 1105; 1109; 1110
222(5)(b)	203(4); 310; 505; 507; 509; 510; 516; 1031
222(6)	514(1), (4); 515
222(6)(a)	203(3); 510; 514(2)
222(7)	204(2); 314(2), (4); 609
222(7)(a)	204(3); 314(3); 708(5)
222(7)(b)	204(3); 314(3)
222(8)	203(5); 609; 610; 611(1); 612; 613; 614(1); 616; 1028
222(8)(a)	614(1)
222(8)(b)	614(2)
222(8A)–(8D)	610; 614(1)
222(8A)(a)	614(1)
222(8A)(b)	615
222(9)	203(5); 615
222(10)	318(2); 707(1), (2); 708(4); 710; 713; 1022
223–226	314(2)
223	202; 205; 206(2); 707(2), (5); 804(1); 807(1)
223(1)	202; 204; 205(1); 305(6); 307(2); 416(2); 519; 701; 707(3); 708(1); 902; 903(3), (4); 904(1); 1002; 1003(3); 1007
223(2)	205(2); 305(4), (6); 410(7); 413; 604(3); 711(1); 804(1); 902; 1022
223(2)(a)	618
223(3)	205(3), (4); 305(6); 602; 606(1); 607; 616; 804(1); 1003(4); 1009(3); 1019
223(3)(a)	205(3); 603; 604(1), (2); 608; 609
223(3)(b)	205(3); 602; 603; 604(3); 606(3); 609; 1009(3)
223(3)(c)	205(3); 314(3); 603; 604(2); 605(2), (3), (5); 606(3); 609
223(4)	206(2); 322(2); 609; 613; 708(1), (2), (3), (4), (5), (6); 709; 710; 711(1); 714(1); 806; 1011
223(5)	205(1)
223(7)	204(1); 314; 609; 618; 708(2); 1024(2)
224(1)	206(1); 308(2); 410(7); 701; 702; 704; 705; 707(1), (2), (3), (5), (7); 713; 805; 1102; 1103; 1104; 1111
224(2)	207(1), (2); 305(4); 308(2); 318(2); 410(7); 707(1), (3), (4), (5); 1107
224(3)	208(2); 306; 307(2), (3), (4), (5), (6); 308(2); 314(2); 322(5); 411(4); 418; 708(3); 1003(6)
224(5)	307(5)
225	312; 708(1); 801; 802; 803(1), (2); 804(1); 806; 807(1), (2); 808; 810; 811; 813; 905(2), (3); 907; 1010; 1013; 1016; 1024(3)
225(a)	804(2)
226	201; 322(3); 1022; 1023; 1024(1), (2), (3); 1025; 1105
226(1)	1022
226(2)	1022; 1024(2)
226(3)	1024(3)
226(4), (5)	1022
226(6)(a)	1022; 1023(4)
226(6)(b)	1022; 1023(4)
229(9)	615
241	711
241(6)	711(2)
241(6)(b)	711(3)
247	1026; 1027; 1028
247(1)(c)	1028
247A	1027
248	1028
248(1)(a)	1027
248(1)(b)	1027
248(2)	1027
251(1)	906
260	804(2); 811; 1016
260(1)	411(5)
262	305(6)

Provision	Paragraph
277	1008
286(2)	903(2)
286(3)	905(3)
288(1)	322(6); 402
288(3)	514(6)
Sch. A1, para. 5(1), (2)	1104
Sch. 2, para. 2(3)	807(2)
Sch. 5	807(2)
Sch. 5, para. 2	411(5)
Sch. 6, para. 10(1)(c)	1102
Sch. 7, para. 6(1), (2)	1015(1)
Sch. 7, para. 7, 7(3)(a)	1015(2)

Taxes Management Act 1970

34	1027
46	412(6)
46D	1009(1)
46D(1)(b)	412(6)
47	410(7)
56(1)	316(4)
95	1031
Sch. 3	412(6)

Town and Country Planning Act 1971

112(1)	409(3)

Town and Country Planning Act 1990

226(1)(a)	409(3)

Trusts of Land and Appointment of Trustees Act 1996

12(10)	803(2)

Value Added Tax Act 1994

Sch. 8, Grp. 5, item 1, 2	1109
Sch. 9, Grp. 1, item 1	1109
Sch. 10, para. 2(3)(b)	1109

Value Added Tax Regulations 1995 (SI1995/2518) 1109

Inland Revenue Extra-statutory Concessions

D3	604(5); App. B
D4	606(3); 607; App. B
D5	813; 814; App. B
D6	409(4); 904(1), (2), (3); 905(1), (3); 909; App. B
D20	1023(2); 1024(3); App. B
D21	520; 521; 612; 615; 617; App. B
D26	715; App. B
D33	1018; App. B
D37	1020; App. B
D49	414; 415; App. B

Inland Revenue Statements of Practice

D4	415
10/79	809; App. C
14/80	708(6); 709; App. C
4/92	1006; App. C

Index

All references are to paragraph numbers

A

Abandoned houses .... 305(3)
Absence from only or main residence – see **Period of absence**
Accommodation
. job-related – see **Job-related accommodation**
Acquisitions and expenditure for gain
. gifts, inheritance or appointment from a trust .... 307(6)
. practical implications .... 307(4)
. tainted acquisitions .... 208(1); 307
.. dual purpose acquisitions .... 307(3)
.. sole purpose acquisitions .... 307(2)
. tainted expenditure .... 208(2)
.. dual purpose .... 308(1)
.. practical implications .... 308(2)
. trading transactions .... 307(5)
Addresses
. factual main residence 504
Agricultural property – see also **Farmers and landowners**
. hold-over relief .... 1015(1)
Annexes 317
Appeal commissioners
. main residence, determination 505
. part of dwelling house, determination .... 316(4)
. permitted area, determination .... 412(6), (7)
. staff or servant accommodation, determination .... 323(3), (4)

B

Barges – see **Houseboats**
Beach huts .... 305(1)
Beneficiaries
. deed of variation 814
. occupation by 813
Boiler houses 319
Boundaries – see **Permitted area**
Business rates 1111
Business use of home
. apportionment of consideration .... 707(1)
.. alternative methods .... 707(4)
. authority for restriction of relief 701
. change of use .... 707(3), (5)
. farmers and landowners – see **Farmers and landowners**
. generally .... 206(1)
. landlords – see **Residential lettings**
. losses .... 707(6); 1003(5)
. residential lettings – see **Residential lettings**
. retirement relief 706
. roll-over relief 705
. Schedule D 702; 703
. Schedule E 702; 704
. settlements 805
. status of property .... 707(2)

C

Change of use .... 305(4)
Capital sums derived from assets
. compensation and damages 1017; 1019
. interest in a dwelling-house 313
. relocation agencies, sales through 1020
Caravans
. case law 304
. chattel exemption .... 305(6)
. generally .... 305(1)
Chalets .... 305(1)
Change of occupation .... 207(1)
Change of use .... 207(2)
Chattel exemption
. caravans or houseboats .... 305(6)
Commercial lettings – see **Residential lettings**
Compensation and damages
. capital sums derived from assets 1017; 1019
Compulsory purchase
. deferral relief 1026
.. restriction 1027
.. traps and problems 1028
. generally .... 409(3)
Converted properties .... 305(1); 308(2)
Co-ownership – see **Joint ownership**

Index   253

	Paragraph
Council tax	504; 1110

Curtilage – see **Garden or grounds**

D

Death – see also **Beneficiaries; Personal representatives**
. generally 812
. main residence election .... 514(4)

Deed of variation 814

Deferral relief – see **Compulsory purchase**

Definitions and meanings
. dependent relative .... 1023(4)
. dwelling-house 302; 303; 304; 315
. garden 406
. period of absence .... 205(4); 601
. period of ownership 204
. permitted area 401
. required area for personal enjoyment 409
. residence 502
. residential accommodation .... 708(3)

Demolition
. loss of relief .... 305(3)

Dependent relatives
. abolition of relief .... 1024(1)
. meaning .... 1023(4)
. rent-free and without any other
    consideration .... 1023(2), (3)
. sole residence .... 1023(1)
. transitional relief 1021
. . availability .... 1024(2)
. . combination of reliefs 1025
. . conditions 1012
. . termination .... 1024(3)

Derelict houses .... 305(3)

Destruction or damage .... 305(3)

Discretionary trusts
. gifts of business assets 1016

District Valuer – see **Valuation**

Divorce – see **Marital breakdown**

Doctor registration
. factual main residence, indication of 504

Domestic servants' accommodation – see **Staff or servant accommodation; Subsidiary dwelling-houses**

Double taxation relief
. overseas property 1008

Dower-houses .... 322(3)

Dwelling-houses – see **Main residence**
. abandoned houses .... 305(3)
. acquisitions and expenditure for gain – see
    Acquisitions and expenditure for gain
. change of use .... 305(4)

	Paragraph
. derelict houses	305(3)
. destruction	305(3)

. garden or grounds – see Garden or grounds
. general law 302
. interest in a dwelling-house – see Interest
    in a dwelling-house
. meaning 315
. . capital gains tax law 304
. . general law 302
. . non-capital gains tax law 303
. . part of a dwelling-house 315
. parts of
. . case law .... 316(3)
. . concept .... 316(2)
. . determinations .... 316(4)
. . entity test .... 319(2)
. . extensions to the main residence 317
. . general law .... 316(1)
. . mansion houses .... 318(2)
. . meaning 315
. . separate outbuildings 319
. . subsidiary dwelling-houses – see
    Subsidiary dwelling-houses
. . unused or seldom used parts of main
    house 318
. permitted area – see Garden or grounds
. subsidiary – see Subsidiary
    dwelling-houses
. tax case law 303
. unconventional accommodation .... 305(1)
. unfinished houses .... 305(2)

E

Elections
. main residence – see Main residence
. re-basing to 31 March 1982 .... 1004; 1005
. . time-limit 1006

Employee occupation – see **Job-related accommodation; Subsidiary dwelling-houses**

Employment outside the UK – see **Period of absence**

Enjoyment test
. generally 405
. overseas property .... 1009(2)
. reasonable enjoyment
. . moderation, concept of .... 409(4), (5), (6)
. . objectivity, concept of .... 409(6)
. . subsidiary dwelling-houses .... 320(2)

Entity test
. contentious hearings .... 323(4)
. curtilage determination .... 322(1)
. garden buildings .... 322(6)
. separate outbuildings .... 319(2)
. subsidiary dwelling-houses 320

Paragraph

Estate management – see **Farmers and landowners**
Expenditure for gain – see **Acquisitions and expenditure for gain**
Expenses
. business use of home 702; 703
Extensions to houses 317
Extra-statutory concessions
. capital gains tax on compensation and damages, Zim Properties Ltd (D33) .... 1018; 1019; App. B
. private residence exemption, late claims in dual residence cases (D21) .... 520; 521; 615; 617; App. B
. private residence exemption, periods of absence (A) (D3) .... 604(5); App. B
. private residence exemption, periods of absence (B) (D4) .... 606(3); 607; App. B
. private residence exemption, property held by personal representatives (D5) .... 813; 814; App. B
. private residence exemption, relocation arrangements (D37) .... App. B
. private residence exemption, residence occupied by dependent relative (D20) .... 1023(2), (3); 1024(3); App. B
. private residence exemption, separated couples (D6) .... 904; App. B
. private residence exemption, short delay by owner-occupier in taking up residence (D49) .... 414; 415; App. B
. relief for exchange of joint interests in land (D26) .... App. B

F

Family trading company
. gifts of business assets .... 1015(2)
Farmers and landowners
. agricultural buildings, redundant use ..... 322(5)
. estate management 713
. exchanges of land 715
. farmhouse 712
. manor houses 713
. worker's cottages 714
Farmhouses 712
Final 36 months – see **Three-year time-limit**
Flats – see **Residential lettings**
Foreign expatriates – see **Non-domiciliaries**
Franchise operators
. job-related accommodation 615
Furnished holiday lettings 711

Paragraph

G

Garages and storehouses .... 315; 319; 322(4)
Garden buildings .... 319; 322(6); 402
Garden or grounds
. acquisition before the house 413
. . extra-statutory concession D49 .... 414; 415
. bringing land within the garden 418
. curtilage, determination .... 321(3)
. grounds, meaning 407
. land, meaning 402
. losses .... 1003(1)
. meaning 406
. paddocks and wild land 407
. permitted area – see **Permitted area**
. retained and sold after sale of house 416
. . crystallising exempt gain 417
. . problems .... 416(1); 419
. . Revenue's practice .... 416(4)
Gardeners' cottages 315
General commissioners – see **Appeal commissioners**
Gifts
. part disposals of land .... 411(5)
. property .... 307(6)
. settlements 811
Gifts of business assets – see **Hold-over relief**
Government departments
. compulsory purchase – see **Compulsory purchase**
Granny flats .... 315; 317; 708(6)
Grounds – see **Garden or grounds**

H

Historical background
. generally 101
. legislation 103
. post-1965 developments 102
Hold-over relief
. abolition of general hold-over relief 1015
. . agricultural property .... 1015(1)
. . family trading company .... 1015(2)
. . discretionary trusts 1016
. marital breakdown .... 903(2)
Holiday lettings – see **Furnished holiday lettings**
Hotels .... 708(3)
Houseboats
. chattel exemption .... 305(6)
. generally .... 305(5)
Houses – see **Dwelling-houses**; **Main residence**

Index

	Paragraph
Husband and wife	
. inter-spouse transfers	314(3)
. living together	510
. main residence election	
. . anachronistic rule	515
. . both spouses having a residence	511
. . death	516(4)
. . divorce	514(3)
. . end of marriage	514
. . fiscal unit, treatment as	510
. . generally	516
. . living together	510
. . more than one jointly owned residence	512
. . one spouse owning electable properties before marriage	513
. marital breakdown – see Marital breakdown	
. office or employment outside the UK	604(5)
. period of ownership, successive interests	204(3)
. separation or divorce – see Marital breakdown	

I

Improvements to property for gain – see **Acquisitions and expenditure for gain**

Inheritance tax	
. co-ownership schemes	1107
. deed of variation	814
. interest in possession, avoidance	808; 809; 810
. leasehold carveouts	311; 1106
. marital breakdown, inter-spouse transfers	903(2)
. non-domiciliaries occupying UK residential property	1012
. . non-resident companies	1014
. . non-resident trusts	1013
. shared occupation schemes	1107
Inherited property	307(6)
Interest in a dwelling-house	
. assignment of a life interest	312
. capital sums derived from assets	313
. different interests at different times	314(1)
. extending ownership period	314(2)
. husband and wife	
. . inter-spouse transfers	314(3)
. . successive interests	204(3)
. inter-spouse transfers	314(3)
. joint freehold owners	309
. leasehold interests	310
. marital breakdown	314(4)
. occupation under licence	313
. restrictive covenants	313

	Paragraph
Interest in possession – see **Settlements**	
Inter-spouse transfers – see **Husband and wife**	
Investment use – see **Residential lettings**	

J

Job-related accommodation	
. conditions for relief	
. . intention to occupy owned property as main residence	614(2)
. . residence	614(1)
. generally	610
. main residence election	521
. . scope	612
. permitted absences	616
. residence status, imputation	611(1), (2)
. residential letting	613
. self-employed	615
. time-limits for relief	617
Joint ownership	
. farmers and landowners, exchanges of land	715
. inheritance tax, co-ownership schemes	1107
. interest in a dwelling-house	309
. married couples – see Husband and wife	
. residential lettings	708(5)

L

Land – see **Garden or grounds**	
Landlords – see **Residential lettings**	
Landowners – see **Farmers and landowners**	
Large plots – see **Permitted area**	
Leasehold interests	
. generally	310
. inheritance tax, carve-outs	311; 1106
Legislation	
. acquisition or expenditure for the purpose of disposal	
. . tainted acquisitions	208(1)
. . tainted expenditure	208(2)
. availability of relief	
. . additional periods of deemed only or main residence status	205(3)
. . longer absences	205(2)
. . only or main residence status lacking during last three years of ownership	205(1)
. . period of absence	205(4)
. changes in status	
. . change of occupation	207(1)
. . change of use	207(2)
. historical background	103

Legislation – continued	Paragraph
. Inland Revenue extra-statutory concessions – see Extra-statutory concessions	
. Inland Revenue statements of practice – see Statements of practice	
. Inland Revenue Manuals	210
. mechanism for relief	201
. occupation under the terms of a settlement	209
. partial business or investment use	
. . business use	206(1)
. . residential letting	206(2)
. period of ownership	
. . different interests at different times	204(2)
. . husband and wife, successive interests	204(3)
. . temporal limitation	204(1)
. principal relieving provisions	202; App. A
. scope of relief	
. . job-related accommodation	203(5)
. . only or main residence	203(4)
. . permitted area	203(3)
. . principal qualifying assets	203(2)
. . principal qualifying gains	203(1)

Letting – see **Residential lettings**
Licences
. occupation under 313; 520

Listed buildings
. permitted area .... 412(2)

Living together – see **Husband and wife; Unmarried couples living together**

Local authority
. compulsory purchase – see Compulsory purchase

Lodge-houses 315

Losses
. allowable 1002
. business use of home .... 707(6); 1003(5)
. main residence election 522
. planning for 1001; 1003
. . business use .... 1003(5)
. . development or hope value .... 1003(2)
. . intention to realise a gain .... 1003(6)
. . non-permitted absences .... 1003(4)
. . non-permitted land as garden or grounds .... 1003(1)
. . withdrawal of elections .... 1003(3)

M

Main residence
. absentee owners – see Period of absence
. business use – see Business use of home
. election 506
. . conclusive 507

	Paragraph
. . delaying decision	517
. . dual residence cases	520
. . final 36 months exemption	519
. . interests by way of licence only	509(3)
. . in writing	508
. . job-related accommodation	521; 612
. . late claims in dual residence cases	520
. . licences, occupation under	520
. . losses	522; 1003(3)
. . married couples – see Husband and wife	
. . necessity	516
. . time-limits	509; 518; 519
. . variation facility	519
. . which property	516
. . withdrawal of, losses	1003(3)
. factual residence	502; 503(1)
. . planning	504
. . Revenue determination	515
. . time test	503(2), (3)
. garden or grounds – see Garden or grounds	
. meaning	502
. multiple owners	501; 502
. ownership – see Period of ownership	
. permitted area – see Permitted area	

Mansion houses .... 318(2)
Marital breakdown
. deferred charges 906
. formal trusts 907
. generally 901
. interest in a dwelling-house .... 314(4)
. inter-spouse transfers 903
. . connected persons and hold-over relief .... 903(2)
. . extra-statutory concession D6 904
. . spouse exemption .... 903(1)
. . three-year time-limit .... 903(4)
. . timing of .... 903(3)
. main residence election
. . divorce .... 514(3)
. . ending of marriage preceded by separation .... 514(2)
. Mesher orders 905; 908
. ownership of marital home
. . beneficial ownership 910; 911
. . difficulties 909
. . non-owning spouse 910; 911
. postponed sales and Mesher orders 905; 908
. sale after both parties have left 902

Married persons – see **Husband and wife**
Meaning – see **Definitions and meanings**
Mesher orders 905; 908
Mobile homes – see **Caravans**

Paragraph

Mortgage interest relief 504; 1101
Multiple ownership 501; 502; 503

N

Non-domestic use .... 305(4)
Non-domiciliaries
. UK residential property
. . inheritance tax planning 1012
. . non-resident companies 1014
. . non-resident trusts 1013
Non-resident companies
. non-domiciliaries occupying UK
   residential property 1014
Non-resident trusts
. non-domiciliaries occupying UK
   residential property 1013

O

Office or employment outside UK – see **Period of absence**
Only or main residence – see **Main residence**
Outbuildings
. generally .... 319(1); 322(4)
. subsidiary dwelling-houses .... 319(2)
Overseas property
. appropriation by foreign power .... 1009(3)
. double taxation relief 1008
. enjoyment test .... 1009(2)
. foreign legal concepts 1010
. permitted area .... 1009(2)
. political upheavals .... 1009(3)
. residential lettings 1011
. territorial limitation 1007
. valuation .... 1009(1)
Ownership – see **Period of ownership**

P

Paddocks and wild land 407
Part disposals of land
. effect on relief 411
Part of dwelling-house – see **Dwelling-houses**
Period of absence
. additional periods of deemed only or main
   residence status .... 205(3)
. long periods of absence .... 205(2)
. losses, planning for .... 1003(4)
. meaning .... 205(4); 601
. permitted absence
. . additive conditions 607
. . before and after rule 606
. . exceeding specified periods 608
. . job-related accommodation 616
. . not exceeding three years 603

Paragraph

. . office or employment wholly outside
   UK 604
. . period of ownership, relevant dates 618
. . sale of home to a relocation agency 609
. . work-related absences up to four years 605
. planning, importance of 602
. timing of elections and variations 602
Period of ownership
. additional periods of deemed only or main
   residence status .... 205(3)
. change of occupation .... 207(1)
. different interests at different times .... 204(2)
. husband and wife, successive
   interests .... 204(3)
. interest in a dwelling-house
. . different interests at different times .... 314(1)
. . extended ownership period .... 314(2)
. long periods of absence .... 205(2)
. meaning 204
. only or main residence status lacking
   during last three years of
   ownership .... 205(1)
. permitted absence relief, relevant dates 618
. re-basing to 1 April 1982, effect 618
. residential lettings .... 206(2)
. temporal limitation .... 204(1)
Permitted area
. areas exceeding 0.5 hectares
. . character of dwelling-house .... 409(9)
. . compulsory purchase cases .... 409(3)
. . larger area .... 409(1)
. . less than 0.5 hectares sold .... 410(2), (3),
   (4), (5)
. . objective test .... 409(10)
. . physically separated garden land .... 409(7)
. . reasonable enjoyment .... 409(4), (5), (6)
. . required, meaning .... 409(2)
. . size of dwelling-house .... 409(8)
. basic rule 408
. calculating taxable gain .... 410(7)
. comparables .... 412(4)
. contentious cases .... 412(7)
. determining size .... 410(1)
. District Valuer, attitudes and
   practices .... 412(3), (4)
. establishing 410
. identifying physical characteristics
   and layout of plot .... 410(6), (8)
. losses .... 1003(1)
. meaning 401
. . enjoyment 405
. . for his own occupation 404
. . land 402
. . which the individual has 403

258 Capital Gains Tax and the Private Residence

Permitted area – continued	Paragraph
. negotiations	412(1)
. . failure	412(6)
. overseas property	1009(2)
. part disposals of land	411
. . changes to plot boundaries	411(4)
. . circumstances in taxpayer's favour	411(3)
. . Revenue's argument	411(1), (2)
. . tax planning	411(5)
. pre-sale planning	412(2)
. professional advisers, co-operation between	412(8)
. valuation	412(3), (4), (5)

Personal possessions
. factual main residence 504

Personal representatives
. generally 811; 812
. occupation by beneficiary of estate 813

Property development – see **Acquisitions and expenditure for gain**

Public utilities
. compulsory purchase – see **Compulsory purchase**

Publicans
. job-related accommodation 615

R

Rates – see **Business rates; Council tax**

Re-basing to 31 March 1982
. election 1004
. . effect on other assets 1005
. . time-limit 1006

Relatives – see **Dependent relatives**

Relocation
. agency, sale of employee's house through 1020
. expenses .... 605(5)
. generally 609

Rent-a-room scheme 709

Replacement of business assets – see **Roll-over relief**

Residence – see **Main residence**

Residential lettings
. commercial lettings 710
. computation .... 708(4)
. co-ownership .... 708(5)
. flats 317
. . conversion into .... 308(2)
. . mansion houses .... 318(2)
. . part of owner's house .... 708(6)
. furnished holiday lettings 711
. generally .... 206(2); 708(1)
. job-related accommodation 613
. lodgers .... 708(6)

	Paragraph
. overseas property	1011
. physically distinct buildings separated by properties in different ownership	320(6)
. pre-1 April 1982	708(2)
. rent-a-room scheme	709
. residential accommodation, meaning	708(3)
. reverse premiums	1105
. settlements, letting by trustees of	806

Restrictive covenants 313

Retirement relief
. business use of home 706
. property partly used for trade 1102

Returns
. entries on 1030
. generally 1029
. records, maintaining 1031

Reverse premiums 1105

Roll-over relief
. business use of home 705; 1103
. furnished holiday lettings .... 711(2)

S

Sales of associated land 412

Schedule D, Case I and II
. assessments .... 307(5)
. business use of home 702; 703

Schedule D, Case VI
. assessments .... 307(5)

Schedule E
. business use of home 704

Self-employed
. job-related accommodation 615

Separations – see **Marital breakdown**

Service wings – see **Staff or servant accommodation**

Settled property – see **Settlements**

Settlements
. acquisition and expenditure for gain ..... 307(6)
. availability of relief 209
. business use of, restrictions 805
. disposal of settled property 801
. entitled to occupy
. . meaning .... 803(1)
. . under the terms of the settlement ...... 803(2)
. generally 209
. gifts 811
. interest in possession 808; 809; 810
. marital breakdown, formal trusts 907
. offshore trusts .... 807(2)
. qualifying asset 802
. residential lettings by trustees 806

Index

Paragraph

. residential status of property
. . duration of occupation rights .... 804(3)
. . let property relief, interaction 806
. . occupation .... 804(1)
. . ownership .... 804(2)
. . settlor interest rules 807
. . user-related restrictions 805
. UK resident trusts .... 807(1)
. user-related restrictions 805
Special commissioners – see **Appeal commissioners**
Spouses – see **Husband and wife**
Stables .... 319; 322(4)
Staff or servant accommodation – see also **Subsidiary dwelling-houses**
. contentious cases .... 323(3), (4)
. dwelling-house, meaning 315
. integral flats .... 320(5)
. tax planning
. . during ownership .... 323(1)
. . pre-sale .... 323(2)
Stamp duty 1108
Statements of practice
. capital gains tax, rebasing elections
 (4/92) .... 1006; App. C
. capital gains tax, relief for owner-occupiers
 (14/80) .... 708(6); App. C
. power for trustees to allow a beneficiary
 to occupy dwelling-house
 (10/79) .... 809; 810; App. C
Storehouses 319
Subsidiary dwelling-houses
. current law 321
. curtilage .... 320(4); 321(3)
. dower-houses .... 322(3)
. employees of the owner occupier .... 322(1)
. enjoyment test .... 320(2)
. entity test .... 321(1)
. . emergence of .... 320(1)
. . reinstatement and development .... 320(3)
. garages, stables and other
 outbuildings .... 322(4)
. integral staff accommodation .... 320(5)
. non-employees occupying .... 322(2)
. physically distinct buildings separated
 by properties in different
 ownership .... 320(6)
Summer houses .... 322(6)

T

Tainted acquisitions and tainted expenditure
 – see **Acquisitions and expenditure for gain**

Index 259

Paragraph

Tangible movable property – see **Chattel exemption**
Taper relief .... 307(5); 708(4); 1104
Tax Bulletin .... App. E
Tax returns – see **Returns**
Technical releases .... App. D
Tenant's rights .... 308(2); 313
Three-year time-limit – see also **Period of ownership**
. inter-spouse transfers .... 903(4)
. marital breakdown, inter-spouse
 transfers .... 903(4)
. only or main residence .... 205(1)
. separation prior to sale 902
Tied accommodation – see **Job-related accommodation**
Time-limits – see also **Period of absence; Period of ownership; Three-year time-limit**
. job-related accommodation 521; 617
. main residence election 509; 518; 519
. . job-related accommodation 521
. . re-basing election 1006
Tradesmen
. job-related accommodation 615
**Trading transactions in residential
 property** .... 307(5)
Trustees – see **Settlements**
Trusts – see **Settlements**

U

Unfinished houses .... 305(2)
Unmarried couples living together
. main residence election .... 516(5)
Unused parts of a dwelling-house 318

V

Valuation
. calculation of taxable gains .... 410(7)
. overseas property .... 1009(1)
. part disposal of land .... 411(2)
. permitted area .... 412(3), (4), (5)
. servant's houses .... 323(4)
Value added tax 1109
Voting registration
. place of as evidence of factual main
 residence 504

	Paragraph		Paragraph
W		**Worker's cottages** – see **Farmers and landowners**	
Wasting assets	305(6)	**Working abroad** – see **Period of absence**	
Willed property			
. acquisitions or expenditure for gain	307(6)	**Y**	
. inter-spouse transfers	314(3)	**Yachts**	305(5)